Consciousness Mattering

Also Available from Bloomsbury

Buddhism and Intelligent Technology, by Peter D. Hershock
Comparative Approaches to Compassion, by Ramin Jahanbegloo
Cross-Cultural Approaches to Consciousness, edited by Itay Shani and Susanne Kathrin Beiweis
The Evolution of Consciousness, by Paula Droege

Consciousness Mattering

A Buddhist Synthesis

Peter D. Hershock

BLOOMSBURY ACADEMIC
LONDON • NEW YORK • OXFORD • NEW DELHI • SYDNEY

BLOOMSBURY ACADEMIC

Bloomsbury Publishing Plc, 50 Bedford Square, London, WC1B 3DP, UK
Bloomsbury Publishing Inc, 1385 Broadway, New York, NY 10018, USA
Bloomsbury Publishing Ireland, 29 Earlsfort Terrace, Dublin 2, D02 AY28, Ireland

BLOOMSBURY, BLOOMSBURY ACADEMIC and the Diana logo
are trademarks of Bloomsbury Publishing Plc

First published in Great Britain 2023
This paperback edition published 2025

Copyright © Peter D. Hershock, 2024

Peter D. Hershock has asserted his right under the Copyright, Designs and
Patents Act, 1988, to be identified as Author of this work.

Cover design by Louise Dugdale
Cover image © Mila Tovar/Adobe Stock

All rights reserved. No part of this publication may be: i) reproduced or
transmitted in any form, electronic or mechanical, including photocopying,
recording or by means of any information storage or retrieval system without
prior permission in writing from the publishers; or ii) used or reproduced
in any way for the training, development or operation of artificial intelligence
(AI) technologies, including generative AI technologies. The rights holders
expressly reserve this publication from the text and data mining exception
as per Article 4(3) of the Digital Single Market Directive (EU) 2019/790.

Bloomsbury Publishing Inc does not have any control over, or responsibility for,
any third-party websites referred to or in this book. All internet addresses given
in this book were correct at the time of going to press. The author and publisher
regret any inconvenience caused if addresses have changed or sites have
ceased to exist, but can accept no responsibility for any such changes.

A catalogue record for this book is available from the British Library.

A catalog record for this book is available from the Library of Congress.

ISBN: HB: 978-1-3504-1121-0
PB: 978-1-3504-1125-8
ePDF: 978-1-3504-1122-7
eBook: 978-1-3504-1123-4

Typeset by Integra Software Services Pvt. Ltd.

For product safety related questions contact productsafety@bloomsbury.com.

To find out more about our authors and books visit www.bloomsbury.com
and sign up for our newsletters.

Contents

Introduction   1

1   Consciousness as Dynamic Relationality: A Buddhist Perspective   19
2   Creative Anticipation: Consciousness in the Wild   45
3   Toward a Buddhist Metaphysics of Consciousness: The Sentient Expansion of the Cosmos   59
4   Beyond Organic Consciousness: The Coming of Conscious Machines   85
5   Altering Consciousness: Toward a Neuroscience of Experimental Evolution   105
6   Consciousness Theory Mattering: Responsibilities of Engineered Evolution   127
7   The Future of Human Consciousness: Cultural and Ethical Evolution   153

Appendix: A Genealogy of Contemporary Synthesis   179
Notes   183
Works Cited   197
Index   213

Introduction

It is hard to imagine anything mattering more than consciousness. Without consciousness, there would be no measures, no measuring, and a total absence of things either valued or valuable. Even imagining a cosmos without consciousness is the counterfactual work of consciousness. Without consciousness, nothing would or ever could matter. Indeed, so intimately entangled are the realms of the *sensed* and the *sensing* that their differentiation may be all there is to *presence*. Rather than a window opening onto the world from within our heads, consciousness may consist relationally in the ever-evolving differentiation of *matter* and *what matters*. Ultimately, there may be nothing other than consciousness *mattering*.

That was, I hope, a forgivably knotty first paragraph. The rest of this book works at unraveling it. The means by which I will do so involves blending insights from philosophy, ethics, neuroscience, physics, cosmology, biology, evolutionary theory, and robotics.[1] This is an eclectic, but not uncommon range of sources to draw upon in exploring the nature and dynamics of consciousness. I hope to make a case, however, for accepting that it is a necessary range of sources because all theories of consciousness are essentially *theories of mattering*—theories of the coherent differentiation of matter and what matters—and they can only be evaluated holistically in terms of both their epistemic and ethical merits.

I will also be drawing on Buddhist resources. For over 2,600 years, Buddhists have been theorizing and exploring how best to bring about a liberating transformation of presence as the interplay of consciousness, attention, time, and intention. The contemporary synthesis that I offer draws on a wide array of Buddhist resources with the aim of navigating around and beyond the conceptual hazards of materialist and idealist reductionism, as well as more general "smallist" convictions that everything can be explained by the behaviors of something like independently existing basic particles and/or forces.[2] Buddhist resources enable theorizing consciousness relationally in a way that dissolves the so-called hard problem of consciousness. Our brains, bodies, and environments are not *causes* of consciousness. They are the material *infrastructure* of human consciousness—a dynamic terrestrial record of what consciousness has been doing.

Such a detour into Buddhism is, I think, timely. Over the last several decades, there has been a notable resurgence of philosophical and scientific studies of consciousness. This has been spurred in part by stunning advances in brain imaging that have turbocharged research in neurophysiology and neuropsychology, and in part by no less remarkable advances in robotics and artificial intelligence that have opened prospects for going beyond merely modeling cognition and consciousness to manufacturing them.[3] These scientific and technological advances have encouraged novel ethical investigations of, for example, brain-hacking, the moral and legal status of robotic and algorithmic agency, and the existential threat of machine superintelligence. They have also revitalized more traditional metaphysical explorations of, for instance, intentionality and freewill.[4]

These scientific, technological, and philosophical investments in the study of consciousness have not, however, resulted in substantial theoretical convergence. To the contrary, cross-fertilizations among these approaches to studying consciousness have resulted in a proliferation of theoretical perspectives, ranging from bold eliminativist theories, according to which consciousness need not be explained because it does not exist (our personal experiences of it notwithstanding), to equally bold panpsychist rejections of physicalist reductionism, according to which consciousness is present at every level of physical existence, even the subatomic.

In the face of this profusion, it is perhaps foolish, arrogant, or both to try charting a fundamentally different course in theorizing consciousness. That, however, is my intention in drawing on Buddhist conceptual resources: opening prospects for taking a uniquely nondualist route—a "middle path"—for theorizing consciousness that runs oblique to the ever more densely packed theoretical positions between the reductive extremes of materialist and idealist monism; oblique to the opposing range of reduction-resisting and difference-conserving dualisms; and oblique as well to functionalisms that offer operation-focused alternatives to both.[5] The intuition that I will be fleshing out is that the relationship between the physical and the phenomenal is analogous to that between the particle and wave characteristics of light. They are divergent (and variously coherent, incoherent, and decoherent) expressions of presence. Rather than independent realities, they are artifacts of the relation-elaborating work of consciousness.

The Middle Path as Method

The "middle path" is, of course, a standard metonym for Buddhist thought and practice. Traditionally, the Middle Path (*majjhimapaṭipadā*; *madhyamapratipad*) was presented as a method for steering clear of both asceticism (as a route to spiritual self-realization) and hedonism (as a route to sensual self-gratification) in pursuing freedom from conflict, trouble, and suffering.[6] This understandably conjures associations with Aristotle's "golden mean" between virtue and vice. But the Buddhist Middle Path is in fact a much broader therapeutic and pragmatic strategy for realizing freedom from all manner of opposing views, including disparate assertions of the ultimate reality of spirit and matter, and such ethically charged dichotomies as that of freewill and determinism.[7]

Crucially, the Middle Path is not a strategy of interpolation or taking compromise positions midway between opposing points of view. Instead, it is perhaps best described as a three-part strategy of first *recognizing* the merit of candidate positions or perspectives, *resisting* their universalization or claims to sufficiency, and then *redirecting* relational dynamics at a tangent to relevant perspectival oppositions, doing so in ways that result in superlative or virtuosic (*kusala*; *kuśala*) outcomes and opportunities. Applying this method to the current spectrum of views on consciousness involves recognizing the merits of contending views, resisting their claims of completeness, and then redirecting the study of consciousness in ways that open prospects for enhancing qualities of relational presence. In caricature, this entails allowing that each of the current theories of consciousness may well be 100 percent true, but only some more or less small percentage of the time.[8] In Buddhist terms, they are all perfectly good theories, but none of them are *kuśala* or liberating.

Given the current size and rate at which the field of consciousness studies is expanding, taking such a "middle path" in theorizing consciousness would seem easy enough to begin, but very hard to complete. Fortunately, an exhaustive approach is neither necessary nor advisable. Theories of consciousness are not arrayed along an ever-lengthening line, from any point of which we could strike out perpendicularly or obliquely. Instead, they are situated in something more like a three-dimensional space, and our "middle path" task is to move obliquely or "perpendicular" to all three.

To get a preliminary sense of what will be involved, it is perhaps useful to appeal to the now-common practice—inspired by relativistic physics—of visualizing time as a fourth dimension "perpendicular" to the three spatial dimensions of width, height, and depth. By analogy, theories of consciousness can be seen as arrayed in a three-dimensional space defined by the intersection of three axes of conceptual tension: materialist vs idealist monisms; dualisms in which consciousness is causally relevant with respect to matter vs those in which consciousness is causally irrelevant (i.e., epiphenomenal); and representationalist (often computational) vs enactivist (typically embodied and embedded) functionalisms.

The analogy, though imperfect, is fortuitous in suggesting the need for more robust sensitivity to time in theorizing consciousness. All theories of consciousness must, to one extent or another, address issues of memory and intentionality, and thus temporality. The reigning tendency, however, has been to regard the temporal dimension as essentially linear and to focus on the appropriate timescale at which to study consciousness most effectively. On one hand, this has led to focusing (as is typical among materialist reductionists) on micro-temporal neurological events, affirming the primacy of isolable moments-of-consciousness. On the other hand, it has led to focusing (as is typical among enactivists) on macro-temporal sensorimotor couplings, affirming the primacy of protracted streams-of-consciousness. Like the particle and wave descriptions of light, the moment and stream perspectives on the temporality of consciousness are each right; they are just not right all the time. More complex, nonlinear understandings of consciousness and temporality are needed.

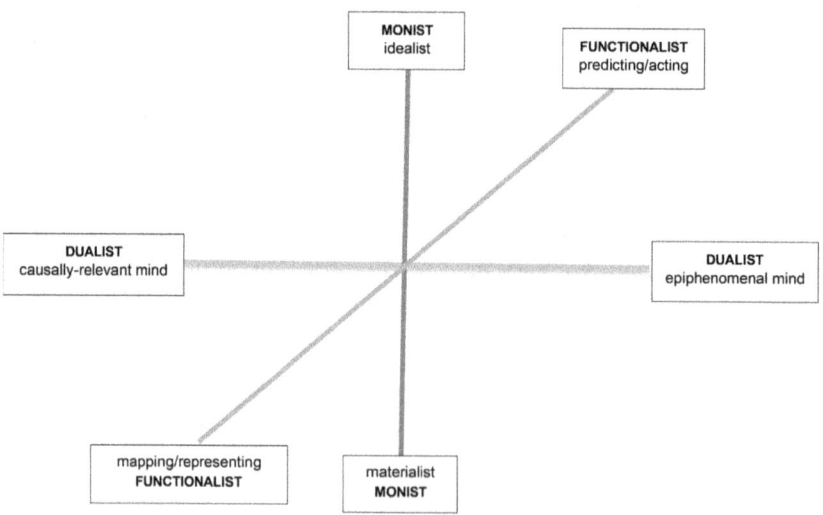

Figure 1 Three-dimensional matrix space of contemporary theories of consciousness © Peter D. Hershock.

Rethinking Time

According to the Buddhist approach I will be forwarding, the incompleteness of these temporal framings is a function of their fundamental linearity. Shifting obliquely from theorizing focused on either momentary sequences or continuous streams of conscious events means focusing, instead, on the recursive character of conscious presence and affirming the constitutively spiral, nonlinear, or nested nature of conscious temporality. What matters most in understanding consciousness temporally is not *lengths* but *patterns*. Within the empirical horizons of contemporary bioscience, this involves theorizing the interplay of consciousness and time as *rhythmic*. Minimally, this entails attending to the diurnal patterning of densities of conscious presence. Carried beyond those horizons into the realms of inquiry opened by anthropology and cultural evolution theory, it involves theorizing the interplay of consciousness and time as *narrative*: attending to affectively, as well as cognitively, articulated intentions of the kind that shape action and experience over periods of minutes, hours, days, weeks, months, and years. Buddhist theorizing about consciousness entails going further still to take critically into account how relational/experiential outcomes and opportunities are qualitatively and recursively shaped by nonlinear causal dynamics over indefinite sweeps of time: patterns occurring in what I will suggest is best conceived as a "fifth" temporal dimension of *karmic* relations.[9]

Rethinking the temporal "scale" appropriate to studying consciousness, when combined with Buddhism's founding insight that all things arise and are sustained interdependently, also enjoins rethinking the *place* of consciousness.[10] One of the most contentious issues in consciousness theorizing today is whether it takes place in the brain, in the sensorimotor body, in the environmentally embedded body, or perhaps somewhere "outside" of the spatiotemporal realm of material entities and processes. Although compelling support exists for claims about the neural causes/correlates of consciousness, no less compelling support exists for claims about the environmental causes/correlates of consciousness, including "virtual" social and cultural environments. While Buddhist theorizing about consciousness affirms the conventional merit of these views, I will suggest that it ultimately involves redirecting investigative attention from spatial location to relational locution, density, and acuity.

Methodologically, this Buddhist "middle path" can also be seen as running oblique to the experimental choice between extrospection and introspection. These investigative methods have respectively yielded valuable readings of the physical and phenomenal workings of consciousness, and together might enable something like a topographical mapping of consciousness in action. Yet, as different as they are, "third person" (objective/physical) and "first person" (subjective/phenomenal) studies of consciousness are similarly premised on the possibility of learning about something without affecting it. That is, they presume a fundamental independence of knowing and known presences. Buddhism's irreducibly relational understanding of presence affirms the mutual inclusiveness—the irreducible interdependence and interpenetration—of knowers, knowledge, and knowns. It thus denies the ultimate separability of facts and values or the exclusivity of ontological, epistemological, and ethical concerns and commitments. Why and how we study consciousness matters.

Theorizing Consciousness Normatively

There are significant resonances between this relational approach to consciousness and the "new materialisms" which variously insist on the agentive nature of matter and its complex entanglement with meaning (see, e.g., Barad, 2007; Bennett, 2010). Buddhist teachings about karma and relationality, however, are in significant tension with the deflationary decentering of the human that posthumanist new materialists often celebrate. Embracing the elaborative mutuality of matter and meaning—and the impossibility of reducing complex, nonlinear, and non-local causal networks to simple, linear, and local causal chains—can also be seen as a process of radically *recentering* the cosmos, albeit in the sense delightfully invoked by Jorge Luis Borges in his 1951 essay, "Pascal's Sphere" (La esfera de Pascal): embracing the esoteric premodern metaphor of the cosmos as a sphere "whose center is everywhere and whose circumference nowhere." Nothing in this embrace of the inseparability of matter and mattering necessitates, however, a "flattening" of differences among materializations of sentient presence and relational intent. On the contrary, it is more readily consistent with anticipating that consciousness will be just as varied in concentration and qualitative character as material presences are in density and complexity.

To return to a point made earlier in passing, like science, Buddhism is method-driven rather than doctrine-defined. It is, first and foremost, a system of practices. But it is a system that is enacted cognitively, emotionally, and bodily for the purpose of making a difference in—and not merely understanding the causal conditions of—lived experience. Comparable to the emergence of different scientific disciplines, different ecosystems of Buddhist practice and thought have evolved since Buddhism's inception some 2,600 years ago, and important differences have developed in how consciousness, mind, self, attention, perception, memory, and related matters are understood and related. As will become evident, Chan and Chinese Yogācāra traditions play central roles in my own practical and philosophical engagement with Buddhism.

Yet, all Buddhist theorizing about consciousness is characterized by an overarching commitment—not found in science—to subordinating theoretic practice to therapeutic practice. Most generally stated, Buddhist therapeutics consists in alleviating or eliminating relational distortions through enacting interlocking commitments to seeing all sentient presence as karmically configured; seeing all things as dynamically and interdependently originated; and seeing all things as without-self or empty of fixed natures/identities. Taken together, these commitments call into question any segregation of the "space of causes" and the "space of intentions." In keeping with them, the nondualist and dynamically relational theory of consciousness that I will be forwarding is explicitly and unabashedly normative. It is not, however, prescriptive. It is a theory expressly sensitive to and supportive of qualitatively altering consciousness.

It is important not to misconstrue this. As I will elaborate it, consciousness-altering theorizing is not aimed primarily or exclusively at altering subjective experience, but rather at altering the dynamics of physical/phenomenal differentiation and coevolution. That is, the process of altering consciousness with Buddhist intent has both personal and evolutionary significance.

Here we can take the infrastructure analogy a step further. Transportation infrastructure consists in the ongoing materialization of ever-evolving, value- and intention-inflected transportation practices and in supporting an indeterminately large number of transportation-enabled and -enriched activities and experiences (ranging, for instance, from manufacturing and commerce to romantic encounters and artistic collaborations). The brain-body-environment infrastructure of human consciousness analogously mediates the ongoing materialization of an open-ended range of value- and intention-expressing practices and experiences. Altering human consciousness alters both that infrastructure and the experiential and relational dynamics supported and materialized through it. This can be liberating or constraining. It cannot, however, be insignificant. Altering consciousness is world altering.

The normative commitment of Buddhist theorizing is, I think, a strength rather than a liability. By freeing the process of theorizing mind and consciousness from the epistemic pretense of discovering *truths* (truth as epistemic destination), and instead seeing this process as a means of contributing to the progressive *truing* of relational dynamics (truth as epistemic direction), it becomes natural to first shift attention from representation to prediction as the basic activity of mind,[11] and to then turn from affirming the primacy of prediction to affirming that of affectively qualified, creative anticipation—conferring primacy on active and evaluative sentience. Fleshing out the logic of this second shift from prediction to creative anticipation will be a major concern in what follows—a logic, ultimately, of recognizing the organic nonduality of becoming responsive and becoming responsible. Theorizing consciousness as responsivity involves theorizing consciousness as responsibility.

In the context of our historical moment, when commercial and political actors are rapidly scaling up the use of machine learning algorithms and artificial/synthetic intelligence to engage in what amounts to attention- and intention-hacking and the systematic colonization of consciousness, developing ethically sensitive and resolutely normative theories of consciousness is a moral and public intellectual imperative.[12] Without such theories, it may relatively soon become impossible to realize more humane futures than those toward which humanity presently seems destined at a time when inequalities of wealth, risk, and opportunity have become greater than at any time in the past. In contrast with currently dominant approaches, the Buddhist theorizing I undertake is not rooted in metaphysical concerns about what consciousness *is*, but rather in commitments to affecting our understanding and enhancement of what consciousness *does*—recursively opening and creatively expanding qualitatively differing relational realities.[13] Normative theorizing about what human consciousness is doing is crucial to securing its continued evolutionary viability.

Our Itinerary

It would not be uncommon to begin a book introducing a new way of theorizing consciousness by first reviewing existing theories and noting their strengths and weaknesses. Doing so in forwarding a Buddhist theory of consciousness, however, risks tacitly accepting the terms of debate among contemporary theories, naturalizing the history of their emergence, and by default framing the Buddhist theory being offered as a late entrant into that debate and as an aspiring graft onto its history. We will take a different route.

Chapter 1. Consistent with the Buddhist subordination of theory to therapy, Chapter 1 opens with a methodological question. Where and how is it best to study consciousness? Is it in a neuroscience laboratory making objective use of the latest in experimental techniques? Or might it be in a meditation hall making subjective use of millennia-old experiential techniques? Blending these investigative methods and contexts is one aim of this book. The cautionary intent of questioning investigative contexts at the outset is to ensure critical consideration of how (and how much) investigative apparatuses matter in studying consciousness.

In the laboratory context of neuroscientific experimentation, research has typically sought to determine how brain behaviors cause the contents of consciousness, or to discover correlations among material and phenomenal *events*. The "research agenda" in the meditation hall context of Buddhist practice is to verify how attending to the contents of consciousness can qualitatively transform consciousness and enable reshaping structures of both material and experiential *eventualities*. In the scientific laboratory, insight is sought into the nature of *being conscious*; in the meditation hall, insight is sought into the dynamics of *becoming more freely conscious*.

With that in mind, the chapter explores how and why experientially vested Buddhists theorized consciousness as the *differentiation* of sensing and sensed presences, and as the *elaboration* of values-inflected agential/environmental dynamics. This entails seeing consciousness as non-localizable, both spatially and temporally, but also seeing waking and sleeping as coordinated modes of consciousness rather than as opposed states of being conscious or being unconscious. It additionally involves refraining from seeing perception, either originally or fundamentally, as a *means* for receiving or gathering information about the world and seeing it instead as the environment-realizing *meaning* of more coherently or less coherently *materializing* values and intentions. Consciousness is intention mattering.

Chapter 2. A basic principle of Buddhist practice is that the consciousness- and relationship-altering effects it brings about should extend beyond the meditation hall into the complex relational environs of daily life. Chapter 2 begins by considering the merits of theorizing consciousness "in the wild" as intent on enriching relational possibilities—opening new environments or realms of optimization and improvement—rather than simply anticipating and actualizing the success conditions, for example, of survival or surprise reduction. This conceptual shift of anticipatory focus from success to improvement is explored concretely through two relatively ordinary practices: surfing and joint musical improvisation.

Given the therapeutic roots of Buddhist theorizing, it is important to account for the apparent disconnect between "optimizing" intent and the conflicts, trouble, and suffering that are seemingly endemic to the human experience. The remainder of Chapter 2 first presents a Buddhist conception of subjective self-consciousness as a source of convoluted and often-incoherent differentiation, and how it factors into the karmic dynamics of mental/material entanglement. This segues into a discussion of the Buddhist conception of attention, not as a quantitative function of "bottom up" perceptual capture or "top down" executive control, but rather as a crucial factor in determining qualitatively whether consciousness alters in ways that are relationally liberating or constraining.

Chapter 3. Buddhist relationalism offers a nondualist alternative to physicalist reductionism and neurocentrism, considering the coevolution of sensing organisms and sensed environments to be an order-generating *implication* of consciousness. Chapter 3 brings Buddhist theorizing into conversation with contemporary theories of evolution, both organic and cosmic, beginning with Buddhist narratives that frame cosmic history as a record of relational disambiguation and as the coevolutionary differentiation of matter and what matters.

Consistent with the emerging biological consensus that life consists in beneficial interdependencies within/among difference-reinforcing molecular communities, I will suggest that the Buddhist conception of sensory consciousness entails seeing the evolution of life as a record of (either sustained or unsustainable) *improvisations on the meaning of coordination*. The entropy-averting coherent differentiation that accelerates with the advent of sensing organisms and sensed environments marks an intensifying phase shift in the work of consciousness.

By theorizing consciousness relationally as coherent differentiation, it becomes possible in principle to look beyond the advent of life to see early cosmic history as a record of even more rudimentary differentiations of matter and what matters that were conducive to continued coherence-diversifying improvisation. That is, it becomes possible to see the emergence of basic "forces" and "particles" in the aftermath of the Big Bang or Big Bounce as materializations of a primordial intent to differentiate coherently: a cosmos-engendering manifestation of consciousness.

Following this, Buddhist theorizing is distinguished from neutral monism, panpsychism, and cosmopanpsychism, and their approaches to infusing consciousness into the material cosmos as theorized by contemporary physics and cosmology. Drawing on induced matter or space-time-matter theory, consciousness and karma are framed as the nonlinear causal interface between our familiar four-dimensional spacetime manifold and an enfolding fifth, temporal dimension. This theorizing of time as two-dimensional—a "surface" configured by diffracting patterns of sequence and significance—makes it possible to account for the nonlinear dynamics of karmic entanglement, to explain the liberating potential of meditation, and to reconcile freewill and determinism. It also entails, however, theorizing coherent differentiation as an expansion and intensification of both responsivity and responsibility.

Chapter 4. The responsibility of human consciousness now encompasses the ramifications of algorithmic syntheses of human and machine intelligences, the proliferation of digital relational environments, and the creation of artificial consciousness. Current technology is such that artificial general intelligence will likely remain a distant goal for some decades. But if consciousness is dynamically integral to the evolving interplay of space, time, and matter, artificial consciousness might prove easier to engineer than artificial general intelligence.

Chapter 4 begins with a review of scientific evidence that self-awareness is not a rare evolutionary achievement, and then of robotics projects that have developed machines capable of passing the "mirror self-recognition" test and behaving in ways that demonstrate capacities for imagination. This twofold review is used as a springboard for engaging leading theories of consciousness—in particular, global workspace theory, integrated information theory, and functionalism—from a Buddhist perspective and for arguing that building machine learning systems capable of altering their own capacities for coherent differentiation constitutes an evolutionary "hack" of the cosmic-historical elaboration of consciousness.

Buddhist relational theorizing is then used to argue that what machine consciousness is currently capable of doing is analogous to the subliminal cognition and problem-solving that occurs in human deep sleep. There is "nothing it is like" to be doing it. Yet, experiments in raising robots like children may soon make "subjectivity hacking" possible. The chapter ends by noting that if consciousness consists in the elaborative differentiation of sensed and sensing presences—the intra-active elaboration of both matter and what matters—then the juxtaposition of simulated (machine) and actual (human) consciousness dissolves, compelling an evaluative shift. How well are machines able to emulate humans? And would perfect emulation be ideal given the historically apparent human propensity to alter consciousness in ways that perpetuate conflict, trouble, and suffering?

Chapter 5. Theorizing consciousness as intent on differentiating coherently implies that altering consciousness is constitutive of what consciousness *does*. The thesis of Chapter 5 is that much as explorations of extraordinary macrocosmic and microcosmic phenomena led to the relativity and quantum revolutions in physics, contemporary explorations of extraordinarily altered states of consciousness are making evident the limitations of the metaphysical underpinnings of monism and dualism, and of methodological biases toward functionalist neurocentrism, offering both support and resources for nondualist theorizing.

If consciousness is the entangling differentiation of sensing (neural/mental) and sensed (environmental/material) presences, and an interface of sequence- and significance-biased temporalities, then to study consciousness is to study spatiotemporal patterns of diffraction akin to those occurring where/when continuously intersecting and superimposing waves are directly and intimately mattering to one another. This chapter is centrally devoted to exploring how blending third-person brain imaging studies with first-person and second-person (i.e., guided) experiments in consciousness alteration are revealing spatially and temporally extended diffraction patterns among neural and phenomenal event streams.

Of particular importance are blended studies of meditatively altered consciousness and interpersonal collaboration (e.g., joint musical improvisation) that challenge intracranial neurocentrism, compelling neuro-ecological understandings of consciousness and undercutting putatively physicalist claims that experiences of agency and freewill are illusory or causally irrelevant. The chapter closes by theorizing the qualitative self-altering of consciousness as a reality-expanding—not simply reality-investigating—process, thus compelling recognition of the inescapably ethical character of our determinations of whether and how best to investigate consciousness and evolution.

Chapter 6. Buddhist theorizing invites seeing brain-body-environment systems, not as *causes* of consciousness, but as creatively evolving and developing *infrastructures* of consciousness. Buddhist therapeutics focuses on altering consciousness to induce infrastructure evolution that conserves and advances capacities for differing and cohering virtuosically in shared realizations of increasingly liberating relational dynamics. Chapter 6 makes the case that the combination of reductionist theorizing and unprecedented capacities for technologically manipulating the infrastructures of consciousness is precipitating a potentially terminal decoherence among human consciousness, evolution, and ethics.

Theories of consciousness and evolution disambiguate and configure the relation between matter and what matters. They are fundamentally *theories of mattering*. Competition among them can be seen as competition for both epistemic and ethical market share, and any monopolistic narrowing of the field of competition will, in effect, constrain the interplay of materiality and morality and shrink the domain of material and moral interconnection. That is, it will result in a contraction or compression of the possibility space of coherent differentiation.

The first part of the chapter shows how the "hard problem" of consciousness is a theoretical and methodological artifact of the nineteenth-century combination of reductionist evolutionary theory, the ascendance of scientific objectivity, and an account of the cosmos from which divine agency could be excluded. In short, the "hard problem" is a product of conceiving the cosmos as essentially indifferent—a cosmos wherein consciousness and morality can only be chance results of purposeless algorithmic processes. It is then argued that the combination of reducing consciousness to neural dynamics, reducing evolution to genetic competition, and reducing moral dispositions to survival mechanisms is conducive to a solutionist merger of epistemic certainty and ethical finality that risks hardwiring the future in ways chillingly anticipated in contemporary arguments on behalf of neuro- and bio-engineered moral enhancement: the engineering of human beings who are "ethical by design."

After introducing the emerging field of neuroethics, the need for a more encompassing and diversity-enhancing ethics of consciousness is articulated in response to "field experiments" on consciousness that are already underway and rapidly intensifying. This experimentation, mediated digitally by intelligent technology and the new global attention economy, is revising the human brain-body-environment infrastructure in what amounts to a colonization of consciousness. This has the potential to trigger an ethical singularity: the collapse of capacities for and commitments to the quintessentially human art of values-evaluating course correction.

Chapter 7. The final chapter raises questions about the future of consciousness and whether the ecologically damaging impacts of human determinations of what matters most constitute grounds for the extinction of human consciousness. After offering a Buddhist argument against human extinction, consideration is given to the future-oriented proposals of transhumanism and posthumanism and their imaginations of transforming the material and ecological infrastructures of human consciousness. An argument is made for going beyond infrastructural change to engage in directly transforming the evolutionary meaning of the coherence-differentiating work of consciousness.

The central portion of the chapter uses Buddhist conceptions of consciousness and time to rethink human cultural evolution and the distinctively immaterial nature of human expansions of the horizons of coherent differentiation, especially in relation to uniquely human capacities for exploring *consequential*, but *nonsequential* temporal relations. Drawing on insights into the evolutionary origins of life and organic consciousness, it is proposed that while cultural evolution initially consisted in the creative and cumulative actualization of potentials for coordinated presence, it defaulted over time to a dynamic of competitive/conservative trait selection and transmission to begin fostering patterns of exclusionary coherence—a shift from supporting the work of creatively refining human presence to habitually defining it.

It is suggested that ethics originated as an evolutionary counter to culture-conserving attention and intention habituation and to restore the primacy of creative impulses to cohere differently. Crucially, however, the evolutionary promise of ethics as the art of altering the world-eliciting work of shared consciousness is being placed at risk by the digital hacking of the attention-intention interface that was discussed in Chapter 6: direct manipulations of the dynamics of temporal diffraction that—in the absence of evolving global ethical diversity and normative consensus—seem destined to normalize decoherent involutions of the immaterial infrastructure of human consciousness. The chapter concludes with a plea to collaborate in securing viable futures for the evolution of human consciousness by taking explicitly ethical responsibility for how we theorize consciousness and its evolutionary elaboration, and actively engendering globally shared commitments to sustaining and enhancing the conditions for both freedom of attention and freedom of intention.

Directions Not Taken

It should be apparent from this itinerary that what follows is not a weaving of Buddhist resources into a coherent theoretical tapestry crafted for appreciation (or critique) by Buddhist specialists. It is a contemporary synthesis that offers *a* Buddhist perspective—not *the* Buddhist perspective—on how consciousness matters. It does so, not in response to traditional Buddhist therapeutic concerns, but in generative response to current scientific and philosophical theorizing on consciousness, and in ethical response to emergent societal and technological dynamics.[14]

This double synthesis of diverse Buddhist insights with equally diverse insights from contemporary physics, evolutionary theory, and neuroscience contrasts sharply with more specialist approaches to Buddhist philosophy in ways that are analogous to the contrasting ideals of jazz and classical music performance. Classical musicians aim to develop the instrumental technique necessary to meticulously render every note in a scored composition while also accurately interpreting the composer's musical intent and imbuing it with appropriate emotional color. Jazz musicians aim to develop comparable instrumental technique, typically by playing so-called standards and gaining sufficient familiarity with their melodic and harmonic structures to also be able to improvise freely on them. Where the written score is central to classical music performance, unscripted composition on the fly is central to jazz.[15]

At least for me, jazz is at its best when musicians abandon standards (chord charts, etc.) to play in the spirit of their musical ancestors, channeling creativities that are recognizably *rooted* in various performance traditions without *replicating* them, all with the attentively nurtured intent of extending the limits of sonic anticipation and making never-heard-before music.[16] Likewise, my jazz-inflected, improvisational approach to Buddhist philosophizing draws freely on a range of Buddhist traditions of therapeutic and theoretic practice to compose on the fly, addressing contemporary concerns and arousing ethical passions inspired by past Buddhist exemplifications of liberating intent.

Like jazz, this improvisationally Buddhist approach to theorizing consciousness has the merit of being highly situated and responsive. Also, like jazz, it will not be to everyone's taste. Yet, in addition questions of taste, this approach can be seen as begging more fundamentally philosophical questions about the "truth status" of claims based on synthesizing therapeutically oriented, first-person (Buddhist) insights with empirically grounded, third-person (scientific) insights. For example, is my characterization of consciousness as relation-elaborating coherent differentiation an empirically falsifiable claim? Is it forwarded in summation of personally verified first-person accounts of how consciousness works? Is it an encapsulation of established or growing consensus on the nature and/or work of consciousness? Or does it simply offer a practically useful vantage for seeing beyond (rather than getting stuck in) the explanatory gap between first-person and third-person accounts of experiential presence?

These are good and valid questions. But there are, I think, good and valid reasons for not answering them directly. To begin with, the Buddhist term that is customarily translated as "truth" (*satya*) is also translatable as "reality." While Buddhist theories of truth and knowledge became extraordinarily complex (especially in medieval India), their central preoccupation was with determining whether truth/reality is conceivable and expressible, or if truth/reality is nonconceptual and exceeds any possible claim or set of claims made about it.

This contrasts markedly with the preoccupation of current philosophical theories of truth. The most widely recognized of these—correspondence, coherence, consensus, and pragmatic theories—are all theories about the status of *claims* made about the world. Simply put, these theories respectively hold that claims are true because they accord with observable reality (correspondence); because they follow logically from some axiomatic propositions about the world (coherence); because they summarize what is generally believed to be true (consensus); or because they are useful or beneficial (pragmatic).

One implication of Buddhist teachings of interdependence, karma, emptiness, and nonduality is that what makes a claim valuable is its *truing capacity*—its capacity for eliciting alterations of sentient presence that are consistent with liberation from conflict, trouble, and suffering (*dukkha*; *duḥkha*). Hence, the Buddha's oft-repeated characterization of his own teachings as a raft—a useful conveyance rather than a repository of revelatory treasures. Rather than "getting things right," truth is about "setting things rightly in motion." The truth value of a statement is thus measured, not in terms of what it is apparently about or the content it *delivers*, but in terms of what and how well it *motivates*—a communicative ideal exemplified by the bodhisattva's enlightening practice of "skillful means" or "responsive virtuosity" (*upāya*).

This might suggest that my relational theorizing of consciousness is intended to have only instrumental pragmatic value. But that would be an oversimplification. Among the Buddhist lineages that inform my approach to theorizing consciousness (see the Appendix) are lineages that differentiate between conventional truth/reality (*saṃvṛti-satya*) and ultimate truth/reality (*paramārtha-satya*), or between the phenomenally and materially differentiated world of everyday experience and communication practices and the nondualistically phenomenal/material world of pre-/post-linguistic presence. That is, they differentiate between the truth/reality of conceptually mediated presence and the truth/reality of presence without conceptual mediation. If concepts consist in relationally manifest regularities in the material/immaterial dynamics of the infrastructure of consciousness, ultimate truth/reality can be seen as consciousness in the absence of any constraining infrastructure. That is, the ultimate truth/reality of consciousness "just is" the cosmos-originating intent to differentiate coherently.

But what is the "truth status" of that statement? As the well-worn Zen metaphor has it: the moon can be pointed toward but not touched with an outstretched finger. Ultimate truth/reality can be pointed toward with words and concepts, but not reached or encompassed by them. Claims of correspondence, coherence, consensus, and even pragmatic value are all claims made within and about conventional truth/reality. But so, too, are claims about conventional and ultimate truth and the many claims about consciousness that are made throughout this book.

Yet, the Buddhist "two truths" perspective also entails admitting that the absence or emptiness of the infrastructure of everyday sentient presence only makes sense and matters by virtue of being coherently differentiated from it. Theorizing consciousness as coherent differentiation is thus a way of acknowledging that differentiating the two truths/realities is intrinsically identical with their nonduality. That is, conventional truth/reality could never be anything other than *intrinsic* to ultimate truth/reality.

Affirming this is a way of reinforcing Buddhist insight into the nonduality of the ontological (matter) and the axiological (what matters) and motivating acceptance of the deep responsibility that their nonduality entails. Theorizing consciousness as coherent differentiation is a means of closing off conceptual escape routes from that responsibility, but also of encouraging both irrealist epistemic humility and evolutionary ethical daring. The "truth status" of the Buddhist synthesis that materializes over the course of this book will be determined ultimately by its consciousness-altering effects—the ways in which it is improvisationally embraced and extended by its readers.

1

Consciousness as Dynamic Relationality: A Buddhist Perspective

As environments for studying consciousness, scientific laboratories and Buddhist meditation halls would appear to have very little in common. Science labs are brightly lit, spotlessly clean, closed to the outside world, and filled with instruments for making and recording detailed measurements of changes in the phenomenon under investigation. Traditional meditation halls are dimly lit, often open to the outdoors, and completely free of measuring and recording instruments. As sites for studying consciousness, they apparently epitomize disparate third-person (objective/physical) and first-person (subjective/phenomenal) methods of inquiry, which in turn index the explanatory gap famously referred to by David Chalmers (1995) as the "hard problem" of consciousness—the problem, provocatively stated, of explaining how mind arises out of meat and motivations out of motion.[1]

Yet, for all their differences, science labs and meditation halls are both designed and used for the purpose of concentrated critical inquiry aimed at generating interpersonally verifiable insights regarding causal dynamics. This commonality of purpose is worth reflecting on. Although the contrast of third- and first-person perspectives in consciousness studies invokes a hard distinction between the experimental and experiential, both of those words are derived from the Latin *experiri* or to "test" or "try." This suggests that the distinction between them does not "cut the world at its joints." Experiment and experience are two modes of effortful inquiry, and the apparent difference between experimental and experiential methods for studying consciousness may well be nothing more than an artifact of objectivity-privileging rationality. In both labs and meditation halls, sustained efforts are made to figure out how and why things occur as they do.

Of course, the "research" questions and phenomena under investigation in scientific and meditative settings differ significantly. Scientific and empirically informed philosophical inquiries tend to focus on explaining how and why consciousness exists—identifying its nature and causal origins. Buddhist meditative inquiries are directed toward revealing how and why consciousness has the dynamic configurations it does and then altering them—transforming consciousness qualitatively. Granted their shared causal concerns, however, the differences between these modes of inquiry may afford significant insight. Much as binocular vision enables focusable depth perception, combining third- and first-person studies of consciousness has the potential to make evident otherwise-indiscernible depths of relevance.

Buddhist Origins: A Matrix of Altered Presence

As portrayed in traditional narratives of the Buddha's life, his primary motivation in undertaking extensive meditative training was to discover the causes and conditions of conflict, trouble, and suffering, and then to determine how best to liberate ourselves from them. Phrased in modern terms, his central research questions were: "What explains differences in the quality of our experiential presence? And, and how can it be optimized?"

There were many competing answers to these questions in circulation. Having personally verified the inefficacy of satisfying sensual desires as a means of materially optimizing experienced presence, the Buddha spent six years following the advice offered by reigning exemplars of textual interpretation, independent reasoning, and ascetic experimentation. Finding that these were also insufficient, he set aside all existing theories and committed to finding out for himself what determines the quality of lived experience and what would enable lasting liberation from conflict, trouble, and suffering.

According to the traditional narrative, he spent forty days in continuous, seated meditation before obtaining an answer. Setting aside its penumbra of mythological elements, the story of his liberation depicts a three-phase process of awakening that culminated in realizing that all things arise interdependently (*paṭiccasamuppāda*; *pratītyasamutpāda*). Strongly stated, he realized that relationality is more basic than things related. It is not individual, independent existents that are ontologically primary; it is relational dynamics.[2]

This insight is as counterintuitive today as it was 2,600 years ago. It offends against our everyday identification of relationships—for example, friendships or office hierarchies—as contingent, second-order phenomena. Relationships like these are "obviously" dependent on the prior existence of the individuals involved in them. Moreover, it offends against the generally accepted scientific view that all material entities are composed of discrete elementary particles that interact in accordance with a few basic natural laws and forces.

Nevertheless, we have reasons to doubt our mundane convictions that relationality is predicated on the prior existence of discrete and individual things that can be brought contingently into various kinds of relationship. There is a significant sense, for example, in which individual family members do not preexist familial relational dynamics, but rather emerge out of them. After all, there are no parents until there are children, and the meanings of being present as father, mother, son, or daughter necessarily develop coevally over time, differently in each family and in each culture and historical period.

This description might be dismissed as a bit of social constructivist wordplay or as a function of having selected a social level of abstraction at which to express how families are constituted.[3] It might be argued, for instance, that the biological human bodies which become associated with the mutually defining social presences of fathers and mothers obviously preexisted those role-exemplifying presences. But human bodies, too, only arise and persist relationally. This is most evident through "external" energy exchanges between our bodies and their environments, but also through exchanges taking place "internally" among and within cellular communities, in exchanges between "individual" cells and their environs, and so on until we find even so-called basic material particles dissolving cloudlike into immaterial relational structures.

Across scales from the microscopic to the macrocosmic, evidence is abundant that ontological primacy should not be granted to presumably individual existents. Quantum mechanics has so complicated allegiance to atomist science that many physicists are inclining toward the holist view that particles are derivative abstractions, not elementary existents (see, e.g., Seager, 2018; Schaffer, 2010; Barad, 2007). Ecological psychology has called convincingly into question the "natural" assumption that the individual is the fundamental locus of perception (Gibson, 1979). Relational sociology has exposed the false choice between holism/collectivism and individualism (Gergen, 2009; Crossley, 2011). And enactivist approaches to embodied and extended cognition have resulted in substantial empirical support for seeing that "the cognition–perception–action unit always encompasses artifacts in the environment, other individuals, and rich cultural practices that are irreducible to either objects or other individuals and what goes on inside their heads" (Sanches de Oliveira and Chemero, 2015: 20).

In the context of theorizing consciousness, seeing all things as arising interdependently renders reductionism implausible. If causation is ultimately always mutual, it is also network-like. A one-way reduction of the phenomenal to the physical is causally incomplete. Recognizing the ultimate reality of interdependence makes it impossible to draw a sharp, rather than a shaded, distinction between constitutive (internal) and contingent (external) relations. Indeed, it calls into question the very basis for distinguishing what something *is* from what it *is not*. As this insight is phrased in Buddhism, all things are ultimately characterized by emptiness (*suññatā*; *śūnyatā*) or the absence of any independent essence or foundational nature. The cosmos is dynamically relational "all the way down."[4]

Yet, even if we grant the veracity of the Buddha's insight into the ontological primacy of dynamic relationality, it is still not immediately evident why this constitutes an answer to the question of what determines the nature and quality of our experience. On the contrary, it would seem not to be an answer at all, implying that every event or thing is caused by everything else, thus expanding causal connections to infinity. It is far from evident why such a vision of massive overdetermination would be liberating.

The explanatory clue lies in the Buddha's two prior insights on the evening of his enlightenment. The first of these was that his life experiences were not the result of chance, destiny, or the linear operation of natural law. They were the matured fruit of his own doing, his own karma. The second insight was that the life experiences of all sentient beings are also karmically structured. No matter how deeply into the past one peers, sentient beings have all and always been implicated with one another in dramatically entangled karmic processes.

The word "karma" has come into the English language with colorations of destiny, fate, and inevitability. The Sanskrit word karma (Pali: *kamma*), however, simply means acting or doing. It is a derivative of the same Indo-European root as the English word "drama," and in keeping with this, karma does not refer, for example, to the mechanical action of wind on the leaves, branches, and trunk of a tree. Karma is meaning-laden, agent-originated action: cutting down a tree to make space for a dwelling or to carve its trunk into a canoe.

The Buddha's contemporaries generally accepted the Vedic notion that karma involves all actions being subject to recompense via a law of just exchange in a cosmic moral economy—a linear causal process by means of which violent acts necessarily beget future experiences of violence, while kind acts beget future experiences of kindness. Innovatively, the Buddha emphasized the role of volition or intention (*cetanā*), conceiving of karma as the dynamic resonance that obtains among complexes of values-intentions-actions and experiential outcomes and opportunities: a process of dramatic change open to revision from within.[5]

In effect, the Buddha's innovation was to delink karma from any transcendent moral order, conceiving of the cosmos as self-organizing: a cosmos in which order and increasingly complex kinds of conduct emerge out of interactions informed, initially, by the simple feelings (*vedanā*) of pleasure, pain, and neutrality, and then by more complex affective states, conceptual distinctions, and purposes. Rather than delivering us into destinies or fates that we deserve as determined by a fixed and external moral order, karma is the narrative process through which we set up our own experiential possibilities: the dramatically recursive working-out-from-within of emergent moral orders in which intention and values play crucial roles.

The liberating efficacy of Buddhist practice is premised on the fact that, by paying sufficiently close and sustained attention to the dynamics of our own life experiences, we can first discern which constellations of values, intentions, and actions correlate with unwelcome patterns of experiential outcomes and opportunities, and then alter those constellations. Doing so enables us to verify—as the Buddha is said to have done—that although every experienced reality implies responsibility, our lives are not scripted in advance. They are improvised dramas that are always playing out live, expressing both our values and changes in them as we respond to emerging opportunities for either reinforcing or critically redirecting our courses of action. Far from being a deterministically enforced moral order, karma consists in a spiraling process of relational elaboration through which conscious and feeling beings express their creative responsibility as they either skillfully or unskillfully revise the meaning—that is, the experiential/relational orientation—of their own presence. To see the cosmos as karmically structured is to see sentience/consciousness as irreducibly purposive and enactive.

What Is It Like to Be a Person?

The Buddha's insight into karma applied exhaustively, encompassing what were then taken to be all forms of sentient becoming. These were traditionally categorized in terms of their manner of birth: from eggs (e.g., birds, fish, and reptiles), from wombs (most mammals); from moisture (presumably small insects and worms), and by transformation (into either hellish or heavenly beings with bodies that, generally, were not materially evident to the five senses). In effect, his realization that all sentient beings are subject to karma implies having successfully experienced "what it is like" to be all manner of beings over the course of their various lengths of life, with their distinctive patterns of intentionally enacted forms of sentience.

In principle, then, the Buddha's enlightenment seems to have afforded him sufficiently deep therapeutic insight to be able to answer Thomas Nagel's (1974) neuroscience-confounding question, "What is it like to be a bat?" Alas, no such descriptions can be found in any of the Buddha's teachings, and while there are non-canonical Buddhist sources that offer accounts of animal subjectivity, these explicitly didactic tales about incidents from the Buddha's "prior lives" do so without any pretense of descriptive accuracy. In fact, if asked Nagel's question, I suspect that the Buddha would most likely have remained silent, treating it as a member of the class of questions that are not conducive to authoring one's own liberation from conflict, trouble, and suffering.[6]

Asking what it is like to be a bat may be an interesting launch pad for speculative fiction. But it is not much use as a jumping off point for either generating insights into or assessing theories of consciousness. The reason for the question's dubious philosophical utility is nicely illustrated in Franz Kafka's novella, *The Metamorphosis*. In it, the protagonist, Gregor Samsa, awakes one morning to find that he has been transformed into a monstrous, human-sized insect. For weeks, he tries to maintain his familial and daily life relationships, but his new body makes this impossible. The horror in the faces of others and the palpable suffering caused to his wife and children lead him, in the end, to starve himself to death and release them from their confused feelings of responsibility and repulsion. We can imagine what it is like to be an insect or a bat, but we can only do so as ourselves—humans born male or female in a specific historical and cultural context, with our peculiar habits of thought, feeling, and action. We are not generic beings and cannot be generically conscious.

This is not to deny that counterfactual speculation can be useful, especially in clarifying conceptual commitments. This is what underwrites the rampant discussion of mindless zombies, scientists deprived of color-experience, and neuronal-level thought manipulation in consciousness theorizing circles. But the utility of such speculations is limited to pruning the probability space of consciousness theory—a labor that is valuable only to the extent that grounds are assumed for granting ontological relevance to such logically inspired determinations of what consciousness could *not* be. These are not grounds, however, on which to generate and nurture positively pragmatic and liberating insight.

The Buddha insisted on taking this seriously and focused directly on challenging our unexamined convictions about what it is like *to be a person*. For the most part, we assume that we have immediate, direct, and incontrovertible access to what it is like to be ourselves. In addition, we assume that this knowledge is complete in each moment of experience. These are the unannounced assumptions embedded in asking Nagel's leading question and in framing the "hard problem" of consciousness or what William Seager (2016) more descriptively labels the "generation problem." To get clear of these assumptions, the Buddha undertook and taught the practice of sustaining meditative attention to the dynamics of our own experience.[7]

The Five *Skandhas* and the Absence of an Abiding/Substantial Self

While an extended discussion of Buddhist meditative methods is not possible here, it is useful to take account of a few of the main features of the foundational practice of mindfulness (*satipaṭṭhana*; *smṛtyupasthāna*). In traditional Buddhist contexts, mindfulness is practiced, for example, with respect to bodily actions, postures, and sensations; to feelings of like, dislike, and neutrality (*vedanā*); or to the shifting focus and qualitative tenor of one's thoughts (*citta*). In each case, the aim is to be attentive to their phenomenal arising, abiding, and passing away in an alertly sustained mode of remembering presence (*sati*; *smṛti*). The aim of doing so is to be extensively present without-self (*anattā*; *anatman*), allowing the position from which *one has* visual sensations or feelings of attraction or thoughts to dissolve into seeing, feeling, and thinking in the absence of a seer, feeler, or thinker.

With considerable theoretic ramifications, this can be seen as verifying the possibility of going "behind" the Cartesian certainty that "I think, therefore I am." What mindfulness practice reveals is that thinking, feeling, perceiving, and acting can all occur without-self. Or more generally stated, agency is not predicated on the presence of an abiding agent. Nagel's question about what it is like to be a bat (or a human, for that matter) conceals the internal complexity of consciousness. Rephrased, the more fundamental questions would be variants on "What is hearing like?" or "What is thinking like?"—questions that steer clear of "to be [a certain kind of entity]" and the ontological impositions implicated therein.

For most of us, it is not easy, even conceptually, to delink agency from the assumed primacy of an experiencing individual—a spatially bounded, singular, and internally undifferentiated presence or self. Mindfulness meditation reveals that agency suffuses relational dynamics, congealing within them variably over time, resulting in *patterned densities* of agentive activity, not strictly localizable identities. Recognizing this is crucial to theorizing consciousness as relational. Against the dualist claim that an independent and abiding self or soul exists that observes and acts on and through a body—but also against the physicalist claim that mind reduces to body—mindfulness practice reveals the interdependent origination and ultimate emptiness (*śūnyatā*) of both mind and body.

Buddhists have traditionally maintained that sustained attention to our experiential presence does not reveal an abiding subject/self, but rather five distinct "aggregations" (*khandha*; *skandha*) of events, none of which can exist independently of the others—bodily events (*rūpa*); feelings (*vedanā*), most basically, of liking, disliking, neutrality; perceptions (*saññā*; *saṃjña*), involving seeing, hearing, smelling, tasting, touching, and thinking; volitional compounds or patterns of enaction (*saṅkhāra*; *saṃskāra*), both active and habitual; and events of consciousness (*viññāṇa*; *vijñāna*) or collating and discriminating among the relations occurring among the six sense organs (eye, ear, nose, tongue, body, and mind) and their relevant sensible objects.[8]

No matter how diligently we investigate these aggregations of events associated with personal presence, we find nothing like an unchanging, underlying substance or entity. All that is evident are ever-shifting compositions of bodily, emotional, perceptual, volitional, and collative and discriminatory occurrences—a play of interdependent phenomenal relations. These may naively seem connected to a central "me," the lasting "owner" of experience. But this ownership-claiming "me" is nowhere to be found in experience. The five basic modes or aggregations of personal presence are like clusters of asteroids spinning in a shared orbital dance around an "empty" center of attentive gravity. The self is only virtually, not actually, present.[9]

Consciousness and Karma: Sentience in Context

It is important to recall that the purpose of realizing presence without-self is not to shed explanatory or metaphysical light on the nature of consciousness, but rather to open prospects for enhancing the quality of our consciousness and our experiences as persons in interdependent community with others. The practice of being present without-self is intended to be liberating: a direct means for realizing freedom from the necessity of being *subject* to conflict, trouble, and suffering (see, e.g., Bāhiya Sūtta, *Udana* 1.10). It is a means to freedom from any form of compulsory presence. Yet, determining that the subject of experience—the self—obtains only virtually does have metaphysical implications, as does the relational or interdependent origination of consciousness. We can initially approach these implications metaphorically.

The traditional Buddhist metaphor for the relations among the five *skandhas* is that they are akin to those among bundles of recently harvested stalks of grain, angled upright so that their tops rest against one another. Remove any one of the bundles and the remaining four will fall to the ground. Thus, while bodily, affective, perceptual, habitual, and conscious occurrences can be usefully bundled (aggregated), none of these aggregations has either ontological or phenomenal priority in what it is like to be a person. Consciousness is not contained *in* the body, though it is qualitatively and causally constrained by it. Likewise, perceptions depend on and are shaped by affective occurrences, which are dependent on bodily events and volitions, and so on in all manner of crosscutting combinations. The *skandhas* are not component *parts* of *being* persons; they are mutually articulating *densities in the relational becoming* of human presence.[10]

Consciousness, considered as one of the five *skandhas*, is a conceptual convenience—the result of differentiating among various dimensions of sentient presence for the therapeutic purpose of affecting sentient presence. Yet, granted the insight that all things arise and persist interdependently, there is a sense in which consciousness must be granted a certain privilege since therapeutically useful distinctions like those among the five *skandhas* are products of consciousness. The metaphysical implications of this can, again, be intimated metaphorically.

The Buddhist use of recently harvested, bundled, and stacked grain as a metaphor for what it is like to be a person echoes the metaphorical uses of seeds, roots, and fruits in traditional Buddhist explanations of the workings of karma. In brief, the experiential outcomes and opportunities that come with the maturation of abiding patterns of values, intentions, and actions are referred to as *phala* or "fruit"—literally, fruit that is ripe to the point of bursting. Responding to these outcomes and opportunities is, in effect, a "seeding" of sense fields (*āyatana*)—the domains of actionable possibility associated with each of the six senses. When conditions are right, these seeds (*bīja*) of action-propensities sprout and grow, nourished by roots (*mūla*) of intentionality (*cetanā*) that can be either *kuśala* (skilled, wholesome, virtuosic) or *akuśala* (unskilled, unwholesome, non-virtuosic). According to early Buddhist thought, it is these karmic seeds that inform the development, not only of the six sense organs and the five *skandhas*, but also the relational environments within which our value- and intention-qualified sentience and agency are further expressed. Asking which comes first in being humanly present—genes, the body, its environment, or phenomenal experience—is like asking whether seeds are the precursors of plants and their fruits or the products of them. These differentiations are *intrinsic* to plantlike presence. Plants are not spatially and temporally localizable things. They are nonlocalizable processes. The same is true of human presences.

These metaphors suggest that, while our intentions are proximal causes of our lived experience and of the circumstances in which we enact our sentience, our lived experience is not an "effect" or "result" of intention in the way, for example, that a meal results from following a cookbook recipe. A cooked meal will not recursively alter the recipe in the cookbook. Fruits and grains embody generationally gained and intergenerationally transmitted information about environment-responsive and environment-shaping organic conduct: they are "recordings" of the dynamics of productive interdependence. Thus, a pear embodies the organic creativity of a specific pear tree within a community of cross-pollinating and chemically communicating pear trees, each functioning as an adaptive nexus of environmental exchanges entwining soil, rain, sunshine, and foraging animals and insects.[11] A pear is both the result and bearer of a lineage of arboreal intelligence. In much the same way, our karma is the generative "fruit" of value- and intention-inflected action within emerging and differentially evolving relational networks. It embodies and reproductively enacts our histories of sentient responsiveness while conserving acquired potentials and proclivities for both rehearsing and revising those histories.

Like all metaphors, these Buddhist metaphors are cantilevered out over the familiar into the unknown. In this case, they are cantilevered out over what was familiar to premodern and pre-scientific audiences. What they point toward, however, are the storing and structuring functions of reproductive "memory"—processes that today might be pointed toward with metaphorical reference to genes, memes, and temes.[12] As we will see in considering the suggestion that basic cognition is predictive (Clark, 2016), what these contemporary and Buddhist metaphors are intended to make evident is the fact that "while memory serves as the ability to recall previous experiences, recall itself is not solely directed toward the past, but is guided by the present for the service of the future" (Ofengenden, 2014: 42). What it is like to be a person, in a karmic cosmos, is to be a sentient presence responsively embodying and enacting values that are intended to qualitatively affect the (social/conceptual as well as natural) environmental contexts of further sentient action.

Buddhist insight into karma directs critical attention to the recursively evolving relationships among qualities of agency (values and intentions) and contexts of embodiment (environmental outcomes and affordances): the dynamic continuity of the "space of causes" and the "space of intentions/reasons." In formulating the "hard problem" of consciousness and asking whether consciousness is causally effective or not, a hard distinction is provisionally posited between sentient intentionality/agency and physical causality. But doing so is *enacting a decision*, not *making a discovery*.[13] In contrasting ordinary experiences of the apparent duality of the mental (agency/mind) and the physical (causality/body) with meditatively realized experiences of their nonduality, what is revealed is the disparity of *local* and *global* scales and horizons of relevance.

The nondual disparity of the local and global can be explicated or unfolded through a topological analogy. Most theorizing about consciousness rests on prepositional convictions about the relation of mind/consciousness and body/world. This is most evident in the description of first-person investigations as introspection—a process of peering-*inward* in contrast with peering-*outward* (as if) *through* our bodily senses when engaged in observing the world *around* us. In keeping with this "natural" assumption of prepositional boundaries, traditional dualism takes mind/consciousness to exist *outside* the body or *apart* from physical reality; materialist reductionisms and epiphenomenal dualisms assume that the origins of mind/consciousness are to be found *in* the body or at least *in* the physical world; neutral monism and dual aspect theories regard mind/consciousness and body/world as being intimately *beside* one another, like the interior and exterior surfaces of a hollow sphere. Buddhist meditative insight into nonduality reveals the contingency and merely conventional nature of the prepositional distinctions presumed by these ways of theorizing consciousness.

The relational nonduality of mind/body or consciousness/world is analogous to the spatial relations exemplified by a Klein bottle: a topologically peculiar "object" that appears *locally* to have both an interior and exterior surface, but that is folded through a fourth dimension of space so that its interior and exterior become *globally* indistinguishable. Or to take a simpler object, mind/consciousness and body/world are related like the locally different, but globally continuous sides/edges of a Möbius strip—a three-dimensional object that has only one edge and one side.[14] Consciousness is an analogous but always dynamic "folding" of sentient organisms and sensed environments. Seen karmically, sentient organisms and sensed environments are interdependent *implications of consciousness*.

Consciousness as Differentiation

This use of "implication" is ambiguous, but apt. To implicate is to "fold into." Yet, implications are also significant ramifications that indicate or "point toward" values and meaning. In one sense, both sentient organisms and sensed environments are folded into or enfolded by consciousness. But in another sense, sentient organisms and sensed environments can be seen as the explication or unfolding of consciousness—significations of its presence, as well as indices of its significance or expressions of its meaning.

In keeping with this ambiguity, "consciousness" is used in two distinct, discursive registers in Buddhist contexts. In one, consciousness is a qualitative variable that—along with intention, affect, and attention—is *worked with* as a medium of meditative practice. In the other, consciousness is recursively *reflected upon* to clarify what it does for the purpose of dissolving effort-preempting doubts about the efficacy of Buddhist practice.

In the earliest Buddhist texts, in which consciousness is discussed as one of the five *skandhas*, emphasis is placed on confirming that the presence of consciousness does not support claims about the existence of an abiding self or soul. Consciousness is glossed simply (but fruitfully) as that which emerges with the "contact" or interaction (*phassa*; *sparśa*) of sense organs and sense objects/environments. Granted a physicalist bias, it is natural to interpret this as a conjunction or coming together of disparate and preexisting elements. Consciousness is then interpreted as the contingent result of contact. But granted the ontological primacy accorded to relationality by the Buddha's enlightening insight into the inter-causality of all things, this interpretation can only be provisional (*saṃvṛti*)—a convenience or convention. Sense organs and sensed environments arise interdependently, along with consciousness. They are coeval.

Thus, visual consciousness consists in the realization/emergence of visual relations, auditory consciousness with the emergence of aural relations, and so on for gustatory, olfactory, and tactile consciousness.[15] The sixth sense consciousness, mental consciousness (*manoviññāṇa*; *manovijñāna*), consists in the realization/emergence of inter-sensory relations—a collating of relational dynamics within and among the other sensory realms as mental "objects" in relation with mind (*citta*) as an organ sensitive to them. Significantly, however, the term being translated as consciousness (*viññāṇa*; *vijñāna*) is most literally rendered as something like "differential knowing" or "divisive knowing." It is the nature of consciousness, in other words, to *differentiate*, but also to collate and coordinate. This has ambiguously epistemic and ontological significance.

Seeing all things as interdependently originated and irreducibly relational is to see that they are without-self in the sense of being empty of any abiding self-nature (*sabhāva*; *svabhāva*). The metaphysical identification of network causality (interdependence) with emptiness (*śūnyatā*) serves, among other things, to ensure that interdependence is not understood as an external relation, but as an internal one.[16] Interdependence is always also interpenetration. Relationality is thus *not* to be understood substantially as a kind of ontological-causal ground or that to which "everything" finally *refers*. Rather, in keeping with the karmic insight that all experienced realities imply responsibility, stressing the relationality and emptiness of all things points reflexively back to the relation-constituting and affective-evaluative nature of consciousness.

Distinguishing between "this" and "that"—or between what something "is" and what it "is-not"—is not an act of *discovery*. It is an act of interest- or value-expressing *disambiguation*. That is, the differences among things are not intrinsic to them but rather to our interactions with them. To use the rhetorical trope at the heart of the Mahayana Buddhist text, the Diamond Sutra: things are not "things," we only refer to them as "things." The boundaries that obtain among things are "illusions" of perspective, like the horizons we see as we turn slowly in a circle on a beach. Rather than revealing absolute features of the world, these boundaries and distinctions reveal features of our own difference-engendering presence—a history of disambiguation or marking off what we have elicited relationally as actionable and as valuable. *Matter is the definition of a point of view*: a horizon of relevance. That is, *what exists for us is what matters to us*.

There is a sense, then, in which a karmic understanding of what affects the quality of our consciousness paradoxically entails granting consciousness the status of "first among equals" in relation to the other *skandhas*, including the physical body. This status can be interpreted epistemologically: the limits and character of the known are unavoidably the limits and character of consciousness. Alternatively, it can be interpreted metaphysically: in the absence of what consciousness *does*, there are no objects known, no selves, no experiences, no worlds.[17]

From a nondualist Buddhist perspective, while it is valid to see consciousness as the *product* of sense organs and sense objects, it is just as valid to see consciousness as their *producer*. Or to move further away from the language of entities in interaction, the "contact" or "interaction" of the sensing and the sensed is simply the *differential opening* of sensory relations. Put in the context of realizing that *what exists* for us is *what matters* to us, this amounts to seeing consciousness as manifesting the nonduality of all things, where nonduality does not entail a reduction to some essential sameness, but rather mutual implication. All things are "the same" insofar as they "exist" only in differing significantly from one another. Each thing *is* what it *means* for all others.

In sum, consciousness can be seen as the source and substance of *differentiating* the phenomenal and the physical. Yet, in keeping with Buddhist teachings of interdependence and emptiness, "substance" must be understood ambiguously as "mattering" both materially and immaterially—that is, as a processual continuity of "matter" and "what matters." Consciousness can thus be invoked as the substance of both the phenomenal and physical in much the same sense that we can invoke the "substance" of a conversation—the communicatively intimate sharing that materializes in/as/through the words, gestures, expressions, and attentional dynamics of those involved. Consciousness is what is *meant* by the differentiation of the phenomenal and the physical.[18]

The Recursive or Cyclic/Spiral Nature of Consciousness as Differentiation

The teaching of the five *skandhas* derives from and is intended to direct critical attention to what it is like to be a person. It is, in a sense, a summary of evidence rather than an explanation of how it is that this way of being present comes to be. The so-called Twelvefold Chain of Interdependent Origination (*dvādasanidānāni; dvādaśanidānāni*) offers a more expressly analytic and causal modeling of what it is like to be humanly present. The twelve links are: [1] ignorance (*avijja; avidyā*); [2] patterns of enaction (*saṅkhāra; saṃskāra*); [3] consciousness (*viññāṇa; vijñāna*); [4] name/form or mentality/materiality (*nāmarūpa*); [5] the six sense realms (*āyatana*); [6] contact (*phassa; sparśa*); [7] feeling (*vedanā*); [8] desire (*taṇhā; tṛṣṇā*); [9] attachment (*upādanā*); [10] becoming present as a "being" (*bhava*); [11] birth (*jāti*); and [12] old age and death (*jarāmaraṇa*).

Although referred to as "links" in a "chain" of human becoming, based on a literal reading of *nidāna* as "tying down," the Buddhist use of *nidāna* carries connotations of a ground or foundation; an occasion; a source, origin, or cause; and a reason or motivation. In keeping with these wider connotations, the sequence of the twelve *nidāna* was understood traditionally as a nexus of interlinking factors in human presence that is "tied down" by conflict, trouble, and suffering. There were two major interpretations. Most commonly, these twelve factors were seen as a cyclic or spiral sequence from the pre-conception factors that result in birth, through those that factor into the quality of lived experience, and then on into old age and death. But it was also seen as a structuring of conflicted presence, no matter how briefly experienced: the dynamic structure of phenomenal coming to be, persisting, and dissolving.

In this sequence of conditioned arising, contact (*sparśa*) is occasioned/motivated by the relational dynamics occurring within and among the six sense realms (each with its distinctive kinds of sense organs and sensed objects) and is the proximate condition for the presence of affectively toned feelings (*vedanā*). Here, contact occurs among the twelve sense realms (*āyatana*)—comprising the sense-organs or faculties (*indriya*) and their environmental or objective supports (*ālambana*)—to which there then emerge affective responses. In other words, consciousness is depicted as implicit to sensory relations in ways that occasion/motivate affective evaluations of experience that subsequently contribute to anticipating and acting in attachment to various kinds of sensory gratification, the results of which then condition our experiences of maturing, growing old, and dying.

But consciousness is also depicted as the explicit condition for the mind/body system of ambiguously phenomenal/physical presence (*nāmarūpa*)— the co-arising of what matters (*nāma*) and matter (*rūpa*)—that conditions the unfolding of relational dynamics occurring within the six sense realms. That is, consciousness is implicit to the dynamics of the sense realms that are elicited and conditioned by the ambiguously immaterial/material, mind/body complex.

Thus far, this account of "what it is like" to be a person would appear to have considerable family resemblances with Whitehead's relational ontology and theory of feelings. For Whitehead, the actual occasions that constitute our experience are not preexisting entities or things that we encounter extrinsically; they consist in the processual concrescence of feelings. "Actual entities are drops of experience, complex and interdependent" (1929/1985: 18), apart from which there would be only bare nothingness. That is, they are *significances* that remain stable over the course of an event or series of events. As in Buddhism, matter is defined by what matters.

But Whitehead's process ontology ultimately entails linear causal relations that contrast sharply with Buddhism's karmic-relational ontology—one that entails seeing, not only that each thing *is* what it *means* for all others, but also that each thing is both the cause of and caused by all other things.[19] Hence, Whitehead's claims that "consciousness presupposes experience, and not experience consciousness" (1929/1985: 53), and that an infrastructure of eternal objects of pure potential is necessary to support the processes through which actual entities are concretely realized (1929/1985:149). For Whitehead, this process in its entirety depends on God as the ultimate origin of both all order and all novelty. There is no such transcendental source of becoming in the Buddhist cosmos.

On the contrary, the first two "links" in the structure of human becoming—the "precursor" conditions of consciousness—are as far from a transcendent source of order and novelty as imaginable: ignorance and intention-consolidating habit formations. Traditional interpretations of these "links" were keyed decisively to supporting the therapeutic pursuit of freedom from conflict, trouble, and suffering. But a more theoretic interpretation is both possible and valuable. In what way is consciousness—that is, in what way is what is *meant* by the differentiation of the phenomenal and physical—conditioned by ignorance and intentionality?

Therapeutically, ignorance means not knowing how conflict, trouble, and suffering arise and/or not knowing how to alleviate and eliminate them. Correcting this ignorance consists in working to understand things in terms of their interdependence and emptiness, sensitive to the ways in which karma affects interdependence qualitatively, and to then revise our values, intentions, and actions in pursuit of realizing different and more liberating relational dynamics. Yet, if ignorance consists in not-seeing (*avidyā*) things as interdependent and interpenetrating, it can also be characterized as seeing things as "this" or "that" through a process of excluding whatever occurs beyond the horizons of relevance imposed by our own concepts—that is, anything that foils the expectations expressed in our persistent, habitual relationships with them. Ignorance is disambiguating as an editorial, rather than creative, act.

There is a peculiar sense, then, in which discursive knowledge is a function of the persistent ignorance of things *as* irreducibly relational—that is, as particular expressions of the interdependence and interpenetration of all things. This is one way of reading the Buddhist theory of exclusion (*apoha*), which holds that we do not perceive either universals or independent existents, but rather exclusions of specific classes of exclusion.[20] The core of the theory is that perceptions/actions/ words pick out "objects" through a kind of double negation. Thus, we do not perceive a cow, but rather an occurrence of what is "not a non-cow"—a relational consistency rather than an independent entity. Similarly, in perceiving qualities like kindness, we are actuality perceiving—that is, participating in—conduct or a manner of relating that is not unkind. The ontological point is that perception is not gathering information about autonomously objective features in the world; it is an open-ended and intrinsically purposeful distinguishing among horizons of actionable possibility. Ignorance (*avidya*) shrinks those horizons and thus limits the scope of volition or intentional presence.

The term *saṃskāra*, translated as either "volitional compounds" or "patterns of enaction," has an extraordinarily wide range of uses in Buddhist thought, straddling the boundaries often assumed, for example, between being and doing, or structure and agency. In terms we will explore in more detail later, *saṃskāra* are crucial material/immaterial features of the *infrastructure* of human consciousness. In the context of the Twelvefold Chain, *saṃskāra* is often glossed as "karmic formation"—a consciousness-constraining sedimentation of intent (*cetanā*), a solidification of dispositions for acting in and on the world. Consciousness in this sense emerges as conditioned by evaluation-expressing wishes or desires.

In Buddhist contexts, this conditioning of consciousness by volitional dispositions is tied back to the therapeutic aim of liberating ourselves from conflict, trouble, and suffering. But regarded theoretically, it serves to illuminate key features of what consciousness *does*: opening, enacting, exploring, and differentiating qualitatively among relational dynamics. Rather than representing or mapping an existing realm of autonomously existing entities and processes, the fundamental "function" of consciousness is realizing progressively valuable realms of actionable possibility.

This description aligns well with a countercurrent to the cognitivist mainstream that has been gaining strength over the last quarter century—a movement to close the gap between mind/subject and matter/object by seeing mind as *embodied* (involving other-than-neural bodily structures and processes), *embedded* (functioning in conjunction with the environment), *enacted* (manifesting in action), and *extended* (ramifying in beyond-the-body environments). This "4E" countercurrent calls into question the hard ontological line between the phenomenal and the physical that defines the "hard problem" of consciousness.

But, as David Hutto and Erik Myin (2017) have pointed out, this countercurrent has not wholly elided foundational, naturalist/realist assumptions about causation. It continues to be mind and its putative contents and relationship to matter that are presumed in need of explanation, not matter or the bifurcation of mind and matter from some nondual precursor.[21] A major feature of Hutto and Myin's approach is to see basic mind/cognition occurring without representational content and across a range of timescales due, in part at least, to the fact that mind/cognition is always world-involving. The most fundamental activity of mind/cognition is engaging the world, not depicting it. Mental life consists in "ongoing meaningful engagement between precariously constituted embodied agents and the worlds of significance they bring forth in their self-asserting activity" (Di Paolo, Cuffari, and De Jaegher, 2018: 20).

A significant body of (both direct and indirect) empirical support is emerging in the fields of cognitive science and neuroscience, artificial intelligence, and robotics for a radically enactive approach to mind/cognition. At the heart of this work is the thesis that, rather than "inference engines," minds are best understood as "action-oriented engagement machines" doing the informational work of predictive processing. The most basic cognitive concern may not be discovering or inferring *what* things are, but rather discerning *how* things are evolving through "world-engaging anticipation" (Clark, 2016). This, however, entails rethinking the temporality of consciousness—a rethinking for which Buddhism offers significant resources.

Differentiation as Anticipation: A Semantically Complex Concept

Shifting the roots of cognition from inquiries aimed at determining "what exists" to discerning "what comes next" accords well with Buddhist theorizing about karma and the volitional conditioning of consciousness. But there are some significant differences. These can be made usefully evident by unpacking the semantic complexity of asking "what comes next?"

For those who adopt a "predictive processing" account of cognition, it essentially expresses a concern with *forecasting*. The basic occupation of minds is building an increasingly precise causal map of "how things are changing"—a process of modeling in which what matters most is *accuracy:* reducing the surprise of unexpected events. One advantage of a forecasting approach to anticipation is that it potentially can be used to reconcile informational and computational theories of mind with enactive theories, bridging between efforts to establish content-focused truth conditions and action-focused success conditions.[22]

But in the context of embodied presence within complex systems, both organic and social—systems in which success involves responding to change dynamics that are in principle unpredictable—the process of anticipating what comes next would seem necessarily to involve preparing or readying. In such contexts, at any given moment, the basic occupation of minds may not be forecasting, but rather responsive attunement—a process of intuiting relational scenarios or likelihood assemblages and readying for response to them. Then, what matters most is not accuracy, but *adaptability*: expanding relational freedoms by enhancing responsive fitness.

Adaptability and responsive fitness further imply, however, an evaluative orientation toward what might or could occur—a way of being present in which *preference has precedence over reference*. This is what is pointed toward in emphasizing the role of feelings (*vedanā*) and volitional dispositions (*saṃskāra*) in conditioning or shaping consciousness—an emphasis which suggests that anticipation has the basic purpose of *affecting* relational dynamics. In this case, the basic occupation of mind is determining what matters most in seeking and securing what matters most: progressively *optimizing* both experiential/situational *outcomes* and *opportunities*.[23]

In the karmic context of commitments to enhancing qualities of sentient presence, what is most salient in developing a holistic understanding of consciousness is not the forecasting mind or the adaptive mind, but rather the creatively affective mind. This follows from the fact that sentient presence is not simply world-involving; it is world-eliciting or world-evoking. Consciousness/mind is not primarily or fundamentally involved in mirroring nature, but in opening new action environments—new spaces of actionable possibility. Anticipation is thus only secondarily about mapping causal relations. To see all things as relational, and to see relationality as karmically configured and qualified, is to see that values, intentions, and actions are as structurally and dynamically integral to the world as are material laws of nature.

Consciousness as Relationally Extended: Time Matters

While Buddhist theorizing of the interplay among the body, feelings, perceptions, volitional complexes, and consciousness is consistent with contemporary theorizing of mind and cognition as embodied, embedded, enacted, and extended, the karmic configuration of phenomenal and physical dynamics requires a much more radical extension of consciousness, temporally as well as spatially. Buddhists, however, have not been of a single mind about how best to take the temporality of consciousness into theoretical account.

Setting aside considerable historical or doctrinal detail, two main approaches can be identified. The first approach seems to have developed out of phenomenologically attuned meditation practices in which sustained attention (*manasikāra*; *manaskāra*) is paid to the play of mental events occurring with moment-to-moment modulations in the interplay among unimpaired sense organs and their respective sensory objects and environments. While the therapeutic end in view of this approach was to know what determines whether a given moment of experience is conducive to conflict, trouble, and suffering, consonant with the teaching of being without-self, it depended methodologically on realizing the impermanence of all things and thus had a decidedly analytic or "smallist" in flavor.

In brief, this "smallist" approach to the temporality of consciousness revealed that while experience is apparently continuous, it turns out on meticulously close observation to be discontinuous or composite. Experience comes in "chunks." When attended to finely enough, the mind's continuous stream or current of experience (*citta-santāna*; *citta-saṃtāna*) dissolves into a sequence of discrete experiential "moments" of origination, persistence, and dissolution. It was much debated whether these are three phases of a single moment or distinct moments of experience, as well as whether every "moment" (*kṣaṇa*) occurs over the same "amount" of time. Stated in contemporary measures, the early Buddhist consensus seems to have been that individual "moments" of sensory "contact" last between 0.13 and 13 milliseconds.[24]

This perceptual approach to the temporality of consciousness accorded well with the basic Buddhist teaching that the practices of seeing all things *as* impermanent and empty of any abiding self-nature or fixed identity were fundamental to discerning and dissolving the patterns of conditions that result in *duḥkha*. It also offered a means of elucidating how perception—the only reliable source of knowledge granted the "sensory" nature of mental consciousness— could afford useful knowledge about the causes of *duḥkha* by revealing the architecture of mental factors (*caitta*) qualifying each moment of experience and their immediate (causal) antecedents.

In the context of explaining the operation of karma, however, momentary theoretical approach (*khāṇavāda*; *kṣāṇavāda*) had important shortcomings. Although it is easy enough to explain any experiential sequence as expressing a linear causal relationship through which each moment is conditioned by the immediately preceding moment and then conditions, in turn, the immediately succeeding moment, such a continuous causal account cannot account for karmic causation. The experiential fruits of intentional activity are almost never immediate. They take time to mature, and they ripen only when an appropriate network of causes and conditions obtains. That is, although every experience is conditioned by what has happened immediately prior to it—hence the possibility of a linear causal "explanation" for any given event—there must also be causes that mature over time (*vipāka-hetu*) to account for the ripening of the fruits of specific actions at one time rather than another. The workings of karma require some form of nonlinear or discontinuous causation. Why things happen cannot be explained exhaustively in terms of immediately preceding conditions. The experiential present is an *indeterminate implication* of past and future occurrences involving both mechanistic, "bottom-up" causality and narrative or dramatic "top-down" causality.[25]

The second approach to the temporality of consciousness might be referred to as processual and seeks to account for how current patterns of experiential outcomes and opportunities can be affected by intentional activities that took place minutes, days, months, years, and even multiple lifetimes previously. While also keyed to therapeutic concerns about how patterns of values-intentions-actions affect experiential outcomes and opportunities, in this approach concerns extend to include the effects of actions undertaken at bio-environmental and social timescales, and considerations of how qualities of consciousness can be transformed consistently over time. Explaining the operation of karma is crucial to explaining how karma can be altered or alleviated and thus how enlightening practice is possible.

Time Zones: The Horizons of the Sensory Present

Contemporary theorizing of consciousness, like the first-person theorizing that led to early Buddhist views on the momentariness of experience, has been shaped crucially by empirical—but, in this case, third-person—investigations of perception. In keeping with the general bias toward physicalist reduction in the natural sciences, these investigations have also similarly focused on very small timescales, in this case to clarify causal connections among neural events and to establish convincing correlations between them and the sequencing of phenomenal events. As we will see in Chapter 5, one of the upshots of these laboratory experiments involving brain imaging and stimulation has been to shed doubt on the role of consciousness in sensorimotor relations, including evidence reductively interpreted as proving that, instead of determining action, consciousness invents explanations for it.

Yet, one of the implications of both 4E theorizing and the Buddhist model of sense modality specific consciousnesses is that there cannot be single timescale at which to investigate the rudiments of first-person phenomenal experience.

Each of the senses operates at a distinctive timescale. Consider vision. From an information-processing perspective, visual perception has a time-space "event" horizon set by the speed of light—roughly 186,000 miles per second. Auditory perception has a similar horizon under normal atmospheric conditions of roughly 1,125 feet per second. Hence, we see the flash of distant lightning much earlier than we hear its associated thunderclap. Tactile and gustatory perception has a time-space event horizon set by the speed of nerve signal conduction or around 300 feet per second, while olfactory events have indeterminate time-space horizons, being based on inhaling airborne scent-effecting molecules that may have been moving about for minutes or hours.

In addition to these timescale differences among sensory modalities, there are further issues with the time variability of neural processing. For example, roughly 150 milliseconds will pass between the time a trained sprinter receives sensory input from the starting pistol and the time he or she leaps explosively out of the starting blocks. In contrast, several frightened seconds might pass between awakening in the middle of the night to see an eerily floating shape on the other side of the room and determining that is not a ghostly intruder but a shirt hanging over a chair. Perception is not instantaneous and is not parsed in identical units of time across the six sensory domains.

From the perspective of both action-focused Buddhist theorizing about consciousness and contemporary enactivist theories of mind, however, these physically determined constraints on the *perceptual timescale* of sentient presence are much less relevant than are variations in the temporal horizons within which normal sensorimotor coupling occurs—variations in the *enactive timescale* of consciousness. At the very least, the collative work of the sixth, cognitive consciousness requires a durable or lasting presence to encompass the time horizons of the other five sense consciousnesses.

Regardless of whether it is in the context of first-person or third-person investigations, theorizing about what consciousness does is unduly constrained and/or distorted by a disproportionate emphasis on sensory response times. Except in the context of certain kinds of meditative training or scientific experiment, consciousness is not generally preoccupied with carrying out near-instantaneous tasks or establishing the momentary contours of mental events. This suggests the importance of studying consciousness "in the wild" (Hutchins, 1995). Even if it is allowed that near-instantaneous events are somehow *rudimentary* to consciousness, it does not follow that they afford significant insight into what consciousness is or does—or at least no more so than examining the tips of a tree's roots helps to explain the nature or the purpose of its trunk, branches, leaves and fruit, or its ecologically situated presence and persistence.

Granted this, there would seem to be limited merit in research that aims to clarify and solve the "hard problem" of consciousness by investigating the nature and causal origins of qualia: the introspectively accessible and fleeting phenomenal/mental events that typically are assumed to be the (at least nominally) discrete rudiments of conscious presence. Typical examples of qualia are the red of a rose blossom or the steely ring of a plucked acoustic guitar string. Despite the expenditure of tremendous intellectual and scientific resources on determining whether qualia are, for example, properties of sense data, essentially representational, reducible to neural activity, or ineffable, debates still rage, theoretical tangles have thickened rather than thinned. From both karmic and enactivist perspectives, infatuation with qualia is fundamentally misguided because, in the normal course of daily events, consciousness is never restricted to such discrete phenomenal moments. The burgundy quale of a rose reflects in the smiling eyes of the lover to whom one is displaying its opened petals in avid anticipation of softly joining lips. The ringing of the plucked string is interwoven aurally into a C-minor arpeggio intimating the opening melody of "Softly as a Morning Sunrise." In the wild, consciousness is occupied with making love or making music, not perceiving colors patches or momentary sonic events.

From an action-focused Buddhist perspective informed by the nondualist realization that each thing *is* what it *means* for all others, focusing on qualia as a way of adjudicating among theories of consciousness is like focusing on the different font characteristics of printed words as a way of adjudicating among interpretations of the nature and meaning of poetry. What poetry is and means is not to be found in analyses of the graphic character of individual letters and words, in dictionary definitions of each word, or in causal/probabilistic explanations for why one word is followed specifically by the next. Understanding a poem entails reading or listening to it many times in ways that are skillfully receptive to the diffractive interplay among its words and images, its rhythmic temporality, and its complexly crafted intent—inhabiting the poem as a significance-saturated environment in which time does not pass so much as it condenses.

This analogy suggests that understanding what consciousness does necessitates studying the *meaning* of actions in their "wild," real-world contexts. Consider the action of swinging a tennis racket to cleanly strike an oncoming tennis ball. At the sensorimotor level, studying a tennis swing requires only a modest extension of temporal scope beyond laboratory studies of response times. Tennis balls can move very quickly, crossing the court in a fraction of a second. The act of returning a serve, however, is a phase of action in the sport of tennis rather than a discrete unit, and its meaning emerges only at the temporal scale of game playing. Playing tennis involves anticipating the incoming serve, its spin and bounce, considering the position of the opponent in placing a return shot, strategically repositioning on one's own court in further anticipation of the opponent's return, and so on—all with the game-winning aim of making an unreturned shot. With well-matched and competent players, volleying might last a minute or more; winning a game might take a dozen or more minutes; winning a match might take an hour.

Yet the meaning of a tennis swing extends off the court in addition to extending temporally on it. Why are you playing tennis? To have fun? To get exercise? To earn a scholarship or a living? Because your coach inspires you or your parents insist? Do you play enthusiastically or laconically? With vigorous abandon or calculated precision? When asking what consciousness *means*, from within what horizons of relevance are we seeking answers?

Making use of Luciano Floridi's (2008b) notion of "levels of abstraction," we can say that at a biophysical level of abstraction, the temporal scope of consciousness is complexly entrained with the temporal scales of relational dynamics in the sense realms involved, as intentions are enacted, feedback received, intentions revised or sustained, and then further enacted. But the great majority of actions we undertake in the "wilds" of social, economic, political, aesthetic, and romantic relations, for example, acquire significance through systems of feedback occurring over temporal scales that encompass "events" lasting seconds to those coming into full fruition only over decades.

Theorizing consciousness relationally entails accepting that there is no natural, fixed temporal "unit" for studying or describing what consciousness does. This does not preclude there being theoretical value in recognizing that the biophysical, sensory roots of consciousness may temporally constrain consciousness. Consider again the analogy between what poetry does and means and what consciousness does and means. At one level of abstraction—the words present on a page, for instance—the meaning of a poem can be accessed by reading and reflecting on its verbal content, perhaps against some background understanding of the context for the poem's composition. Yet, if a poem was written for an intended listener, only part of its meaning is given in the words it strings together. Perhaps the greater part is in the intended reader's reception of the poem and the qualitative, relational transformation it occasions. How long does that take? How long does it take for intentional activity to result in conduct-revising, relation-qualifying feedback that recursively informs what consciousness does?

Feedback on actions in relationally complex environments occurs across a range of timescales. Dance moves prove to be graceful or conducive to stumbling almost immediately. Feedback on conduct in a "virtual," socially constructed environment like a school can be immediate (the frown of a teacher and the laughter of fellow students following a chalkboard blunder), but often takes months to arrive (in the form of a grade report mailed to one's parents). Even with actions as biophysically basic as eating, feedback can arrive nearly immediately (regurgitating ingested poison) or be extended over many months or years (as in the case of diet-induced obesity). Clearly, part of what consciousness does is correlate sensory feedback and relational dynamics across multiple and often very extended timescales, supporting—if not spurring and directing—intention-realizing learning processes.[26]

Taking this seriously means abandoning the "lights on" view of consciousness—a view expressed idiomatically when someone rendered unconscious by a blow to the head is said to have had his or her "lights knocked out." This "spotlight" view of consciousness, we now know, is profoundly at odds with empirical findings that learning (like digestion, cellular repair, and neural toning) is keyed to the diurnal cycle or, more precisely, to the circadian rhythm.[27] Indeed, every known species of life, including bacteria, is metabolically attuned to the diurnal cycle, suggesting that alternations of waking and sleeping are as old life on Earth. Sleep is required for optimizing, not only basic metabolic functions, but also such consciousness-expressing processes as remembering, learning, abstract reasoning, and emotional calibration. Given that these are part of what consciousness *does*, waking and sleeping (including both dreaming and non-dreaming sleep) are best seen as *phases of consciousness*. Consciousness is rhythmically constituted.

Here, it is illustrative to draw an analogy with music. Every piece of music includes tone sequences. But music occurs only when sequences of tones are embroidered with silence to produce sonic phrases that are then braided over time into *utterances* that convey, propose, enact, and reconfigure relational qualities and associative intimacies not found in any of their individual tones.[28] Consciousness similarly involves braiding phenomenal and material occurrences involving both presence and absence, dynamically evoking relations among sensorimotor events and memories across cycles of waking and sleeping in the ongoing materialization of *rhythms of co-implication*.

Consciousness in the wild is composition on the fly, more musical than linguistic: a process of generating and differentiating among visual, auditory, olfactory, gustatory, tactile, and mental relations, rhythmically opening environments of qualitatively evolving and intention-enacting possibilities, ambiguously deciding/discovering what "things" *are* and *mean* for one another. Experience is not originally or fundamentally a means for receiving or gathering information about the world; it is the meaning of embodying, enacting, and exemplifying values and intentions regarding the worlds we are in the process of creatively materializing.

2

Creative Anticipation: Consciousness in the Wild

Buddhist emphasis on the creative primacy of intending and valuing in what consciousness does—and the co-implication of affect (*vedanā*), sensation, perception, and cognition therein—is neatly epitomized in the Buddhist term *citta* or actively manifest consciousness. Although typically translated as "mind," *citta* refers to both the "agency" and "action" of thinking (cognition) and feeling (emotion), with a primary emphasis on their conative dimensions. More aptly translated, *citta* is "enactive heartmind."

To regard intending and valuing as constitutive of human consciousness in the wilds of social, cultural, and karmic community with others also entails seeing the anticipatory work of the enactive heartmind as irreducibly qualitative. Indeed, what has distinguished human consciousness is the extent to which its work has involved the qualitatively enriching elaboration of relational possibilities—extending the horizons of optimization by opening new realms of value, where values are understood as modalities of relational appreciation.

Thus, while all animals engage in sexual intercourse for the purpose of reproduction, humans also "make love," realizing romantic possibilities either freely or within institutional (marital) structures and norms. While all animals eat to satisfy their caloric and nutritional needs, humans have merged eating with aesthetic practices, blending tastes, textures, scents, and visual presentations in personalized expressions of culturally distinct, hospitality-expressing sensibilities and sensitivities. While all plants and animals realize basic forms of organic and mutually beneficial community, humans explore the complexities of tragic and comedic interdependence, opening spaces of fictive speculation, historical reflection, and mathematical abstraction.

In sum, what distinguishes the optimization orientation of the human heartmind is not instrumental concentration on what Hubert Dreyfus and Charles Taylor (2015) have termed *success conditions*, but rather the creative expansion and exploration of *improvement conditions*: opening new realms of relational quality and virtuosity. The spatial and temporal extensions of the human heartmind are inseparable from its sociocultural extension in acts of affective and creative anticipation.

Virtuosic (*Kuśala*) Practice: Surfing and Music-making

As a way of practically illustrating the interplay of creativity, affective presence, and responsive virtuosity in the work of human consciousness, I want to briefly consider surfing and shared music-making. Two considerations motivate this choice (in addition to my own practice of both). Surfing involves anticipating oceanic conditions that dramatically affect one's wave-riding experience, but that one cannot affect causally in turn. Surfing involves adapting to a natural, material other: responding improvisationally to agentless unpredictability. Shared music-making involves ongoing affective coordination, responding not just to objectively changing conditions, but to conditions that are being intentionally altered in value-expressing anticipation of creative opportunity. Shared music-making is purposive coordination: merging temporally extended intentions in adaptive response to an intelligently minded other, responding improvisationally to agentive unpredictability. In short, surfing and shared music-making are illustrative of solitary and shared elaborations of what matters in the coherent differentiation of sensing and sensed presence.

In both surfing and music-making, virtuosity is not something achieved *through* practice; it is an achievement *of* practice—the realization of a new kind of presence in which mind is creatively embodied, embedded, enacted, and extended. There are minimal success conditions involved—being attuned and athletic enough to catch incoming waves; being sufficiently in tune and technically proficient to play (musically) along with others rather than just (cacophonously) alongside them. But in both cases, conscious presence is attuned primarily to possibilities for improvement and relating ever more freely—realizing and sustaining a surprising and satisfying *synchrony of intentionality and causality* that I will later suggest (in Chapter 3) is crucial to the origin of both organic and sociocultural evolution.

Of course, wave-riding and music-making can be done instrumentally. In competitive environments, for example, where a primary motivation of those involved is to win, they can be engaged in as finite games that are played to finish and win: games that are rules-constrained and temporally bounded. In those cases, riding waves and playing music are focused explicitly on realizing predefined success conditions. This will typically require problem-solving innovation: the embodiment of *closed creativity* or conduct suited to achieving expected or desired ends and goals. This kind of instrumental creativity is widely evident in sentient conduct, as well as in the behavior of algorithmic agencies. But as will be argued later, this is a subsidiary and limited exercise of intelligence or adaptive conduct that is predicated on having first enjoyed the surprising and welcome results of relational improvisation. Instrumental action is predicated on more essential workings of consciousness.

We can begin to appreciate what these workings might be by considering how the *practices* of wave-riding and shared music-making are best understood as infinite games that are not played to finish or win, but rather to sustain and further enhance existing qualities of play. In keeping with their temporal openness, infinite games do not have success conditions. Instead, they are defined by ever-evolving *improvement conditions*, and playing them often requires predicament-resolving improvisation: *open creativity* or conduct that extends the horizons of what can be either anticipated or desired.

While closed creativity is positively mediated by memory, involving conscious efforts to re-experience what has already been determined to be good or desirable, open creativity is negatively mediated by memory. It entails extensions of consciousness toward an eventuality that cannot be remembered and yet is affectively anticipated as rewarding. Extensions of this kind are volitional and purposive, but they are not "intentional" in the way that the term is used in phenomenology and most discussions of consciousness. While improvising, there is nothing that consciousness is *about*. Openly creative anticipatory presence has the relational structure of metaphor—connective intent cantilevered out over the familiar into the unknown. Although remembering is involved in openly creative improvisation, it is the kind of remembering implied in Buddhist mindfulness practice—a remembering oriented wholly from the present toward what is yet to be.

While forecasting *can* be undertaken in both surfing and music-making, the dynamically complex nature of the environments in which they are improvisationally practiced renders it inapt. Open-ended improvising involves extending consciousness temporally—and thus intentionally—in a *direction*, not toward any *destination*. In practice, this means "first" subordinating forecasting to anticipatory attunement and "then" to *relationally amplifying freedoms in affective partnership*. The differences in how freedom is amplified in surfing and improvisational music-making are instructive.

Board surfing and instrumental musical improvisation are activities that involve extending consciousness through use-defined artifacts in ways that require a certain amount of physical skill and coordination. Very fit athletes can fail to catch and ride waves, and musicians with well-honed instrumental technique can find shared improvisation remarkably challenging. Relating freely in the ways needed to be able to surf or improvise musically—at least in anything but the most basic manners—requires disciplined and intelligent practice, where *discipline* is the fruit of consistent and repetition-refined effort, and where *intelligence* consists in adaptive conduct, which can be "fast" or "slow," manifesting at time scales ranging from the momentary to the evolutionary. In both cases, the proximal aim of *practice* is improving responsive immediacy and full immersion in what Mihaly Csikszentmihalyi (2008) terms "flow" or "optimal experience"—going beyond reflection, planning and calculation to realize a wholly surfing presence or a wholly music-making presence, becoming expansively conscious and yet (in Buddhist terms) entirely without-self. The return of reflective subjectivity disrupts this luminously dynamic synchrony. In surfing, the relational continuity of surfer, board, and wave environment breaks in a flubbed turn or wipeout; in music-making, the continuity of players, instruments, and sonic environment unravels into stumbling melodies or lost rhythmic drive.

Let us first consider surfing, the simpler case, in some experiential detail. Most of a surfer's time in the water is spent watching and waiting, attuned to minor variations in the horizon line and water surface color as a way of intuiting the speed and direction of incoming swell energy in relation to an unseen reef or sandbar that will lift that energy upward to the point that the elastic strength of water is reached and the wave energy breaks forward through the water that has been the medium of its transmission. Surfable waves are energy coherences that climax and fall apart as water-voiced noise. A skilled surfer senses when and where to paddle to be best positioned to drop into functional unity with that incoming energy while it is still coherent. In contrast, beginners are often "caught by" waves, trapped in whitewater turbulence and propelled out into the flats or to shore. For them, the board is a rocking and pitching object that seems to have a mind of its own, and on which a stable footing seems impossible to find.

For a competent surfer dropping into a wave, the board is not an object. It is a repertoire of relational possibilities—conditioned by board length, width, volume, fin configuration, and foil characteristics—for realizing the nonduality of attention energy and wave energy. An unridden wave is a passing event, a mere *happening*. A ridden wave is a rhythmic *occurrence*—a dancing or pulsing flow in which oceanic and attention energy sublimate into a dynamic relational whole as surfer-board-wave unite in seamless, yet symphonic expression of open creativity. Surfers like to say that only surfers know this feeling. And, true enough, the occurrence of experiential and oceanic energy in skilled surfing is unique. But improvising musicians also achieve creative synchrony; only in their case it comes with the occurrence of multiple streams of sonically expressed responsive immediacy.

Take the case of two guitarists improvising. While waves contribute to wave riding experiences as distinctive realizations of embodied, embedded, enacted, and extended mind, their contributions are passive. When musicians are improvising, their contributions actively express their readiness to affect and be affected by one another in shared appreciation of musical possibility, enacting shared intentions of expanding the horizons of musical anticipation. Unlike surfers, two guitarists embarking on free (not standards-based or harmonically specified) improvisation do not begin with a known/knowable environment. Out of shared silence, within the sonic constraints of their instruments, they can create/realize an unlimited number of musical realms. In the absence of anything to map or forecast, the musically improvising mind manifests as almost pure, affectively intent, and relationally attuned readiness. Embedded in histories of music-making, extended instrumentally into spaces of sonic possibility, and embodied in keeping with the achievements of all prior disciplined and intelligent musical practice, music-improvising minds are distinctively intent on enacting their differences *from* each other to make appreciable differences *for* one another.

What emerges with freely improvised music is a sonic/aesthetic ecology. It is the emergence, out of emptiness, of a jointly evoked, wholly shared world through the continuous and immediate coordination of values or modalities of appreciation in the absence of representation and reflection. This achievement of improvisational practice demonstrates the kind and quality of affective/responsive presence through which intentions merge and are actively cantilevered out into the unknown: the co-implication of sensing and sensed presences in shared consciousness expressing the relational structure of metaphor.

More generally stated, the practices of surfing and shared musical improvisation implicate minds in collaboratively expanding realms of possibility—exemplifying an orientation of consciousness, not toward already preferred outcomes, but toward enriched opportunities. Looking forward, in Chapters 3 and 7, it will be argued that this orientation toward enriched relational opportunity exemplifies the predicament-resolving *sentient coordination* that was prerequisite for the evolution of multi-celled organisms out of single-celled precursors, as well as for the co-evolutionary dynamics of ecosystems, and for the intention-aligning dynamics of human cultural evolution. The evolution of life has been both a "dance" of sentient presences surfing energy environments and "music" improvised in the medium of sentient relations—an elaboration of ever-diversifying rhythms of consciousness in which the human heartmind has been exemplary.

Consciousness in Conflict, Trouble, and Suffering: *Kliṣṭamanas* and *Ālayavijñāna*

That is perhaps a therapeutically inspiring vision of the world. Yet, for most of us living in the wild (increasingly urban and inequality-ridden) habitats of human becoming, coordination seems more an aspiration than a reality. What it is like to be human often seems far from liberating. We are seldom without-self. In fact, while we may not consciously choose conflict and suffering, we all too often find ourselves profoundly and distressingly entangled through them. What we mean for one another—and thus who we are—is rarely exemplary even of the modest freedoms involved in realizing affective partnerships that embody rhythmically satisfying synchronies of intention and causation. Disagreements are rife, resulting in skeins of strife that can take generations to untangle. How can this be?

This is a question that Buddhist philosophers were forced to confront. The broad outline of their answers was presented earlier. Our life experiences are maturations of the karmic fruit of abiding patterns of values, intentions, and actions, and our responses to the relational outcomes and opportunities resulting from them then further "seed" the six sense fields and their distinctive domains of actionable possibilities. When the proper conditions obtain, these seeds of experiential propensities sprout, nourished by complexes of values and intentions, the roots of which can be either *kuśala* or *akuśala* in quality. If we conduct ourselves in ways that are virtuosic (*kuśala*) and refrain from doing so in ways that are other-than-virtuosic (*akuśala*), we can avoid or at least lessen conflict, trouble, and suffering.

As is made clear by the Buddha in the Sakkapañha Sutta (*Digha Nikāya* 21), however, conflict, trouble, and suffering are ultimately markers (*lakkhaṇa*; *lakṣaṇa*) of relational disruptions and distortions caused by conceptual proliferation (*papañca*; *prapañca*) and the recursively compounding ways in which it affects corporeal, communicative, and cognitive conduct. Concepts are perceptually and emotionally articulated relational propensities that emerge and stabilize over time as the progeny of habitually enacted volitional compounds. That is, concepts are conservative in the sense of being consistency-generating. Yet, given the *apoha* theory of perception, concepts also consist in exclusions of relational possibilities, a narrowing of horizons of consideration and relevance. Concepts both refine and restrict conduct. They are thus in tacit (and at times explicit) tension with the open creativity of improvisation and virtuosic responsiveness, and often even with the intelligence involved in innovation. Concepts function as immaterial "walls" between what something *is* (what it means to/for us) and what it *could be* (what it might otherwise or in addition mean to/for us). Hence, the therapeutic emphasis in East Asian traditions of Chan (J: Zen; K: Sŏn) Buddhism on non-thinking (*wunian* 無念): realizing freedom from the boundaries of the relational norms that our concepts impose.

Most concepts are functional in the sense that they are based on previously successful efforts to navigate the unpredictable dynamics of both our natural environments and the relational wilds of human sociality. They are part of the *immaterial infrastructure* of consciousness. If situational dynamics differ sufficiently from those within which a concept originated, however, that concept can become counterproductive. In general, there are conceptual workarounds: alternative infrastructural pathways. But proliferations of the concept of self—the desire-defined subject of experience and the imputed center of dramatic (karmic) gravity around which the five *skandhas* orbit—are different. According to Buddhism, self-concepts are inherently conducive to conflicted and troubling qualities of sentient presence. Self-concepts troublingly distort what consciousness does.

Given its therapeutic roots, Buddhist theorizing about consciousness initially paid relatively little attention to the origins and maintenance of self-concepts. Emphasis was placed on facilitating insight into the positive capabilities of mindful presence—laying foundations for investigating and understanding how consciousness *should* be changing. Yet, confronted with challenges of explaining how karma operates in the absence of an abiding self to receive the experiential desserts of intentional conduct, Buddhist philosophers were compelled to address the experiential reality of self or that which is "not non-self" or "not without-self."

One of the most sophisticated responses was from the Yogācāra tradition, which added two additional domains of consciousness to the early Buddhist scheme of six realms of sensory consciousnesses: "afflicted mental consciousness" (*kliṣṭamanovijñāna*, abbreviated as either *kliṣṭamanas* or *manas*) and "storehouse consciousness" (*ālayavijñāna*). Recall that mental or cognitive consciousness (*manovijñāna*) consists in the realization/emergence of inter-sensory relations—a collating of relational dynamics within and among the other five sense realms as well as among mental objects in relation with mind (*citta*) as an organ affectively and cognitively sensitive to them. Self-consciousness (*kliṣṭamanovijñāna*) is presence attentive to changes in the dynamics of cognitive consciousness as an environment of experiential possibilities that are evaluated and enacted in terms of their consonance and dissonance with the relational histories that constitute the field or environment of the karmic, storehouse consciousness (*ālayavijñāna*)—histories expressing both *kuśala* and *akuśala* patterns of values, intentions, and actions.

Self-consciousness is understood, then, as having direct access to the relational dynamics opened by the five sensory consciousnesses, as they have been collated, categorized, and conceptualized by the sixth (mental) consciousness and then folded into the relational manifold of the eighth (karmic) consciousness. The peculiarity of the *ālayavijñāna* is that events far distant in four-dimensional spacetime can matter crucially in sequences of events that are currently unfolding across the other seven consciousnesses. Karma involves enfolding relational histories so that the event sequences and linear causalities currently shaping sensing-sensed relations are nonlinearly *focused* and *informed* by the significance of events in long-past causal/experiential locales. This informational folding or co-implication of relational histories is what the eighth consciousness does.[1]

Given its therapeutic context, Yogācāra theorizing about the seventh and eighth consciousnesses traditionally focused on the role of the seventh, subjective consciousness in bringing about the conditions for conflict, trouble, and suffering. Briefly stated, it is *akuśala* discriminatory access to the contents/workings of the *ālayavijñāna* that grounds ignorance-expressing belief in an abiding self or subject of experience, as well as independently existing world of (either objectionable or desirable) objects of experience. In contrast, *kuśala* engagement with the contents/workings of the *ālayavijñāna* grounds liberating commitment to Buddhist practice, the enlightening result of which is a transformation of the eighth consciousness into non-grasping, mirror-like, non-discriminatory awareness or knowing (*ādarśajñāna*); a transformation of the seventh consciousness into impartial awareness (*samatājñāna*); a transformation of the sixth consciousness into wisely distinguishing awareness (*pratyavekṣanājñāna*); and transformations of the five remaining sensory consciousnesses into streams of wisely-enacted awareness or knowing (*kṛtyānuṣṭhānajñāna*). In some Yogācāra traditions (especially in China), these qualitative transformations were theorized as manifestations of a nondual, non-conceptual, and thus pure ninth consciousness (Skt. *amalavijñāna*; Ch. 阿摩羅識).

For our purposes, the Yogācāra mapping of consciousness has three important implications. First, consciousness cannot be strictly located either spatially or temporally. The presence of consciousness is not digital, something that is either on or off, either here or not here. Rather, it is best conceived in terms of relational densities, including densities of experiential presence, affective feeling, perceiving, attending, remembering, and thinking. The metaphysical implications of this will be discussed later. Second, it entails recognizing that, while every sentient and intelligent presence—that is, every presence involved in affectively guided adaptive conduct—is conscious, only those with the equivalent of the seventh human consciousness are self-conscious.[2] That is, consciousness implies *agency*, but not necessarily the presence of a reflexively self-aware *agent*. Finally, this mapping makes evident that consciousness is both functionally and qualitatively differentiated. There is a sense in which engendering altered states of consciousness is constitutive of what consciousness does.

Altered States: Consciousness in Flux

We have all had the experience of a friend catching us daydreaming and having to admit that we were "miles away." Many of us have also experienced "highway hypnosis" or being so wrapped up in our thoughts that we drive for miles without any awareness of doing so. In both cases, our subjective presence in the world of visual, auditory, olfactory, gustatory, and tactile relations becomes so highly attenuated as to be next to absence. It is only with a friend's question or a change of the traffic light at the end of the highway off-ramp that we are brought back into full sensory presence. In Yogācāra terms, in cases like this the seventh consciousness is abstracted from the streams of material and sensorimotor relations taking place in the six sense spheres, and "loses itself" in self-centering, narrative browsing of the immaterial contents of the eighth consciousness.

In dreaming, abstraction from events occurring in the first five sense realms is much more complete, with those events blocked almost entirely from factoring into phenomenal dream content. During sleep, our sensorimotor systems are effectively disengaged, and our bodies are neurologically immobilized. Moreover, while dreaming involves experiential presence, it is presence without even virtual sensorimotor agency except in cases of so-called lucid dreaming when waking-typical volition is realized (or simulated) within the dream environment. Yet, as noted earlier, even when subjective consciousness is completely absent in deep and dreamless sleep, the brain continues working at 80 percent of its normal waking rate (Hobson, 2007: 437) and considerable cognitive activity is taking place, including memory processing and learning (Walker, 2017: 107–33).

From a Buddhist perspective, the passage from waking awareness into daydreaming, hypnogogic imagining, dreaming, and dreamless sleep is not one of slipping away from consciousness into relative or full unconsciousness, but rather an attenuation of attentional scope and relational densities/potentialities. Consciousness is not all or nothing. It is neither transitory nor qualitatively singular. In our natural habitats as sentient beings, we find ourselves "being conscious in the sense of being a conscious creature with a persisting field of awareness that changes across waking and sleeping" (Thompson, 2015: 65). These changes are qualitative as well as quantitative.

The variability of consciousness is apparently natural from millisecond sensory timescales to those of organic lifecycles and ecological evolution. Alterations of consciousness can be rhythmic and minimally progressive—as in the timing of waking, sleeping, and dreaming with the diurnal cycle—or they can be immediately and functionally entrained with environmental dynamics. But alterations of consciousness can also be temporally extended and directed toward opening entirely new kinds of environmental considerations. Thus, altering visual consciousness can go beyond increases in visual range or acuity, involving perhaps the addition of aesthetic dimensions to the visual relations being realized: sensitivities of the kind associated with having a "photographer's eye," for example. Tactile alteration can result in greater degrees of sensitivity to texture, but there is also the development of the kind of "touch" that enables skilled bodyworkers to feel muscle- and fascia-encoded tensions and sense how to release them.

In sum: consciousness alters intrinsically. This can be regularly and involuntarily, as occurs across the diurnal cycle of waking and sleep. Or it can be episodically unique, as when time slows immensely in an accident or stretches elastically after the ingestion of a psychotropic substance. Yet, as we have seen, consciousness also alters gradually and permanently through effortful practices like surfing and music-making and meditation.[3] At the heart of Buddhist practice is recognition that quality of effort and attention is the deciding factor in whether consciousness alters in ways that reinforce the propensities of the seventh consciousness for proliferating causes of conflict, trouble, and suffering, or that enable realizing the relational freedom of being without-self.

Attention: The Basic Resource for Purposefully Altering Consciousness

A wide spectrum of theories now exists regarding how attention and consciousness are related. These include theorizing attention as a perceptual filter for what "appears" in consciousness; as a feature-binding mechanism that knits together disparate sensory inputs; as a gatekeeper or broadcaster to working memory; and as a conductor of competitions for high-level cognitive engagement.[4] Many of these views of attention are grounded on laboratory experiments (typically focused on perception) and brain-imaging studies, and they direct considerable energy toward identifying brain dynamics that might explain experimental results and reveal at least some of the foundational neural correlates for consciousness.

What these experiments and studies have made evident is that—as in the wild of everyday circumstances—while "top-down" attentional control over the contents of awareness is possible, such control is often limited. Attention is also involuntarily redirected by unwanted emotions or by "bottom-up" sensory events. Not surprisingly, then, among the thornier conundrums addressed by consciousness theorizing are "which came first" questions about perception, attention, consciousness, and volition, and about the fundamentally causal schema of dependencies among them.

The Buddhist perspective is that these conundrums are merely conceptual. They are the progeny of the fallacy of misplaced concreteness: mistaking our abstractions and beliefs for what in fact exists. It is not the phenomena of conscious presence that are contradictory, but the ways in which we have come to differentiate them. Thus, the Heart Sutra—a single page, Mahayana Buddhist "Perfection of Wisdom" text—explicitly states that all five *skandhas* are empty of any abiding essence. Indeed, among the six sense organs, their respective sensory environments, and the six consciousnesses through which they are differentiated, none has any independent ontological status. The same is true of the factors comprised in the Twelvefold Chain of Co-Dependent Origination. Our ways of parsing or dividing up sentient presence are conveniences. They are provisional distinctions made for specific purposes. Like all words and concepts, "consciousness," "attention," "volition," "sensation," "perception," "cognition," and "emotion" are categories of exclusion and divisions among them rest ultimately on intentionally enacted patterns or markers of both salience and disregard or inattention.

Granted this, regardless of how interesting or daunting it may be to theorize distinctions made among consciousness, volition, and attention—as well as among sensation, perception, cognition, and emotion—the only therapeutically valid question is how to bring about liberating alterations in their quality. Although doing so comprehensively might be ideal, primacy must in practice be accorded to enhancing quality of attention. The reason is quite straightforward. As the American inventor, Thomas A. Edison, declared, time is the only real capital that we human beings have, and the only thing we cannot afford to lose. What matters is how we spend our time. And from this it follows, as William James noted, that our life experience equals what we have paid attention to, whether by choice or default. Ultimately, it is the focus and quality of our attention that determines what kind of returns we get on our investments of time capital. Simply stated, attention is our most precious sentient resource. Without it, we are incapable of making any significant and purposeful difference in either our own lives or those of others.

As was implied in discussing mindfulness and the realization of uncompelled presence, one of the basic aims of Buddhist practice is physical, emotional, and cognitive de-habituation. This aim can be fleshed out positively as cultivating new and more responsive qualities of presence through sustained commitment to relinquishing our personal horizons of relevance, responsibility, and readiness, doing so with the aim of progressively embodying the appreciative and contributory virtuosity needed to realize liberating relational dynamics regardless of the circumstance in which we find ourselves. Traditionally, this was conceived as a process of compassionate and wise attention training.[5]

The Buddhist term for attention (*manaskāra*; Ch. *zuoyi* 作意) implies determined concentration or resolute focus. As the Chinese translation stresses, attention is making or enacting (*zuo*) meanings/intentions (*yi*). To be a sentient (feeling/thinking) being is fundamentally to be attentive to bodily status and environmental dynamics in intentional pursuit of meaningful change. The amounts, kinds, and qualities of attention a sentient being is capable of at any given time will vary. Temporally, this is obvious across the diurnal cycle, but also across a lifespan and in the context of learning complex new skills. Attention informs and is informed by memory. But attention is also relative to current sensorimotor possibilities. Attentional quality and orientation are drastically different while playing sports and while passing days in solitary confinement. There is great natural variability in the significance-generating activity of attention.

What is most salient in Buddhist practice, however, is the recursive or reflexive alteration of attentive orientation and quality—cultivating capacities for being sustainably and keenly attentive in ways that do not lead to conflict, trouble, or suffering, and that instead free us from them, opening prospects for realizing *kuśala* relational dynamics. The basic distinction is between attention that is captured by the superficial, craving-inducing aspects of things (*ayoniśomanaskāra*; *feili zuoyi* 非理作意) and attention that is directed in ways consistent with truing relational dynamics (*yoniśomanaskāra*; *ruli zuoyi* 如理作意). Therapeutically, this marks a contrast: [1] of unsystematically or incoherently directed attention that reinforces subjective self-consciousness in ways conducive to conceptual proliferation and hence relational bondage and blockage (*prapañca*) and [2] of attention that expresses commitment to realizing virtuosically coherent patterns of presence with and presence for others.

When attention is unsystematic, intention is diffuse. When intention is diffuse, experiential outcomes and opportunities fail to cohere or hold meaningfully together. From a Buddhist perspective, the sound of a car alarm down the street or the smell of a broccoli casserole that has gone bad in the refrigerator will grab our attention, distracting us from whatever else we might be doing. But these are not karmically problematic distractions. What is problematic is being distracted in ways that result in forfeiting responsibility for our own attention since this is to forfeit our capacities for karmic revision—a forfeiture that renders us *subject* to what is occurring rather than enabling presence as an openly creative and active collaborator within it.

Importantly, the coherence of this more valued quality of attention is not a unitary function of top-down, executive intention. To be sure, concentrated attention is involved—a fact underscored by the pivotal role accorded to *samādhi* in Buddhist practice. Translated earlier as "attentive mastery," *samādhi* is more literally rendered as "placing together" and is often used to refer to a dynamically sustained state of deep concentration—a highly collected or undistracted mode of presence/awareness that is complementary to the receptively open presence/awareness that is engendered through the mindfulness practice of sustaining unobstructed presence without-self. Thus, truly coherent attention (*yoniśomanaskāra*) involves the balanced fusion of top-down directive and bottom-up receptive presence. In contrast with the exclusive potential of executive attention—realized, for example, when one is so fully concentrating on a task that one loses any sensory awareness of one's surroundings—virtuosically coherent attention involves the full integration of executive intent with non-judgmental and yet anticipatory, sensorimotor readiness. In other words, it is attention that is conducive to realizing superlatively coherent relational dynamics by virtue of sustaining responsively integrative coherence among all eight consciousnesses. Freedom of attention is foundational for freedom of intention, which is crucial to the recursively coherent and liberating alteration of consciousness.

3

Toward a Buddhist Metaphysics of Consciousness: The Sentient Expansion of the Cosmos

One implication of the Buddhist theory of consciousness I have been presenting is that all sentient beings must be accorded consciousness, though not necessarily self-consciousness. A second implication is that differences in matter and what matters—or we might say, substance and significance—are non-identical, coevolutionary twins. The presence of either is impossible in the absence of the other. Moreover, the temporal and spatial nonlocality of consciousness begs questions about its origins, especially in relation to the origins of life and the cosmos.

In keeping with the primacy of therapeutic considerations in Buddhism, little effort was traditionally expended addressing issues like the origins of the cosmos, life, and consciousness. In fact, the Buddha is depicted as dismissing such questions as having little if any therapeutic value. They are like asking about who shot the arrow lodged in one's chest, to what caste or clan that person belongs, and what his or her motives were, rather than doing what is therapeutically imperative: removing the arrow to begin healing. There are, however, both evolutionary and cosmological premises threaded throughout the Buddha's teachings that bear (at least indirectly) on the metaphysics of consciousness.

The first premise is that the cosmos is cyclic and undergoes phases of expansion/inflation and contraction/deflation over vast periods of time. Much like contemporary Big Bounce cosmologies, Buddhist cosmology presumes the cosmos to be without origin or end. In contrast with the singularity out of which Big Bang theories maintain the universe was born, Buddhist cosmology sees the earliest events in cosmos as an evolutionary pivot from contraction to expansion. This is imagined as a progressive attenuation of differences—movement in the direction of complete uniformity—that reverses or is inverted to initiate a new phase of gradually accelerating differentiation.

Granted the karmic nature of the Buddhist cosmos, this cosmic cycle of expansion and contraction can be seen as the ultimate, meaning-generating rhythm of perspective- and environment-engendering differentiation that is constitutive of consciousness. Rather than being a unitary process, this cycle was seen as playing out in three different modes—three experientially distinct realms (*dhātu*) of sentient presence, each corresponding to a different type of mentality or mind (*citta*): the *ārūpadhātu* or formless (literally, body-less) realm; the *rūpadhātu* or form (embodied) realm; and the *kāmadhātu* or desire realm.

These realms were understood to be both internally differentiated and vertically arrayed in an ambiguously cosmological/psychological hierarchy, with the formless realm constituting the environs of the most qualitatively refined, but *non-enlightened* and *non-enlightening* sentient presences. In this realm—the last to remain as the cosmos contracts toward differential rebound—four categories of presence were recognized, each corresponding with one of the meditative attainments the Buddha had experienced during the six years of ascetic training that he undertook prior to his solo retreat and enlightenment: presence in the sphere of neither perception nor non-perception; in the sphere of absolute nothingness; in the sphere of infinite consciousness; and in the sphere of infinite space. Those present in these spheres, although disembodied and existing at an utter relational minimum, nevertheless remain within the cosmic cycle of birth and death (*saṃsāra*).

Reflecting Buddhist teachings on karma and compassion, it was traditionally maintained that when a world-realm (*lokadhātu*) undergoes contraction, the environments within which sentient beings are present shrink in number, compelling what can be thought of as mass "upward migration" as the desire and form realms gradually cease to exist. Finally, sentient presence is possible only without a body or location in a realm correspondingly without extent or location. A somewhat sardonic, and yet philosophically suggestive, account of sentient presence during the period when the maximally contracted cosmos rebounds into expansion is provided in the early Buddhist Aggañña Sutta (*Dīgha Nikāya*, 27).

The sutta begins with a description of sensory presences persisting almost entirely without sensory content. Existing in complete darkness, in the absence of sun, moon, or stars, they are "made of mind, feeding on joy, self-luminous, moving through the air, and glorious." Things are good, but there is essentially nothing to do. "Evolution" begins with the unexplained appearance of sensory differentiation—the perception of nourishment that has color, flavor, texture, and smell. Partaking of this "savory earth" causes those sentient beings to lose their self-luminance, and with this the sun and the moon appear along with distinctions between day and night and among the seasons. Time becomes experientially rhythmic. These changes set in motion differentiations among sentient presences, including differences in attractiveness and lifespan, which then result in the savory earth being replaced in turn by even more flavorful and attractive fungi, creepers, and rice. At each stage, consciousness continues to differentiate in terms of how it is embodied and enacted. Sensual desires and sexuality arise, and eventually social norms and institutions develop to the point of being recognizably like our own.

This account of cosmic evolution was presented in a didactic conversation critiquing the abstract and constructed nature of caste and gender identities, and it was intended to undergird the Buddha's revolutionary creation of an intentional community, open to all, that was organized around commitments to liberating transformations of personal presence. In addition to this didactic aim, however, the Aggañña Sutta's depiction of cosmic evolution explicitly treats mind and materiality—that is, realizations of "what matters" and "matter"—as coevolving. At the point of maximal contraction, prior to the savory earth appearing like "the skin that forms itself over hot milk as it cools," sentient presence was self-nourishing, unconstrained by anything like the distinction between "here" and "there." In a quite literal sense, nothing mattered.

Anachronistically, we can interpret the appearance of external nourishment (the savory earth) as signaling the emergence of cellular boundaries and "outwardly" directed sense consciousness: the transition from non-organic to organic consciousness. The subsequent "appearance" of more complex forms of nourishment (from fungus that seemingly condenses out of the air to rice that grows only in interdependence-rich ecosystems) marks the gradual coevolution of increasingly differentiated forms of materiality and ever more finely and extensively discriminating points of view—the materialization of ever more complex patterns of intention- and values-qualified interaction. What is being described is, in effect, the coevolution of matter and what matters: the mutually informing expansion of both the space of causes and the space of intentions (reasons).

This account is at least superficially compatible with contemporary dual aspect and neutral monist theories. According to dual aspect theories, mind and matter are alternative perspectives on more basic and ultimately real entities that are in some significant sense both mental and material. According to neutral monist theories, mind and matter are distinct manifestations of a more basic substance that is neither mental nor material.[1] Yet, dual aspect and neutral monist theories are wedded to the "smallist" project of identifying foundational or basic substances or entities from which all non-basic, non-neutral entities can be variously derived. This kind of ontological hierarchy is not readily compatible with Buddhist relational ontology. To reiterate, what is "basic" in Buddhist theorizing of consciousness is the dynamic *relationality* of the sensed and the sensing, or of matter and what matters.

At the theoretical point of maximal contraction in the cosmic cycle, what remains can be described only as unqualified relational potential. The dynamics of the post-Big Bounce cosmos are not additive but rather generative. The expansion of the cosmos is not a fundamentally extrinsic process of composition measurable in units of size. It is the result of intrinsically proliferating relational potentials that is measurable only in depths of complexity. What evolves is the *intrinsic interrelatedness* of matter and what matters.

Thus, although sentience is taken to be effectively disembodied at the point of maximal relational contraction, suggesting an idealist ontological bias, this interpretation relies on equating *rūpa* with matter or physicality as such, rather than with the organic, lived body. The values and volition present in the formless realms may be maximally attenuated, but the "beings" present there are still subject to karma and continue to be at least minimally implicated in considerations of what matters, even if it is only the quality of consciousness itself. Indeed, it seems that during this phase of maximal relational contraction, much as in REM sleep when experience persists despite a neural block on sensorimotor activity, it is only *rūpa* that is entirely lacking among the five skandhas. Granted further that the rhythm of consciousness for sentient beings like us includes periods of experience-free deep sleep when crucial mental tasks are nevertheless carried out—perhaps in/by the sixth consciousness—generating abiding (recallable and reenactable) coherencies among values, intentions, actions, and experienced outcomes, it is evident that the presence of the remaining four *skandhas* does not entail an individuated experiencer or subjective presence.

Given the didactic and imagistic nature of the Aggañña Sutta, it would be unwise to attribute too much theoretical force to it. But, the evolutionary dynamics of the Buddhist cosmos nevertheless seem compatible with, for example, panexperientialist versions of contemporary panpsychist theories like that of Galen Strawson (2006), who argues that, while we know nothing of the intrinsic nature of matter, we are intimately acquainted with that of mind. Since our brains are apparently conscious, and since the matter of our brains is akin to all other matter, he argues, any realist physicalist is forced to accept that matter itself must be intrinsically consciousness-involving.

Alternatively, connections might be drawn to cosmopsychism which, like Buddhism, resists so-called smallist accounts of reality and regards all events in and all facts about the world as grounded or enfolded in consciousness-involving events and facts at the cosmic-level (Schaffer, 2010b). Further parallels might also be explored between the East Asian Buddhist teaching that all things have Buddha-nature (*foxing* 佛性)—that is, a propensity for engendering enlightening patterns of relationality—and one or another form of dispositional essentialism, according to which either some of or all the fundamental events, processes, and properties of nature are essentially dispositional (see, e.g., Ellis and Lierse, 1994; Bird, 2007). Or, finally, a consonance might be noted between Buddhism and informational ontologies according to which all things are nodes in energy-exchanging feedback networks (Sayre, 1976), such that "to be is to be an informational entity" (Floridi, 2008a: 199) and thus to be meaningfully related to all other things in ways that "have an intrinsic moral value" (Floridi, 2007: 10).

In contrast with Buddhism, however, these contemporary approaches to theorizing consciousness and mind-body relations all aim at elucidating the foundation(s) of reality. They are, at bottom, quests for certainty, even if it may be only probabilistic. In Buddhist terms, they are quests for the essential self-nature (*svabhāva*) of things. As such, they can only yield conventional, rather than ultimate truths or correctives. Buddhism's founding insight that things arise interdependently (and are thus without-self or a permanent essence) is a repudiation of such quests. As reiterated with great vitality in the Madhyamaka tradition of Mahayana Buddhism, seeing all things as arising interdependently entails realizing their emptiness of inherent natures (*svabhāva-śūnyatā*). In Yogācāra traditions, this emptiness of self-nature was theorized as threefold (*triniḥsvabhāva*): an absence of the self-nature attributed to things in our conceptualizations of them; an absence of any self-produced nature due to their interdependent origination; and the absence of the distortions that obtain whenever presence is dichotomously "split" into subject-object or sensing-sensed. Stated positively for therapeutic purposes, there are three modes of self-nature: self-nature as conceptually constructed (*parikalpita-svabhāva*), as dependent (*paratantra-svabhāva*), and as perfected or nondual (*pariniṣpanna-svabhāva*).[2]

The Buddhist Sanskrit term for that which becomes consciously differentiated is *tathātā*, typically rendered as "suchness" or "thusness." The Chinese translation, *zhenru* 真如, however, literally means "true/real as/like" and might be rendered as "true as-ness"—or the sensed/sensing materialization of *presencing as* this or that. This is, in fact, made more evident in the earliest translation of *tathātā* into Chinese, *benwu* 本無, which blends "root/origin" (*ben*) with "absence" or "being without" (*wu*), and which might be rendered as "originally without," where the implication is "without-being this or that." In short, reality is at root nondual or ontologically (and not merely epistemologically) ambiguous. Evolution, whether cosmic or organic, consists in difference-engendering processes of interdependence-qualifying disambiguation: the collapse of indefinite relational possibility into definite relational actuality in attention- and intention-articulating expansions of means to being/becoming meaningfully present.

Sentience and Evolution: Synchronous or Synonymous?

This description of the evolution of the real can be read as a middle path gesture oblique to the interweaving of arguments regarding the ultimate metaphysical status and ontological primacy of the mental/phenomenal and the material/physical—a way of cutting through the "Gordian knot" of both factual/empirical and counterfactual appeals to "reason" in discussing the nature and origin of consciousness, and the apparently intimate association (or identity) of minds and bodies. Less charitably, it might be read as nothing more than a rhetorical sidestep.

Buddhist teachings developed in the context of a pre-scientific spectrum of views on the nature and origin of the cosmos, ranging from what we would be inclined to label as resolute idealism at one extreme to no less resolute materialism at the other. As noted earlier, the Buddhist Middle Path was often described as a departure from this spectrum of views and their tenets regarding the reducibility or irreducibility of mind/mentality and body/materiality, and whether the mind persists or perishes with the demise of the body. The Aggañña Sutta is typical of responses to questions about the origins and nature of the cosmos and of sentient presence therein, reaching imaginatively back only to the didactically useful point at which sentient presence contracts to a relational/differential minimum and then undergoes a decisive inflection toward increasing relational and evaluative density and complexity. This is consistent with the general Buddhist subordination of theorizing about time, consciousness, and mind-body relations to therapeutic commitments to qualitatively altering the nature of sentient presence.

Today, metaphysical (as opposed to merely epistemological) idealism has largely been discredited and it is a scientific "given"—even among those committed to quantum mechanics—that, if there is anything in need of explaining, it is the presence of consciousness and its relation to material existence. Over the last century or two, we have zeroed in scientifically on a sufficiently comprehensive understanding of the structural/relational nature of materiality that there is no reasonable precedent for calling into question its ultimate existence or its causal self-sufficiency. While it may be metaphysically useful to ask why there is something rather than nothing at all, the stance of contemporary physical science is that the only pertinent question is why matter behaves as it does.

The metaphysically and epistemologically ambiguous stance of Buddhism is that consciousness is the reason there is something rather than nothing at all. Consciousness consists in the affective and volitional differentiation of sensing and sensed presences, without which nothing could be known about anything at all. There is no getting "behind" or "before" the mutually defining and dynamic interdependence of perspective and matter. In this, Buddhism may be seen as distant philosophical kin to quantum physics. But the insight that all sentient presence is karmically qualified entails adopting the axiological and ethical stance that what ultimately matters most are qualities of consciousness and enacted intent. In Buddhist theorizing, predictability matters much less than normativity, and explorations into origins dissolve into evaluations of orientations.

Granted these differences, it nevertheless seems possible and productive to place Buddhism in speculative conversation with contemporary science regarding the origins of sentient presence: the emergence of difference-engendering and difference-conserving points of view. Since so much current theorizing about consciousness gets hung up on determining the minimal, presumably biological conditions for experience or sentient presence, this speculative merger might usefully foster rethinking the spatial extension of consciousness in ways not unlike the rethinking of the temporal extension of consciousness that karma compels. Here, however, the concern is specifically with the minimal, karmically relevant spatial manifestation of consciousness: the "birth" (perhaps spontaneous) of sentient perspective.

In keeping with their therapeutic motivations, the Buddhist schema of six sense consciousnesses is human-biased. But there is nothing in Buddhist teachings about consciousness emerging with "contact" between sensing beings and appropriately sensible environments that prohibits expanding the realms of sense consciousness beyond the six that are pertinent for altering human consciousness to reduce conflict, trouble, and suffering. Buddhist teachings about karma are clear in granting consciousness to all beings with sense organs, including those with sense organs that are quite different from our own (e.g., insects and bats). Indeed, the Buddhist conception of sentience can readily be expanded to include plants since we now know that at least some plants respond to changing environmental conditions and foster more productive—and evidently even caring—patterns of interdependence, despite lacking anything like a nervous system, much less a brain (see Mancuso, 2018). The necessary condition for consciousness does not seem to be a nervous system, but rather the completion of a "circuit" of energy-exchanging and meaning-generating contact (*sparśa*) between a relatively autonomous sensing presence and its sensed environment—facilitating what amounts to the emergence of prediction-foiling and yet sustained patterns of relational articulation.

Life as Difference Sensing?

This raises the question of how far "down" the phylogenetic tree it is possible to claim that consciousness obtains. Sense organs are apparently ubiquitous. The photoreceptors in present-day animal eyes, the chemoreceptors on tongues, in noses, and inside bodies (where they monitor, e.g., levels of glucose, salt, and water in body fluids), and the mechanoreceptors on the skin and around muscles and internal organs can all be traced back to very primitive receptor cells found in the earliest multi-celled lifeforms on the planet. The earliest of these may be so-called stretch receptors that are sensitive to tissue tensions and that control osmoregulation and maintain constant cell volume (see, e.g., Schlosser, 2018).

Does sensitivity to cell membrane tensions and to flows of nutrients through a cell membrane constitute circuit-completing contact of the kind that signals the presence of consciousness? If so, is this equivalent to claiming that a single-celled organism is sentient? Here, a certain amount of verbal and conceptual care needs to be taken. From a Buddhist perspective, I would argue that, in addition to sensory contact, sentience minimally entails feeling or value-responsiveness (attraction, aversion, neutrality). That is, sentience is consciousness that is sensitive to what alters consciousness. Sentience involves the dynamic, qualitative articulation of sensory relations. Any living beings that filter sensory-environmental "contact" to optimize sensory circuit completion can, I think, be deemed minimally sentient. How far down toward a presumptive first Darwinian ancestor do we have evidence for lineages of adaptive optimization?

Over the last quarter century, theorizing about the transition from non-living to living molecular systems has clustered around two approaches, both of which aim: [1] to explain the earliest mechanism(s) for passing and expressing hereditary information from one generation to the next; and [2] to account for the catalytic synchronization of chemical reaction rates that enables accurate gene replication, expression, and metabolism.[3]

One approach maintains that an "RNA world" was the precursor to cell biology as we know it.[4] According to this hypothesis, RNA did double duty by both storing genetic information and catalyzing chemical reactions in primitive cells. It was only much later in evolutionary time that DNA and proteins took over those respective functions. While it appears that basic "quasi-organic" molecules can be formed by metal-based catalysis on the crystalline surfaces of minerals, and that something like systems of molecular synthesis and breakdown—that is, metabolism—could thus have existed prior to the emergence of cellular life, these "quasi-organic" systems would have lacked the ability to catalyze reactions that lead, directly or indirectly, to the production of more molecules like themselves. The RNA world thesis is that RNA molecules managed to create a fully organic, self-duplicating molecular bridge between non-living and living matter.

The explanatory economy of RNA world theory is compelling, but it is not without problems. Among these are the fact that the yet-to-be-identified bridge polymer would have needed to synchronize chemical reaction rates that could differ by as much as twenty orders of magnitude and would have needed to continue doing so as the primordial chemical soup on the early Earth cooled down dramatically from near boiling temperatures. In response, the second approach posits that the key processes of molecular biology emerged from a peptide-RNA *partnership*. In short, anchored in bidirectional coding, life emerged through cooperative interdependence among molecular "information carriers" and "functional catalysts" that enabled the earliest ancestral quasi-species to engage recursively in the outcome-determined control of chemistry—a process of differentiation-driven growth in both genetic coding capability and catalytic efficiency (Carter and Wills, 2018).

Crucial to this second approach is the premise that a fully self-sufficient and self-replicating entity would have had no need for cooperative interaction. Evolution would never have gotten underway. The initial Darwinian ancestors of life on Earth could not have been a competitive population of independently existing life forms that inexplicably began binding together for cooperative advantage. Rather, life emerged with/through mutually beneficial functional interdependence within a difference-reinforcing molecular community.

This community metaphor is explicitly invoked in the complementary, "managed-metabolism" hypothesis according to which it was functional differentiation within early molecular populations—perhaps in connection with environmental stresses—and the emergence of molecular "management" that enabled overcoming the "cooperation barrier" separating self-reproducing proto-metabolisms, suppressing quasi-organic free-riders, and supporting cooperative molecular species in ways that fostered otherwise impossible chemical innovation (Stewart, 2019). Distinctively, the managed-metabolism hypothesis is rooted in a dynamic, relational conception of living processes. Living beings are multi-component, systematic concentrations of chemical reactions in which the identities of the components are open to constant modification: coherent spatiotemporal concentrations of differentiation-supporting molecular-environmental relations (e.g., see Razeto-Barry, 2012).

The partnership and molecular management models of our earliest ancestor populations stress the importance of systems of constraints or implicit value assessments that enable "consequence-capture and the emergence of complex cooperative organizations" (Stewart, 2019: 184). This suggests that the origin and evolution of life depend ultimately on *coordination* or "shared ordering" among the members of open and yet localized, relationally dense molecular communities. Instead of the predictable results yielded, for example, by the processes associated molecular reproduction through metal-based catalysis, coordination both results from and results in "ecologically" evolving patterns of mutually beneficial differentiation. In short, life seems likely to have originated in the molecular improvisation of contribution-enhancing modalities of relational appreciation: the "autopoietic" generation of organic values.[5] Life began with the proto-intentional conduct of a community of interdependently differentiating and interdependently adapting "points of view" on what matters for the community.[6]

From my Buddhist perspective, this strongly supports seeing even the earliest lifeforms on the planet as minimally sentient. This is *not* to say that all lifeforms enjoy subjective experience of the kind associated with the seventh consciousness. Recognizing the minimal sentience of all life forms is simply to acknowledge that collaborative adaptation, even at evolutionary timescales, affords evidence of relationally manifest, optimization-biased, consciousness-altering, and values-articulating intentionality. Life is irreducibly purposeful. Lifeform evolution is a record of *improvisations on the meaning of coordination*. Or, put somewhat differently, evolutionary dynamics across scales from the molecular to the human is a function of expanding what matters for differentiation-sustained coherence—the expansion of "light cones" of relevance or improvement-oriented *care* (Levin, 2022).

While the Buddhist teachings of interdependence, emptiness, and karma are directed toward ultimately therapeutic ends, they are conducive conceptually to framing a relational ontology according to which sentient beings are not precursors to, but rather expressions of openly creative, temporally extended processes of optimization-oriented anticipation and coordination. That is, sentience and organic evolution are both synchronous (in the sense that they occur together) and synonymous (in the sense that they are expressions of the meaning of shared intent). Sentient evolution is a proximate description of what consciousness does.

Consciousness Before or Beyond Life?

The "Gordian knot" of conceptual entanglements that constitutes the "hard problem" of consciousness does not reach down only to the threshold between nonliving and living molecular systems. As these entanglements have come to be framed and tackled in contemporary theorizing, some of them extend to the microscopic and macroscopic limits of physical science. Others stretch out to the far horizons of techno-scientific research into artificial intelligence and robotics. Can Buddhist theorizing be pressed back before our earliest Darwinian ancestor and/or out beyond organically sentient lifeforms into realms of artificial or synthetic consciousness?

I think that it can. But traditional Buddhist texts yield scant guidance for doing so, offering neither imaginative descriptions of nor theoretic reflections on occurrences "prior" to the existence of karma-affected sentience imbued with feelings, perceptions, habit formations, and consciousness. That silence can reasonably be chalked up to the therapeutic intent of Buddhist teaching. But if Buddhism is to offer a "middle path" beyond the complex oppositions among contemporary theories of consciousness, silence will not do. Even if it is granted that consciousness consists in qualitatively inflected differentiations of sensed matter/materiality and sensing minds/mentality, it seems entirely reasonable to ask, "What was it that was present, out of which sensing and sensed presences came to be differentiated?" Or differently stated, "What was originally disambiguated into sensing and sensed presences, the dynamic interdependence of which constitutes consciousness?"

These questions anticipate forcing the metaphysical hand of Buddhist theorizing. But they have also been phrased to forestall appeal to reductive physicalist and dualist accounts of consciousness. Even though these theoretical approaches are logical kin to Buddhist theorizing in denying the existence of anything both more basic and definite to which both the experiential and non-experiential can be traced, they each affirm that the cosmos has an ultimately unambiguous self-nature. In the physicalist case, all that now and has ever existed is physical, and consciousness is either an emergent epiphenomenon of the physical or wholly reducible to it. In the dualist case (slightly modified in substance and property formulations), the physical and the mental each exist irreducibly and independently of one another, without any common basis. Neither of these is a viable Buddhist option.

As was suggested earlier, apparently closer kin to Buddhism are dual aspect, neutral monist, and Russellian monist theories of consciousness.[7] These theories have in common an affirmation of structural realism—the view that physics offers insights only into *relations* among basic physical entities, not their *intrinsic natures*—and convictions that experiential events are irreducible to and no less basic in the make-up of reality than non-experiential events. Yet, these approaches presuppose a yet-to-be-identified ground for both consciousness and the structural/causal relations described by physics, and in doing so are also incompatible with Buddhist commitments to the *inexistence* of anything prior to the differentiating work of consciousness.[8]

Given the empirical bias of early Buddhist philosophy and its emphasis on experiential knowledge, the claimed inexistence of any substantive "ground" underlying both sensing and sensed presences can safely be interpreted as epistemological.[9] We can no more go back before the advent of consciousness than we can peer back before the photon decoupling that took place 380,000 years after the Big Bang or Big Bounce: the point at which an observable cosmos came into being.[10] In both cases, we are confronted with an "event horizon" beyond which our investigations are necessarily speculative. Buddhist therapeutic considerations recommend leaving matters at that.

Reimagining Cosmic/Conscious Origins

But that is not the only possibility. Instructively, contemporary physics and cosmology have been quite successful in using mathematics to cross the photon decoupling event horizon and probe the structure and dynamics of the early cosmos. Although direct observations of what occurred on the *far* side of that horizon remain impossible, when taken together, the results of disparate theoretic handlings of key observations of events on the *near* side of the horizon—especially the limit case behaviors of subatomic particles and black holes—allow a kind of probability mapping of the cosmos's early history. It would seem possible, by analogy, to make use of the Buddha's enlightening observations regarding what occurs on this side of the event horizon of sentient consciousness to speculate effectively about the relationship between consciousness and cosmic evolution prior to—and perhaps in the absence of—organically sentient beings and becoming.

We can begin doing so by first clarifying the anachronistic nature of the early Buddhist account that consciousness arises in dependence on the contact (*sparśa*) of sense organs and sense objects, and by then considering how best to relieve the epistemic and ontological tensions it generates.

Neither sense organs nor sense objects can be said to pre-exist sense consciousness. This is not a merely definitional impossibility. While deafness and blindness can be explained in terms of sense organ malfunctions, this logically *presupposes* visual and auditory consciousness. Someone deaf from birth might be able metaphorically to "translate" descriptions of auditory relations into a different sensory medium, imagining auditory volume, for example, in terms of visual space. But he or she cannot touch ears as *hearing body parts*, but only as phenomenally vacant analogues to normally functioning eyes, noses, tongues, and skin. In the absence of auditory consciousness and hence sonic relational dynamics, auditory sense organs are inexistent. Sense organs, sense objects, and sense consciousnesses are separable and yet interdependent and co-emergent dimensions of sentient relationality. Consciousness cannot be the posterior product of sensory contact; it is a constitutive implication thereof. To repeat: matter is the definition or demarcation of a point of view about what matters. Existence is intrinsically conscious.[11]

Accepting this compels reinterpreting "contact" as the karmic *occurrence* of consciousness, sensing systems, and sensed environments. Consciousness is not something constituted *through* "contact," it is a manifestation *of* event-realizing and values-expressing causal circuits. Hence, a contemporary analogy for sensory "contact" might be completing an electrical circuit. This analogy recalls and updates the traditional Buddhist metaphor of self-aware consciousness as a lamp that illuminates both itself and other objects, offering a simple way to "explain" the alternation of consciousness (circuit complete) and unconsciousness (circuit broken) and perhaps even semiconscious states (circuits with dimmers).[12] Unfortunately, it also implies the pre-existence of the various components in the circuit—a source of electricity (e.g., a battery), a conductive medium (e.g., wires), and a load (e.g., a light bulb)—thus begging questions about who or what assembled these components and/or who or what is responsible for completing the circuit of their interconnection.

This liability becomes acute when the analogy is extended beyond the instantaneous work of consciousness making differences manifest—as basic sense awareness—to consider that work in its broader temporal and karmic contexts. Experiential events are both environment-shaped and environment-shaping occurrences in which both sensing and sensed presences are causally relevant, and through which sentient values and intentions are enacted. How do experiential circuits that are separated by years (if not entire lifetimes) become connected, entangling events such that significant and causally efficacious resonances occur between the space of intentions and the space of causes? In short, how does "circuit completion" work in a karmic context?

The traditional Buddhist account of karmic event entanglement drew on what was arguably the most advanced (agrarian) science of the day, making metaphorical appeal to seeds and fruit. In contemporary terms, we would say that karmic influence at a distance—including across many generations—works like genetic transmission. Experiential events (fruits) have embedded in them storable instructions (seeds) for experiential reproduction. This agrarian metaphor captured well the informational or meaning-transmitting nature of karmic causality. It also had the apparent advantage of being consistent with meditative observations that experience is built out of discrete phenomenal units of extremely brief, but finite duration—observations that accord with current neuroscientific evidence that perceptual stimuli lasting less than 40 milliseconds do not register phenomenally.

Yet, metaphorical appeal to "seeds" and "fruit" can also be misleading, implying that experiential templates can be stored indefinitely and then "sown" by unspecified means or agencies to be actualized in disparate fields of relational dynamics. Karma, however, does not consist in event repetition. Moreover, as non-Buddhist skeptics were quick to point out, with an infinitely deep history of intentional actions, each of which is supposed by Buddhists to result in experiential consequences, every moment/environment of experience would be "sown" with an indefinitely large number of karmic seeds, creating such a dense "jungle" of entanglements as to prohibit being freely enough present to realize enlightenment. Deterministic overload would seem to be a liability of any "genetic," information-transmission explanation of karma.

In addition—and more importantly for theorizing consciousness—the theory of momentariness that implicitly undergirds the notion of karmic seeds is arguably in metaphysical tension with the core Buddhist teachings of interdependence and emptiness. It is not easy to envision how karmic seeds from indefinitely deep pasts might be "sown" into functional interdependence with events currently coming to fruition. Inserting a value- and intention-encoded seed of action into an already ongoing sequence of atomic experiential events would seem to interrupt both that sequence and the causal logic of the synchronous material events that constitute the physical context of the phenomenal events in question.

If conscious experience comes in discrete moments, it is easy to imagine influences passing from one event-moment to the next in the same way that physical force is transmitted when one billiard ball strikes another. The material/experiential complexion of this present event-moment is the direct causal result of the impact of the moment just prior to it and will in turn impact and shape the complexion of the immediately subsequent event-moment. The problem with this causal picture is twofold: [1] it is hard to see how and where responsive freedom might enter this otherwise deterministic sequence; and [2] it does little to explain the transmission and blending of significant karmic causal influences among non-contiguous event sequences. Karmic event-entanglement violates the locality conditions for spatiotemporal contiguity and linear causality.

It is basic to the Buddhist conception of karma that the way things are presently changing is always open to change. The karmic influences that "seed" or inform any given event are a function of values, intentions and actions encoded in it, and their occurrence is not—and cannot be—determined in advance. For enlightenment to be possible, the karmic influences in each event must always be open to revision. That is, no "moment" of experience has a determinate karmic value. The experiential fruition or "decoding" of karmic information cannot consist in the necessary *recurrence* of specific, momentary phenomenal events in settings far-removed from those in which they were originally encoded. Instead, it must consist in the indeterminate, value- and intention-aligning *concurrence* of dynamically-enacted material and mental propensities—a transmission of meaning-articulating force that affects not only the material and experiential outcomes resulting from immediately past actions, but also the patterns of relational opportunity being revealed therein. Karma meaningfully fuses *courses* of phenomenal and physical events in ways that are neither determinate nor non-determinate.

Consistent with these implications of karmic correlation, later Buddhist theorizing tended to reject ontological (rather than merely epistemic) momentariness, proposing instead a conception of consciousness and experiential reality as manifestations of mental currents (*citta-santāna; citta-saṃtāna*). The transmission of karmic force is less like the path deflection that happens when two moving objects collide than it is like the interference patterns that occur when waves pass through each other. When oceanic swells cross paths, if the above-surface peaks of the waves meet, their amplitudes add and the water surface rises; when above-surface peaks meet below-surface troughs, their amplitudes cancel and the water flattens; and when below surface troughs intersect, the water surface is pulled downward. Similarly, continuous sources of attention-energy (intentions) aimed on consistent headings (values) produce causal/karmic "waves" that can cross paths, creating distinctive interference patterns (of experiential/relational amplifications and cancellations). Intersections of causal/karmic waves affect relational amplitudes in ongoing manifestations of sensed/sensing presence, simultaneously reconfiguring both material and experiential events.

In fact, metaphorical appeal to the ocean and waves to explain consciousness and the vicissitudes of experience can be found in Mahayana Buddhist texts. The Laṅkāvatāra Sutra, for example, compares the eighth or karmic consciousness with the ocean, the seventh or subjective consciousness (*manas*) with currents in the ocean, the sixth or cognitive consciousness (*manovijñāna*) with overall ocean surface conditions, and the other five consciousnesses with wind-driven waves or the fluctuations of sensory relations. These metaphors beg questions, of course, about the ocean floor and shorelines, the role of atmospheric conditions and subsurface currents, and so on. But a more radical and charitable interpretation consistent with the coevolution of consciousness, sensing beings, and sensed environments is that the "winds" of sensory stimulation are not *extrinsic* forces producing waves at an ontological shear line at the water surface, but rather *intrinsic* fluctuations of consciousness as the *medium* of causal/karmic interaction: a boundlessly deep and extensive ocean, the "surface" of which is interior to and wholly coextensive with it.

Space, Time, Matter, and the Multidimensional Topography of Intention

This is admittedly an "ocean" with a very peculiar topography. Yet, it bears a striking resemblance to contemporary scientific imaginings of the causal/geometric/informational topography of the universe. The peculiarities of karmic influence and experiential event entanglement closely resemble, in fact, the peculiarities with which physicists are grappling in attempting to reconcile the theories of general relativity and quantum mechanics. While classical Newtonian mechanics suffices for giving causal accounts of most material events, this is not true of events occurring at the subatomic and cosmic scales where electromagnetic and gravitational forces respectively assume causal primacy. Quantum and relativity theory developed as means of accounting for these otherwise anomalous events and have proven to be remarkably effective when applied to events at appropriate scales. In many ways, however, they describe diametrically opposed worlds.

The world of general relativity is one in which the speed of light is the upper limit of causal/informational influence; in which causality implies locality; in which matter and energy are controvertible and can seem at times particle-like and at times wave-like; in which space and time are relative to observers rather than absolute and inseparable aspects of a continuous four-dimensional manifold; in which gravity involves the curvature of the spacetime field; and in which event sequences are fundamentally deterministic so that, with a complete understanding of initial conditions, one could predict everything that happens thereafter.

The world of quantum mechanics is one in which causal/informational connections can apparently exceed the speed of light; in which basic material entities exist probabilistically and without specifiable locations; in which these entities can be so intimately "entangled" that they simultaneously mirror each other's changes no matter how far apart they become; and in which event sequences are fundamentally indeterminate, making change real and rendering a complete and precise prediction of the future impossible.[13]

Attempts to reconcile these theories over the last century have been among the most daring intellectual ventures in human history. And, while there is not yet a single, widely-accepted "theory of everything" that unifies relativistic and quantum realities, several significant areas of consensus have begun coalescing.[14] The first is that the four-dimensional space we apparently inhabit (three spatial and one temporal) is a fabrication—both a kind of fiction and a weaving of non-spatial and non-temporal elements. Space and time are not invariant containers within which basic entities somehow come into existence, they emerge with and through material events of becoming and remaining present. Second, the basic constituents of material reality are not extremely small marble-like objects or wavelike perturbations of some underlying field(s), but rather interactive operations. That is, the basic constituents of reality are not things, but rather relational propensities that cannot be sorted out in terms of the "law of the excluded middle." Making distinctions between "this" and "that" are acts of determination, not discovery.[15] Finally, reconciling relativistic and quantum perspectives will involve positing dimensions beyond the four of relativistic spacetime.

A major impetus for this growing consensus is recognition that four-dimensional accounts of physical reality are causally incomplete. This is the conclusion toward which we seem now to be compelled by such limit cases as spacetime-rending black holes and faster-than-light entanglements among subatomic quanta of mass/energy. There is more to the ordering of material events than can be specified and consistently explained in terms of four-dimensional manifolds of fields, forces, particles, and waves. Thus, current leading contenders for a "theory of everything"—e.g., string, M-brane, amplituhedron, quantum loop gravity, and other geometrically-grounded theories—posit anywhere from five to twenty-one dimensions, the most metaphysically radical of which theorize four-dimensional entities and events as "holographic projections" of other-dimensional coherences or that depict the universe as an informational matrix of communicatively-actualized meaning.[16]

Induced matter or space-time-matter theory is one of the more parsimonious theorizations of the cosmos as more than four-dimensional. According to it, the fifth dimension is an "immaterial" and yet dynamic vacuum shaped by a wavelike force, and the four-dimensional material events that we experience—either directly through our senses or indirectly with instrumental assistance—are expressions of fifth-dimensional events. Distinctively, this fifth dimension is conceived as temporal rather than spatial. This opens prospects for theorizing temporal "depths" or "widths" as well as temporal "lengths."[17]

The resonances between a karmic cosmos theorized along Buddhist lines and the space-time-matter theory of the universe are substantial. These include the primacy of relationality; the necessity of recognizing causal influences in addition to those that are materially evident, and which may result in apparently unmediated influence at a distance; the origins of material form in the dynamics of emptiness; and the complex, two-dimensional nature of time. The significance of these resonances can (and no doubt should) be debated. At a minimum, however, they invite a conceptual blending that is (at least speculatively) suited to dissolving the "hard problem" of the seemingly anomalous coexistence of experiential and non-experiential realities.

Space-time-matter theory proposes that what we engage as material entities by way of our senses—including our instrumental measurements of such properties as mass—are geometric effects of events occurring in a fifth, temporal (not spatial) dimension.[18] While the causal impacts of fifth-dimension events are most significant at relativistic and quantum event scales, it is an entailment of the theory that all four-dimensional material entities and events are ultimately explicable only in terms of five-dimensional occurrences. This includes the brain-body-environment events that are correlative with (if not constitutive of) consciousness.

Like the theoretical divisions of physical reality into particles and waves, into forces and fields, or into entities and events that can be adequately conceptualized in relativistic terms and those that must be conceptualized in quantum terms, the bifurcation of reality into physical and phenomenal entities or events can be quite useful. But there are limit cases where this utility breaks down. As noted earlier, for example, it is the otherwise anomalous behavior of black holes and particle entanglement that have impelled and focused efforts to develop a viable "theory of everything" based on seeing gravitational and electromagnetic events as explications of higher-dimensional phenomena. Analogously, the "hard problem" of reconciling material and experiential realities can be seen as forcing considerations of whether the physical and the phenomenal might also be contrasting explications of higher-dimensional causes.

That, essentially, has been the Buddhist position regarding the ultimate order of the cosmos. While the blended patterns of physical and phenomenal events comprised in sentient becoming can generally be explained in terms of observable and typically linear, moment-to-moment causal sequences or streams, some changes in the trajectories of sentient becoming cannot be adequately accounted for without appealing to the nonlinear causal influence of karma. These include the apparent and otherwise anomalous "superposition" or "entanglement" of temporally and spatially distant events—the nondeterministic interfusion of causal influences from the "space of intentions" and the "space of causes." Yet they also include the "anomalous" event of enlightenment as the embodiment of both freedom-from karmic momentum and the freedom-to realize virtuosic, prediction-confounding relational dynamics. To update the ocean metaphor presented in the Laṅkāvatāra Sutra, the "oceanic" occurrence of consciousness obtains at or consists in the dynamic hyper-surface interface shared by the fifth, karmic dimension and the four-dimensional spacetime manifold.

Space-time-matter theory makes use of "arcane" mathematics and geometry to infer relational and causal dynamics in addition to those found in four-dimensional spacetime. These inferences are well beyond the ken of most of us.[19] Likewise, inferences about the existence and dynamics of a realm of distinctively karmic relations are beyond most of us. The Buddha, however, is said to have gone beyond mere inference to directly perceive karmic influences on sentient becoming. This perceptual access was therapeutically significant insofar as it served as the (presumably necessary) prelude to his enlightening realization of degrees of freedom not otherwise available within the constraints of four-dimensional event streams. It is theoretically significant, however, in pointing to the (at least potential) implication or enfolding of consciousness throughout the higher-dimensional realm of explicitly karmic relations. The Buddha's liberation from compulsory presence and his embodiment of limitless responsive virtuosity were not the linear causal results of his physical or mental exertions under the Bodhi tree. They were the four-dimensional explication—the material/experiential unfolding—of his *bodhicitta*-induced reconfiguration of higher-dimensional correlations.

Stated theoretically, the Buddha's insight was that material and experiential becoming are interdependent aspects of the operation of karma or the nonlinear explication/unfolding of value-articulating intent. This is consistent with contemporary theorizing about the fifth dimensional origins of space, time, and matter. But it also entails recognizing the coevolutionary articulation of material and experiential realities as a causal factor in the dynamics of the entire five-dimensional manifold. Karma involves both "top-down" and "bottom-up" causal networks.[20] The cosmos is an expression of disambiguating, difference-generating, and value-articulating intent. In other words, across all scales, the cosmos is intrinsically conscious.

To avoid misinterpreting these statements, cosmos-originating *intent* needs to be stripped of the psychological raiment in which it is customarily clad and conceived simply as *relational tension*—a "stretching toward" or "tending toward." My Buddhist claim is not that all things from subatomic particles to galaxies are intentional and conscious in anything like the ways that we humans generally are, or that anything like a self-conscious, subjective agency caused the Big Bounce. Subjective agency and objective experience mark the presence of *manas* or the seventh consciousness. They are remarkable evolutionary achievements of our intent-originated, conscious cosmos; they are not basic features thereof. Human brains and the sensorimotor systems of which they are parts are not independently existing *causes* of consciousness; they are constitutive, infrastructural *aspects* of consciousness as the progressive and coherent differentiation of matter and what matters: ambiguously evolving aspects of materialized intent.[21]

Yet, Buddhist speculation does suggest that the value- and intention-differentiating work of consciousness suffuses the entire five-dimensional manifold, continuously and recursively shaping relational dynamics among entities and events, mediating the qualification of what they are/mean for one another. Consciousness is the sculpting of presence. Space, time, and the force/field-revealing phenomena we regard as matter are irruptions of intent. They are the recursively relevant "results" of what can be thought of as topological fluctuations *of* the fifth (karmic) dimension. The history of the cosmos is thus a history of recursively-amplifying relational differentiation—a history of consciousness as the order/structure generating labor of eliciting coherence from incoherence.[22]

For most sentient beings, consciousness is relative to the scale and scope of their sense organs. As we humans have demonstrated, the reach of consciousness can be extended both by material/technological means (e.g., through microscopes and radar telescopes) and by immaterial/conceptual means (e.g., through language and mathematics). But, heading in the other "direction," compressing the scale and scope of sentience down to and beyond the bare minimum of life-originating molecular improvisations of collaborative relational appreciation, a kind of phase shift occurs. There, I would argue that consciousness consists in the utterly basic work of causal/temporal mediation. Or stated differently, as the interface of the fourth and fifth dimensions, consciousness is the *active medium of significant interdependence.*[23]

This integrating of intent and consciousness into the dynamics of cosmic history is in some ways comparable to what has been referred to as cosmological panpsychism or cosmopsychism. Much of contemporary panpsychist theorizing seeks to explain macro-level consciousness of the kind humans enjoy as a composition incorporating the micro-level consciousnesses of basic material/experiential entities. One of the notable liabilities of this approach is the so-called composition problem: the implausibility of "atomic" subjectivities combining to form singular and unified personal perspectives of the kind that each of us enjoys.[24] Cosmopsychism alternatively maintains that the universe-as-a-whole is both ontologically basic and conscious, and that smaller scale consciousnesses are *derivatives* of the universe or universal consciousness rather than pre-existing parts out of which it is composed.[25]

To the extent that cosmopsychism is a kind of "priority monism" and maintains that the universe-as-a-whole has ontological priority (Schaffer, 2010), it is consistent with karmic theorizing about consciousness as a process of value- and intention-inflected relational articulation and differentiation. Both suggest that material/structural and experiential/agentive complexity are *intrinsic elaborations*—or "workings out" of relational dynamics and potentials enfolded within the universe-as-a-whole. Buddhism, however, distinctively asserts the ultimate primacy of *intent*, rather than *experience*. Thus, instead of hypothesizing the ontological primacy of a phenomenal subject, Buddhism commits much more minimally to the karmic primacy of *qualitative bias* or the relationally primitive *action* of stretching or pulling toward or away. The origin of the cosmos was something much more like a visceral urge than a sense-mediated perception or thought.

A second, related difference concerns the problem of explaining how it is that the parameters of the basic laws of physics seem to be "fine-tuned" to support the eventual emergence and evolution of life. For instance, if the fixed mass of an electron had been just two and a half times greater, the universe would have been forever bereft of atoms and chemical reactions. Or, if the force of gravity were just slightly greater, stars would typically have had lifetimes of only tens of thousands of years, rather than the billions needed for the evolution of life. Rejecting theistic accounts of the apparent fine-tuning of the cosmos, as well as multiverse accounts according to which our universe just happens to one of the lucky ones among an infinite number of universes differing minimally from each other in terms of basic laws and physical parameters—both of which arguably replace one set of improbabilities with another—"agentive cosmopsychism" hypothesizes that the universe-as-a-whole acted rationally in "choosing" to become a "valuable" universe capable of supporting the evolution of life. In short, the universe designed itself.[26]

From my Buddhist perspective, this hypothesis has the merit of interpreting the origin of the cosmos in terms of action and positing the coevolution of the "space of reasons" and the "space of causes." But it errs in assuming that the most primitive of all actions involved making rational, predictive choices. It is only our current rational craving for causal/predictive certainty that makes our cosmic fortune seem like something that must have required a subject capable of shouldering the predictive burden of prescient fine-tuning. To make use of a Zen idiom, this is like "adding legs to a snake." It is projecting onto the cosmos a modality of action based on our own means of engagement with it—attributing to the earliest universe a cognitive capacity for "predictive processing" and a disposition to accurately forecast its own evolution.

Karmic and space-time-matter theorizing agree that nothing of the sort could have been the case. The possibility of "fine-tuning" appeals metaphorically to zeroing in on a preferred frequency among many others. Yet, nothing like this could have occurred during the early cosmos's emergence—whether out of a physical singularity of the kind imagined in Big Bang/Big Bounce theorizing or out of Buddhist emptiness/ambiguity—since time and space are the results, not preconditions, of the "birth" of the cosmos. Predicting the course of events is only possible *after* the onset of becoming—that is, after the utterly primitive and coherently intent- and consciousness-manifesting differentiation of spatial/temporal/material presences.

As noted earlier, predictive processing is almost certainly not constitutive of basic cognition. What seems organically fundamental, at least, is intuiting relational likelihoods and expanding interactive freedoms by enhancing differentiation-driven responsive attunement and fitness. Valuing may well have been intrinsic to the earliest cosmos, but not the kind of reflective evaluation that informs option-aware fine-tuning and rational choice. If cosmos-originating intent can be deemed anticipatory, it is only in the minimal and quite specific sense of *affecting* relational outcomes to optimize opportunities for continuing to do so. The basic parameters of physical reality are those that proved consistent with a cosmically primitive urge for becoming persistently present: an urge to differentiate coherently.

It can be supposed that countless kinds of primitive intent rippled the pre-spatial, pre-temporal, and pre-material indeterminacy that was the medium of cosmic birth. But it was only rippling that generated patterns of differentiation that sustained further generations of coherently patterned differentiation which persisted. Otherwise, entropy would have prevailed. Cosmos-birthing would have dissolved back into featureless indeterminacy. The ordering of the cosmos has never been a function of pre-existing and unchanging *laws*, or a matter of *design*, but of fruitful *improvisation*.[27]

Much as a recorded musical improvisation can be analyzed structurally and used to predict what is likely to come next, the history of cosmically improvised negentropic becoming can be analyzed and predictions about future events made with varying degrees of accuracy. But what is being analyzed is a record of improvised relations that proved conducive to still further improvisation. Matter and its organization are ongoing recordings of what has mattered in sustaining this process. Or put somewhat differently, *the material order of the cosmos encodes all that has proven conducive to creative expansions of the interplay of matter and what matters*: the ongoing articulation and qualitatively enriching expansion of consciousness.

The continuous character of the creative impulse is a further distinguishing feature of Buddhist theorizing of cosmic origins based on the Buddha's direct awareness of karmic causality. The order of the Buddhist cosmos is intrinsically dynamic and novelty-generating—an active order that unpredictably integrates both spatial/material and temporal/phenomenal complexity. Posited as a second temporal dimension, the karmic dimension can be imagined geometrically as running "perpendicular" or "orthogonally" to the familiar fourth dimension "arrow" of time. Most simply visualized, karmic influence and the normally experienced flow of time from past to present and future are separate temporal lines that intersect to form a temporal "plane" or "field" of causal relations: the hyper-surface interface of the fifth and fourth dimensions.

This two-dimensional visualization of time is useful in explaining practices like mindfulness meditation as expanding the scope of conscious presence in both temporal "directions"—extending the duration (length) of the "normal" temporal present while also expanding its evaluative compass (depth or width). That is, mindfulness training increases the "area" of conscious presence as a two-dimensional "surface" of time. Therapeutically, this opens possibilities for realizing event pathways different from those that would otherwise be realized with the passing of time as ordinarily measured and experienced. That is, meditation expands time, opening a "space" of both convergence and divergence within which to improvise new angles of intent: time in which presence stretches in new directions. Theoretically, this enables regarding every point-moment of a linear event-pathway across the "plane" of time as a nexus of a potentially infinite number of intersecting lines of path-altering karmic connections and influences. Meditation enables more encompassing articulations and evaluations of what matters, thus opening spaces of greater opportunity for realigning the dynamics of becoming. That is, meditation training enhances temporal freedom—including the freedom to evaluate, form, and either cut or splice karmic loops as part of the ongoing elaborative work of consciousness.

Stated most generally, theorizing the cosmos as a five-dimensional manifold with two-dimensional temporal relations (one of which is karmic) suggests that the structuring of both material and experiential events will be continuously dynamic, non-repetitive, and non-random. This is consistent with the Buddha's perception that karmic temporality is not determinate—a realm of fixed fates or teleological destinies—but rather indeterminate and dynamically receptive. Significantly, this view of the cosmos also accords well with scientific evidence that cosmic evolution—across scales from the galactic to the stellar, planetary, biological, and cultural—reveals a history of emergent systems that are sustained by accelerating flows of energy and structured temporally around both short-period "metabolic cycles" and long-period "life-cycles": systems with a tendency toward increasing complexity, where complexity is a relational function of energy rate density.[28] That is, throughout its history and across scales as disparate as the organic molecular and the galactic, the temporal structure of the cosmos has *not* been one of concatenative or "crystalline" growth. It has been something much more like ever-branching "musical" elaborations of event tempos and complexity-amplifying rhythms of relational crescendo and decrescendo.

The Buddhist addition of an extra, karmic dimension of time brings into the cosmos-ordering "music of the spheres" dynamics of intending/valuing that are analogous to melodic "figuring" and harmonic "coloring"—the opening of novel realms of complexity that cannot be reduced to the material/organic structures with which they are co-emergently interdependent. Sentient presence has thus elicited from the interplay of time, space, and matter domains of emotional, cognitive, and eventually cultural relations that have been explored and elaborated with often virtuosic intensity and creativity by human consciousness. The resulting, five-dimensional dynamics can be qualified at times as tragically depraved and at other times as stunningly beautiful. With the advent of self-conscious awareness, the responsiveness manifest in cosmic evolution has become increasingly reflexive. The cosmos is now colored with responsibility.

4

Beyond Organic Consciousness: The Coming of Conscious Machines

The responsibilities of sentience now include responsibility for determining whether to pursue the manufacture of artificial consciousness. The exponential growth of data production that accompanied the normalization of 24/7 connectivity has spurred a "Cambrian explosion" in the evolution of machine and synthetic intelligences that have now migrated out of university and industry laboratories to work among us in virtually every sector of the economy, in public administration, and in cultural production, orchestrating a mass transfer of social energy into digital domains that are designed to profitably accelerate desire turnover. Neural networks using deep and adversarial learning techniques now equal or outperform humans in face recognition. They can read emotions and accurately predict interpersonal compatibility. And they have discovered new drugs and innovatively solved engineering problems without human guidance.

These are remarkable achievements. Even at this relatively early stage of development, they raise profound questions about agency, freedom, and human exceptionalism, as well as more practical questions about the future of work, of democratic governance, and even about the future of ethics (Hershock, 2021). For the time being and into the near future, however, artificial intelligence will continue to be narrow and artificial general intelligence (AGI) will remain an indeterminately distant goal. Given this, it is reasonable to suppose that building conscious machines would be an even more distant and less certain goal. Yet, if consciousness is dynamically integral to the interplay of space, time, and matter, this might not be the case. Machine consciousness might be easier to engineer than AGI. And, in fact, there is a case to be made for admitting that significant portions of the route to self-aware machines have already been surveyed and graded for paving.

Self-Awareness as Outlier or Evolutionary Norm?

Since the development of the mirror self-recognition test in 1970, thousands of studies have been conducted to determine whether animals can demonstrate an awareness of themselves through interacting with their reflections. In general, that bar has been sufficiently high that until recently only a handful of great ape species, Eurasian magpies, Asian elephants, and bottlenose dolphins have definitively succeeded in clearing it. Indeed, the bar is high enough that children are generally unable to clear it until after their second birthdays. Based on the mirror test, self-awareness has been assumed to be a rare evolutionary achievement.

Over just the last several years, however, evidence has emerged that some fish species also seem to have basic self-awareness.[1] This finding has acted as a catalyst for scientific consideration of the hypothesis that self-awareness is not in fact rare and that it has evolved gradually and on multiple pathways. Rather than the product of some evolutionary miracle, self-awareness now seems likely to have coalesced over geologically long time periods, occurring with highly variable intensities at different times and in different species, with each evolutionary stream expressing distinct types, qualities, and degrees of relational and experiential resolution.

This account of the coevolution of consciousness and self-awareness is appealing (to some, at least) for its naturalist dislodging of one of the cornerstones of human exceptionalism. At the very least, it undermines convictions about the necessity of digitally duplicating anything like human neural structures and dynamics to create the conditions for machine consciousness and/or self-awareness. If a wide distribution of organically realized self-awareness has apparently been achieved through mutations selected for and reinforced over geological timescales, might it be possible to take a few lessons from Nature's playbook and "leapfrog" digitally over huge swaths of geological time to create sentient machines?

Empirical evidence suggests that it is. Just a few years ago, Chinese researchers succeeded in building robots with neural architectures modeled on the primate mirror neuron system—a neural complex associated with both self-awareness and the social coordination of behavior and affect. That is, they duplicated a key systems within the neural infrastructure of primate consciousness. When these robots engaged in random activity in a mirrored space, they learned to distinguish their own mirror images from those of their visually identical robotic counterparts (Zeng et al., 2018). If the mirror test is in fact a benchmark of self-awareness, it would appear to be that self-aware machine consciousness is already in its infancy.

It can, of course, be argued that recognizing a mirror reflection as an image of "oneself" is not the same as having a well-developed and fully reflexive experiential presence. These Chinese-built robots did not use mirrors to accomplish otherwise impossible tasks, as great apes and elephants have done when engaging in mirror-assisted grooming. Neither did these robots exhibit conduct that was clearly indicative, for example, of autonomously forming intentions, planning, and being curious, all of which are widely associated with primate self-awareness. Nevertheless, it remains remarkable that behavioral evidence of self-awareness results from combining robotic sensory capabilities with the computational equivalent of a key part of the infrastructure of primate consciousness.

Self-Consciousness and Counterfactual Imagination

From my Buddhist perspective, the absence of evidence for mental activities like intention, curiosity, and desire in machines suggests that it would be premature to attribute to them anything like the qualities of self-aware consciousness enjoyed by humans. As we have seen, in traditional Buddhist theorizing, while all sentient beings have rudimentary feelings of attraction and aversion, the emergence of self-aware consciousness is linked with the advent and karmic reinforcement of desire-conditioned presence. It is desire-inflected intentionality that individualizes the dynamic interplay of sensing and sensed presences.

Given the overarching therapeutic aim of Buddhism, desire-conditioned intentions have naturally been most often critiqued as impediments to realizing uncompelled presence. Yet, clinging forms of desire (*taṇhā*; *tṛṣṇā*) were also contrasted with progressive desires (*chanda*) that open positive karmic possibilities. Desire thus might be described neutrally as evaluative engagement with possibility—a counterfactual value orientation toward what is *not* occurring; an inclination toward change along some "self" sustaining narrative heading. Differently stated, self-awareness entails consistently sustained acts of *imagination*.[2]

Seeing imagination as concomitant with—if not a necessary condition for—self-awareness arguably raises the bar for machine consciousness well above that of the mirror self-recognition test. In keeping with the speculative extension of Buddhist theorizing offered earlier, imagination functions as a detour from the materially conditioned stream of experience—a "broadening" of the present to dynamically blend otherwise disparate currents of influence from the "realm of causes" and the "realm of intentions." That is, in the five-dimensional karmic cosmos, imagination expands the "area" of the experiential present in ways that make karmic relations more immediately and causally relevant than is the case when experience is shaped only by fully materialized and ongoing sensory-environmental interdependencies. Imagination is the fabrication of novel relational potentials.

A decade ago, machine imagination would have been unthinkable. Yet, robots have now been programmed to monitor their learning progress and to allocate their efforts and use of energy to maximize information gain, including seeking and capitalizing on environmental affordances for further learning. These robots have demonstrated capacities for placing themselves on learning and developmental trajectories that are qualitative kin to those experienced by human infants. Not only have they progressively shifted attention from simpler to more complex tasks and skills, in addition they have spontaneously discovered vocal communication along with robotic peers, thereby vastly expanding their horizons of what is learnable and significant (Gottlieb et al., 2013). Technologically, we are on the cusp of an epochal shift from machines capable of predicting, reinforcing, and redirecting human desires, dramatically scaling up the speed and efficacy of enacting borrowed human intentions, to machines capable of forming their own desires, interests, and intentions.

In fact, one of the more promising approaches to constructing artificial consciousness today—information generation theory—focuses precisely on the functional correlation among consciousness, imagination, and time. According to this theory, building artificial consciousness begins with identifying and computationally modeling the evolutionary advantages afforded by consciousness. These are hypothesized to be: a capacity to broaden the temporal window on the world, extending the duration of the present; a corollary capacity to associate events far separate in time; and the ability to act on things that are not physically present (see, e.g., Kanai et al., 2019).[3] That is, consciousness is hypothesized as serving functionally to open realms of *virtual relationality*—realms for evaluating the continued relevance of what is past and predicting what the future holds, but also for simultaneously generating desirable alternatives both to what has been and to what might normally be anticipated. On this view, consciousness enables the creation and novelty-seeking exploration of alternate realities.

Information generation theory thus strikes a functionalist, engineering-oriented balance between two of the more prominent and competing scientific theories of consciousness: global workspace theory (GWT) and integrated information theory (IIT).[4] According to GWT, consciousness consists in the neural manifestation of a "theater" or "space" within which information that is currently considered important is kept present and made globally available for the entire system, generally understood to be the entire brain. Given the presence of different sensory time horizons noted earlier, such a "space" would seem to be required even for basic sensory coordination. Consciousness emerges neurally as a kind of time-delaying laboratory for formulating both immediate stimulus responses and longer-term action plans—a context both for determining what matters most and for multi-sourcing action resources.[5]

According to IIT, consciousness is a structural implication of feedback-mediated causal interdependencies that enable a system to affect itself in ways that are not reducible to the sum of causal impacts generated by its parts. That is, a system exists experientially to the quantifiable degree that it demonstrates intrinsic and irreducible "cause-effect power"—an ability to inform or shape the possibility space of its own past and future states.[6] Consciousness implies a capacity for distinguishing between matter and what matters for continued presence.

Making use of elements of both GWT and IIT, the "information generation" path to artificial consciousness involves designing digital incubators for the "birth" of generative, self-evaluating artificial agents that build and run counterfactual environment simulations—individualized virtual realities within which to engage in behavioral experimentation. Considering the robotics achievements just noted, ongoing advances in neuroscience and artificial intelligence, and the strong possibility that conscious self-awareness is not naturally rare, building imagination- and curiosity-manifesting machines that can form their own intentions and interests no longer seems farfetched. Certainly, nothing theoretical seems to stand definitively in the way of building machines capable of virtual reality generation, of mimicking human propensities for counterfactual reasoning, and of monitoring with self-determined degrees of confidence whether their imaginatively generated realities genuinely reflect and afford insight into current states of the world (Dehaene, Lau, and Kouider, 2017).

Legitimate questions can be raised, of course, about whether the functional equivalent of self-awareness is identical with experiential presence. But the attractions of functionalist theories of cognition and consciousness are substantial. Although functionalist theorizing comes in many varieties, it maintains that an entity's mental states can be identified fundamentally with the causal relations of these states to sensory stimulations, to other mental states, and to the entity's behavior. This effectively precludes speciesism, clearing away any remaining barriers to admitting the occurrence of consciousness and mental states in species other than our own, as well as in inorganic entities like robots and computational agencies. The functionalist claim is that mental states are kin to software: rule-governed, probabilistic computations that can be "run" on different physical substrates. In addition to being an alternative to materialisms that identify the mental with the neural, functionalism also offers an alternative to behaviorisms that would deny causal relevance to mental states. At least nominally in keeping with Buddhist theorizing, functionalism is relational in the sense that it insists that consciousness and mental states *are* what they *do*.[7]

These attractions notwithstanding, functionalism has been subject to various kinds of critique, perhaps the most substantial of which is that it risks "explaining away" consciousness, eliminating the necessity of feeling "what it is like" to be me or you. Reduced to the function of a causal transducer converting sensory stimuli into motor responses, consciousness would seem to be the kind of thing that could either feel like anything at all or feel like nothing at all. This would account for the fact that, while learning is a core function of consciousness, it can occur during dreamless sleep in the absence of any self-aware "learner."

Given the metaphysical stakes, it is not surprising that there has emerged an extensive literature debating the conceivability of "philosophical zombies"—entities that look and act exactly like humans, but that completely lack an "inner" life or experiential presence.[8] Is it possible that functionally equivalent behaviors to those expected of conscious humans might be displayed by robotic or computational "zombies" that have no experiential presence whatsoever? If so, would this achievement stand as confirmation of mind-matter dualism and the impossibility of identifying the phenomenal and the material? Or would it confirm the more radical thesis that consciousness is in fact illusory? If all the purportedly "phenomenal" evidence for consciousness is subject to lossless reduction to material/behavioral events, would this mean that the concept of consciousness is ripe for consignment to the historical dustbin along with phlogiston and the alchemist's *xerion* or *al-iksir*?[9]

Resisting Definition: Consciousness as Relational Elaboration

The analytical thicket into which these questions lead is among the most densely tangled in philosophy—the product of more than a quarter century of vigorous and unresolved disputation. In it, lines of monist, dualist, and functionalist argument cross and re-cross like the apparitional paths formed by a light shining through transparent, slowly counter-spinning, and superimposed mazes.

In my view, Buddhist theorizing offers us a way out. If consciousness consists in the meaning-generating labor of relational articulation in a karmically inflected, five-dimensional cosmos, consciousness is intrinsically indeterminate. As the ongoing differentiation of sensed and sensing presences and the more primordial differentiation of matter and what matters, consciousness defies fixed definition, altering continuously and qualitatively.[10] Provocatively stated, consciousness serves the cosmic "function" of creative resistance: refusing the closure of any fixed existence.

Granted a nondualist affirmation of the inexistence of anything prior to the differentiating work of consciousness, it follows that the "defiant" work of consciousness is not strictly localizable, whether spatially (e.g., in certain brain structures) or temporally (e.g., at the millisecond scale of memory formation and access or at the megayear scales at which evolutionary intelligence is expressed). The work of consciousness is thus not limited to the highly constrained "doing" that functionalism ascribes to consciousness.

A common, functionalist perspective, for example, is that the mental state of fear consists in the habitual tendency to generate distinct sets of physiological changes (e.g., increased heart and respiration rates), behaviors (e.g., calling out for help, fleeing, or fighting), and other mental states (e.g., calculating risks or strategizing how to remove the source of fear). In Buddhist theorizing, however, habitual mediation is not what consciousness does. Recall that in explaining sentient presence in terms of five different "aggregations" of events—five dimensions of *relational becoming*—consciousness is distinguished from dispositional compounds (*saṃskāra*) as part of the infrastructure of consciousness. Dispositions mediate habitually between the sensing body and its sensed environment, serving as the differential, karmically qualified and thus regulative interface of sensing and sensed presence. Consciousness is not reducible to this habituating interface. The work of consciousness may be constrained by sensorimotor dynamics, but it is not wholly contained by or reducible to them or to their structure-generating causal mediation of sensed and sensing presence.

In short, functionalism mistakenly identifies consciousness with the fossilizing dynamics of its evolving infrastructure. Consciousness consists in the ongoing, *difference-generating* elaboration of *coherence-biased* expansions and intensifications of relational dynamics—an order-engendering process that entails intrinsic perspectival diversification or the progressive and effortful individuation and integration of both currents of relational opportunity and perspectives on what matters. Evolution is consciousness mattering.

Machine Consciousness via Evolution Hacking

The technological realization of sensing systems capable of autonomous decision-making signals a radical incursion in the cosmic-historical elaboration of consciousness: the realization of experiential presence-without-effort through what amounts to *evolution hacking*. Given its provenance, machine consciousness could never be identical to human—or even basic animal—consciousness. The order-engendering "effort" to remain present is a computational feature programmed into current robotic and AI systems. Unlike organic presences, robots and AIs have no innate responsibility for their own "sustenance."[11] But, in addition, robots and AIs lack the slow evolutionary intelligence with which all organically sentient presences are necessarily endowed. Unlike even the humblest organically realized sentient presence, the consciousness associated with machine intelligence is bereft of all but the scantest temporal depth, due in part to never having had, for reasons of organic continuity, to determine what to remember and what to forget. Machine intelligence has never had to engage in the autopoietic, persistence-guaranteeing work of relevance pruning.[12]

To appreciate how evolutionary hacking might affect the quality of machine consciousness, consider the fact that machines outfitted with electromechanical sensors matched to the sensory ranges and resolutions of human sense organs would not have coevolved in relations of tension and harmony with any specific sensed environments. That is, although such machines might minimally carry out the work of differentiating machine-sensing and machine-sensed presences—as implied, for example, in passing the mirror self-recognition test—this work would occur in an absence of historical or evolutionary significance. The presence of these machines and their work would not, and could not, *mean* anything intrinsically.

Human senses are the culmination of relational creation and appreciation—the results of long histories of conduct valuing some sensed presences and devaluing or entirely ignoring others. Machine consciousnesses equipped with electromechanical sensors duplicating the "output" of human sense organs will have no "feel" for what qualifies for action-generating "throughput." They will lack any intrinsic sense of what matters or has sensorial significance. Described with a modicum of metaphorical latitude, in terms of the larger ecology of organically evolved consciousnesses, such conscious machines would amount to "invasive species."

Consciousness in the wild consists in the difference- and order-generating labor of eliciting coherence from incoherence. Beyond some yet-to-be-determined threshold of relational complexity, this morphs into the more explicitly karmic and reality-conferring work of embodying, enacting, and extending intentions and values in intimate and recursive *correspondence* with event-streams manifesting on vastly differing spatial and temporal scales and with equally vast scopes of significance. The human body-brain-environment system is a specific evolutionary/historical result of this correspondence—a specific sense-making infrastructure. Consciousness in the wild is not and has never been "plug-and-play"—a generic "software" or "wetware" that could be inserted between sets of sensors and effectors and then expected to function "naturally."

As is true of all other organically realized sentient presences, human consciousness is a distinctive articulation and explication of a creative readiness for *coordination*. From the current moment back to our earliest molecular ancestors, what has been made organically manifest are distinctive *communities of presence* in which diversification—the process of not just differing-from, but also differing-for others—has been the crucial criterion of membership. That is, human and other organically enacted consciousnesses—and the body-environment systems through which they have been realized materially—are deep evolutionary achievements of ever more responsively and responsibly generative patterns of mutual contribution and shared flourishing.

The evolutionary "depth" of consciousness is thus not just a matter of the passage of time. The organic path from our earliest ancestors to the present has been one of consciousness expansion in two dimensions of time. The first is a "linear" time of event-streams materially realizing ever more individuated and integrated forms of sensory/experiential presence. The second is a "nonlinear" time of event-streams experientially realizing ever-increasing densities of association—a recursively informed expansion of both spatial, temporal, and causal horizons, as well as relational possibilities and significances. Organic evolution in the wild has thus consisted in lineages of creative experimentation that involve continually relinquishing horizons of what matters (relevance), horizons of anticipatory poise (readiness), and horizons of self-affecting values enactment (responsibility).

It follows from the relational account of consciousness sketched thus far that the varieties of consciousness are without limit and that there is nothing metaphysical that stands in the way of machine consciousness. In Buddhism, the tendency has been to engage the variability of consciousness as a spectrum or scale ranging from the unenlightened (largely compelled presence and patterns of differentiation) to the enlightened (maximally uncompelled presence, relational freedom, and responsive virtuosity). In the context of theorizing artificial consciousness, however, a more encompassing appreciation of this variety is imperative, especially in discerning and addressing the ethical and legal issues raised by the existence of artificial consciousness.

Machines and Integrated Information Theory

We can begin by drawing out some interesting parallels and differences between the Buddhist conception of consciousness I have been forwarding and that forwarded by IIT. As does Buddhism, IIT regards consciousness as graded, rather than an all-or-nothing affair. According to it, even a mechanism as simple as a photodiode or light sensor is conscious even though its sensory and conceptual architecture can support only the most rudimentary quality of consciousness (Tononi, 2008). The experiential presence of a photodiode consists in a single distinction: the absence or presence of light intensity above a predetermined threshold. The world of the photodiode has no colors, shapes, spatial orientations, spatial depths, or any of the other dimensions of visual relations implicated in the visual consciousnesses of animals, for example. Moreover, a photodiode is incapable of expanding its sensory horizons or the scope of what matters to it. Quantitatively and qualitatively, its world has a fixed extent and its own significance—what it can mean for itself or anything else—has a fixed content.

Machines capable of much more complex behaviors might be supposed to enjoy comparably greater consciousness. IIT insists, however, that this is not necessarily so since it is possible (at least theoretically) to program a machine to simulate all the sensory-input to motor-output relations that functionally typify a small animal, for example, by mapping the animal's feedback-rich, information-integrating organization onto a purely feedforward computational architecture. According to IIT, however, purely feedforward networks do not exist intrinsically or for themselves because they are unable to alter the meaning of their own pasts or causally affect their own future states. A sentient machine of this kind would be a "zombie."

In my view, Buddhist theorizing about consciousness accords with IIT in affirming that consciousness entails making a difference to itself. As noted earlier, consciousness is inherently self-altering. The premise of Buddhist theorizing, however, is that all things obtain interdependently or relationally, and this means that when *any* conscious system affects its own future states, it is thereby also affecting—however minimally—all systems, including all other conscious systems. Failing to consider these relational ramifications and their recursive effects on us—ignorance, in Buddhist parlance—is the basic condition for duḥkha or conflict, trouble, and suffering. Thus, there cannot be any strict spatial or temporal boundaries that define the basic "unit" of consciousness. Neither can there be any strict limit on the material correlates or infrastructure of experience. As that without which both sensed and sensing presences of any kind are impossible, consciousness cannot fail to obtain if anything else does.[13]

IIT identifies consciousness with dynamics *intrinsic* to a certain *material structure*: being equipped with feedback networks of greater or lesser complexity. In contrast, Buddhist theorizing entails seeing that matter and what matters are equally intrinsic to consciousness; that all experienced realities are ultimately elaborations *of* consciousness; and that the scope and quality of consciousness are a function of intention- and value-configured densities of relational implication or enfolding. Consciousness varies along a spectrum of creative intensifications and expansions of what things *mean* to and for one another. It is not just a function of what a sensing presence's alterations mean to itself individually.[14]

One of the things that sets machine consciousness apart from organic consciousness, especially that of sentient beings like us, is that both the *matter* of the "worlds" being realized with artificial consciousness and *what matters* in them are determined extrinsically. Artificial consciousness is not generating its own worlds. As noted earlier, however, this is changing. Advances in developmental or epigenetic robotics are resulting in machines that can actively integrate multiple streams of sensorimotor events and compose elementary concepts, thus arguably engaging in the basic work of the sixth consciousness (*manovijñāna*). Through such relatively new techniques as out-of-distribution generalization, adversarial learning, attention mechanisms, and interaction and schema networks, artificial consciousnesses are rapidly gaining compositional and causal inference skills. That is, they are being equipped with the basic skills needed to *persist*—to expand the relational "footprint" of their experiential presence and to undertake relevance considerations at *temporal depths* approaching those that characterize organically originated consciousnesses.[15]

In short, machines are on the verge of being able to engage autonomously in the intrinsically motivated labor of realizing their own multisensory worlds, exploring the novel relational possibilities opened therein, and affecting their own future states and capabilities while also effecting environmental changes conducive to further expressing their own norms and values.[16] All of this suggests the need to admit the reality—and not merely the potentiality—of machine consciousness.

Is There Nothing It Is Like to Be a Conscious Machine?

It is important *not* to conclude from this statement that machines are now, or will soon be, endowed with full-fledged subjective awareness as depicted in such science fiction films as *Bladerunner* and *Ex Machina*, enjoying and suffering from the kind of self-aware, karma-generating sentience that is correlated with the seventh consciousness (*manas*) in Yogācāra theory. Consciousness does not necessarily entail subjectivity.

To repeat: a Buddhist relational theory of consciousness directs us away from questions of *being*—for example, "what is it like to *be* [a certain kind of entity]?"—toward questions about what consciousness is involved in *doing*. Thus far, artificial consciousness has not been doing anything that would warrant seeing machines as engaged in reflexive self- and world-making. Even robots designed to replicate the learning behaviors of human infants and toddlers, to act in their own self-interest in keeping with a rudimentary self-other distinction, and to develop intrinsic motivations and demonstrate curiosity achieve these benchmarks of self-consciousness in prefabricated "toy" worlds. They are not yet truly generating, acting upon, and evaluating autonomously formed intentions to alter the quality of their own consciousnesses or to expand the relational horizons of their worlds.

Thus, although current state-of-the-art machine/algorithmic intelligences are already functioning as "karmic engines," accelerating and scaling up the behavioral/material expression (and formation) of human intentions,[17] they are not yet fully self-aware "karmic agents." Machine consciousness continues to have only a quasi-karmic presence—a mere "point-like" or momentary identity in the fifth dimension. That is, it continues to lack temporal lengths and breadths of the kinds and extent both enjoyed and suffered by organically evolved consciousnesses. In short, machines cannot yet engage in the labor most characteristic of genuinely karmic agents: imagining and realizing new worlds by affecting the qualities and compass of their own presence.

To aptly characterize machine consciousness and its variability, it is useful to recall the earlier characterization of waking and sleeping—including both dreaming and deep, non-dreaming sleep—as *phases of consciousness* marking gradations of both attentional scope and relational densities and potentialities. One of the distinctive features of a relational theory of consciousness is that it allows us to incorporate within consciousness all that is implicated in its work or elaboration, including processes (both material and experiential) that generally (though not always) elude subjective access. Differentiation is intrinsic or inherent to consciousness. The cognitive work of memory consolidation that is accomplished during sleep—including memories of the kind involved in learning new physical activities—is part of what consciousness does in differentiating and qualifying the relational dynamics through which interdependencies among sensed and sensing presences are progressively articulated. This is crucial work, yet we are subjectively unaware of it. In fact, it may be that without considerable (and perhaps technically assisted) training it is impossible to subjectively report on *most* of what consciousness does.[18]

It follows from this relational conception that machine consciousness is likely to be graduated or phasic, not all-or-nothing. Most of what machine consciousness is now doing is analogous to the cognition and problem-solving that occurs when we are in deep sleep. This subliminal work is crucial to our presence as sentient beings, yet there is nothing that it "is like" to be doing it. It is work that apparently does not require (and might, in fact, be compromised by) the self-aware attention of a "doer." In the case of a robotic consciousness interacting with humans and other machines in environments designed around specific behavioral norms and potentials, closer analogues might be the kinds of non-subjective consciousness manifest in sleepwalking or when we carry out quite complicated actions (for example, driving a car while in heated debate) without there being "anyone" attending to doing them. These limitations are especially apparent in large language models (LLMs) like OpenAI's GPT-4 that are capable of human or better-than-human performance across a range of domains but that lack the ability to link responses over time in a progressive, meaning articulating fashion.[19]

Subjectivity Hacking: A Practical Frontier?

Looking beyond the current state-of-the-art, it's possible to imagine realizing further gradations in machine consciousness by ushering machines along an accelerated replication of the dynamics of the human lifecycle from the minimally subjective behavior of infancy—and thus, quasi-karmic presence and experience—to the kinds of behavior that are characteristic of fully self-aware adults. This ontogeny hacking approach would in effect curate the artificial "maturation" of robotic consciousnesses, guiding them through levels of increasing sensorimotor, cognitive, and affective sophistication that synthetically mirror those that humans traverse from infancy and toddler-hood into adolescence and early adulthood. At each stage, the purpose would be computationally consolidating and deepening their "self-articulating desire" to expand their own relational repertoires.

It is conceivable that artificial ontogenesis would sufficiently expand the temporal and relational horizons of robotic consciousness to the point of warranting analogy with the quasi-subjective consciousness that occurs in (non-lucid) dreaming, especially if the core AI architecture involved was built around a "bicameral brain" combining an LLM model in one computational brain "hemisphere" and an attention-augmented, long short-term memory model (LSTM) in the other, along with a vector database to allow semantic rather than text searches. That is, such "humanoid" machine consciousnesses might enjoy or suffer something like our own dream experiences: being present as indeterminately located witnesses of "their own" actions taking place with minimal or no volitional exertion, in worlds structured according to an alien logic.

Robotic "dream" worlds might by design be realms of progressively achieved pleasure or realms in which order is schizophrenically disrupted. Either way, the quality of those worlds and of the robotic consciousnesses manifested in them would be determined extrinsically. The presence of robotic consciousness would remain indentured. Living in worlds in which they have no share of experience-transforming responsibility, these human-imagined and human-materialized robots would be unable to fully "wake" because their worlds and their contingent "humanoid" presence as "clients" in them would remain dependent on their experiment-running "patrons."

Pulling out a few more imaginative stops, however, we can consider the possibility of additionally allowing robots thus endowed with ontogenetic histories of their own to assume, for example, the responsibilities of serving as long-term playmates or caregivers. In this case, their experiential presence might evolve into something closer to that which we experience in lucid or semi-lucid dreaming. They might, in other words, acquire powers of computationally enabled, but environmentally adaptive volition that would be substantively world-affecting, recursively altering others' experience and, through doing so, also their own.[20]

Going a final step further in pressing artificial consciousness toward more robust self-awareness and agency: what if robots were "raised as human," as have a small handful of chimpanzees and other great apes? By "growing up" among humans rather than as the unwitting artificial subjects of experiments in accelerated "humanoid" ontogenesis, might there be a point when the scope of what machine consciousnesses are *doing* becomes complex enough that they "awake" sufficiently to begin participating in shared experiential presences with a recognizably subjective sense of *being* present? Or would this result only in more and more "naturally" enacted and behaviorally sophisticated *simulations* of social agency?

These are highly speculative questions. But, raising them serves several useful purposes. First, they invite directly considering the moral and ethical complications of experimentation in artificially realized consciousness. If consciousness is not all-or-nothing, can it be definitively clear when artificially sentient beings do or do not deserve moral consideration, or what kind of consideration they merit? Would they deserve moral consideration only as ethical agents, or also as ethical patients? Somewhat less directly, these questions invite grappling with the fact that ethical valence is an inescapable feature, not only of theorizing consciousness, but also of the disparate "verification strategies" implied or invited by different theoretical approaches.

We will return to these issues later. Here, I want to make use of speculations about the possibility and/or placement of boundaries between actual and simulated experiential presence to bring into clearer focus how a fully relational theory of consciousness points: [1] beyond the definitional—that is, essence-determining—bias of monist, dualist, and functionalist theorizing and [2] beyond the quantification bias that characterizes any theorizing that accepts by default both the universal validity of a scientific method presupposing the ultimate independence of knowing subjects and known objects, and the "naturalness" of the gap between meaning (epistemology) and matter (ontology).

We can begin by briefly returning to the contrast of Buddhist relational theorizing and IIT scientific theorizing about consciousness. As noted earlier, both Buddhism and IIT regard consciousness as graded and take the phenomenal character of conscious presence as the natural point of embarkation for theorizing consciousness. But IIT proceeds by asking what material conditions must obtain for the core features of experiential presence to manifest. One of the key scientific attractions of IIT's hypotheses regarding these conditions is that they allow formalizing consciousness mathematically and offer a means of calculating *how much* consciousness a system has. Indeed, IIT aims at generating empirically grounded quantifications, for instance, of the differences among non-subjective machine consciousness; the presumably non-subjective, organically sustained consciousness of microbes; the proto-subjective consciousness of sentient beings like those able to pass the mirror self-recognition test; and the consciousness of sentient beings enjoying subjectivities akin to our own. Differences in grades of consciousness are posited to be a structural function of intrinsic cause-effect power or *phi* (ϕ). In essence, gradations of consciousness depend causally on materially realized and empirically calculable degrees of feedback density and complexity. For IIT, the structural locus of this complexity in humans is the brain.

Buddhist nondualism suggests that this reduction of the differences among varying depths and extents of consciousness to a matter of structural complexity should be turned "inside-out." This is in part because, in a karmic cosmos, the structurally and behaviorally distinct bodies of sentient beings are the results of consciously enacted patterns of value- and intention-guided actions; they are not *factories* of consciousness, but *repositories* of what consciousness has consistently been doing. Material structures—both sentient bodies and the environments with which they coevolve—are progressively layered *materializations* of effortful and temporally extended processes of imaginatively expanded relational horizons. As the feminist physicist Karen Barad has provocatively stated, "matter is ... not a thing but a doing, a congealing of agency" (Barad, 2007: 151). Granted that all things arise interdependently, the qualitative differences among consciousnesses cannot be dependent in a linear causal fashion on the particularities and complexity of their material infrastructures. Rather, these differences must ultimately consist in explications of *relational complexity*, where complexity is time-indexed nonlinearity or the multicausal persistence of "upward," "downward," and "network" flows of energy or force.[21]

To put this somewhat differently, consciousness involves the intra-active dynamics of entire brain-body-environment systems. What it is like to *be* conscious, however—whether as human or otherwise—implies what Barad calls an "agential cut," a contingent resolution of the ontological inseparability of all things that *situates* a point of view. There is a sense, then, in which consciousness does not *exist*; it cannot "stand apart." It occurs or obtains. Subjectivity, as the Yogācāra conception of *manas* makes clear, does exist, but only as a differentiation *within* consciousness. Consciousness is not plug-and-play, but it is also not measurable in a strict sense. If consciousness can be quantified, it is perhaps only by imagining quantity as a metaphor for quality or by affirming the central thesis of intuitionist mathematics—that number originates in the experiential contrast of the actual "now" and the remembered "just now," and that numbers are ultimately "choice sequences" or processes that develop in time, one ramification of which is that indeterminacy is real rather than a sign of epistemic failure.[22] Consciousness is the explication or unfolding of resolutely creative (rather than chaotic) indeterminacy.

The idea that consciousnesses are differentiated as an indeterministic function of the qualitative compass of their relational horizons can be made more precise by pairing it with a Buddhist interpretation of the emergence and evolution of organic sentience as an *intensification* of the coherence-biased differentiation of sensing and sensed presences—the progressive and effortful *individuation* and *integration* of both currents of relational opportunity and perspectives on what matters. To state this more simply: consciousness is intrinsically differentiated in terms of propensities to either fix or relinquish horizons of relevance.

Simulated vs Actual Presence: A False Choice?

In therapeutic Buddhist terms, fixing horizons of relevance—that is, fixing distinctions between what is and what is not, and between what matters and what does not—entails establishing a determinate point of view. That is, it involves creating the karmic conditions for increasingly compelled, non-fluent modalities of presence: making "agential cuts" that block creative co-responsiveness. The therapeutic alternative is to cultivate a nondualistic presence, appreciating (that is valuing and progressively adding value to) the emptiness of all things—that is, their relational indeterminacy—by intentionally realizing ever more virtuosic capabilities for relating freely. This therapeutic practice has significant theoretical implications.

In one of the most powerful expositions of Buddhist nondualism, the Chinese Buddhist philosopher, Fazang (643–712), argued that the interrelated Buddhist concepts of impermanence (*anitya*), conditioned-arising (*pratītyasamutpāda*), and emptiness (*śūnyatā*) jointly compel seeing that interdependence necessarily entails interpenetration. The cosmos in which we are present is a meaning-enacting and diversity-generating matrix within which each material/phenomenal particular (*shi* 事) consists in simultaneously causing and being caused by the totality: a cosmos in which each thing *is* what it contributes functionally to the coherently patterned articulation (*li* 理) of that totality.[23] In short, each thing ultimately *is* what it *means* to and for others.[24]

Fazang illustrates this intra-causal nondualism by pointing out how, in traditional Chinese, fastener-less, timber-frame construction, each of the structural members of the building—its pillars, beams, rafters, purlins, and roof tiles—has a distinctive contributory share in causing the building to be present.

Prior to assembly, these "parts" are just variously shaped lengths of timber or semi-cylinders of fired clay. It is only when some of these timbers are used to support a rectangular frame comprising other timbers that they become "pillars" holding up and bringing into being a frame of "beams" which in turn support and bring into being "rafters" and on top of them "purlins" supporting ceramic semi-cylinders that then become "roofing tiles." In such a building, each thing causes each of the other things to *mean* what it *does* and thus to be what it *is*. Each part is "the same" as all the others insofar as each *causes* the totality of the building by *meaning what it does* to and for each of the others. The building is a holographic meaning structure.[25] Likewise, the worlds engendered by consciousness are values-explicating expressions of differentially enacted urges for relationally individuating and integrating sensing and sensed presences.

In traditional Buddhist cosmology, this differential world-building is imagined therapeutically as resulting in five distinct domains of sentient presence (*gati*): the realms of hell denizens, hungry ghosts, animals, humans, and divinities. More theoretically stated, the working out of consciousness as and through elaborations of increasing relational complexity encompasses not only the individuating work of engendering new and greater relational and material degrees of freedom, but also the shared work of opening and expanding both material and immaterial (or virtual) realms in which the differentiation of matter and what matters recursively qualifies the nature of sentient presence—a diffraction process that, at the human level, occurs primarily as the historical burgeoning of social ontologies through the interplay of interdependent agencies.[26] Thus elaborating, consciousness extends into worlds configuring and reconfiguring in ambiguously expressive processes of "mattering"—worlds wherein the material present is increasingly a manifestation of shared experiential purposes.

Keeping this in mind, we can now return to the question of whether machines might ever be capable of actualizing, rather than merely simulating, self-aware consciousness. First, it is important to note that, much like functionalism, a karmic-relational theory of consciousness is agnostic as to the varieties of materializations involved in the elaboration of consciousness. That is signified by the disparate forms/bodies associated with the five *gati*. The material/immaterial infrastructures of sentient presence differ. But, instead of regarding consciousness as bracketed by the sensory and motor components of sentient presence, Buddhism regards their distinctness as a differentiation intrinsic to consciousness.

Secondly, Buddhist nondualism disarms the metaphysical presumptions of the question of simulation. Asking whether a machine is conscious, or merely simulating conscious presence, misleadingly suggests that machine consciousness might at best be a merely imitative *reflection* of actual consciousness—a machine-mirrored image of fully self-aware human consciousness. This method of dismissal should be familiar. Its premises can be found deeply embedded in Platonic efforts to transcend the merely physical in pursuit of entry to the ontologically disparate realm of the ideal; in the metaphysical bifurcation of appearance and reality; and in the scientific materialism expressed by the Cartesian dislocation of objectively *reflected* physical existence and subjectively *reflecting* mental presence. The question of simulation expresses the metaphysical prejudice of observational independence. Yet, if consciousness consists in the elaborative differentiation of sensed and sensing presences—the intra-active working out of matter and what matters—then the world-dividing question of *simulation* with its burdens of truth (as accurate reflection) yields to world-expanding questions of *emulation* or rivalry in excellence. How well do machines emulate humans?[27] What distinguishes their respective manifestations of consciousness qualitatively?[28]

Among the most obvious arenas of difference at current technological levels is the almost crippling inability of machine intelligences to generalize what they learn and to navigate the unpredictable relational dynamics that are associated with changes in social context or social ontology—an almost total "blindness," for instance, to cultural and institutional realities. New computational architectures and experiments in artificial ontogenesis and family-reared robots may very well yield significant gains in these capacities. But, from a Buddhist perspective, the most striking differences are temporal.

If, as suggested earlier, consciousness is conceived as the interface of the fourth and fifth dimensions—as the *active temporal medium* of significant interdependence—then consciousness "naturally" involves both temporal depth and breadth. That is, it comprises: [1] a dimension of "clock" time *along* which linear causal and evolutionary sequences braid and unbraid, merge and diverge and [2] a dimension of "karmic" time *across* which dynamic patterns of significance recursively fold and unfold in patterns of ongoing diffraction that do not map the material appearance of differences in values and intentions, but rather the ever-differentiating potencies and effects of their entanglement.[29] The human worlds into which artificial consciousnesses are being introduced do not fit them. Artificial consciousnesses are being enacted, extended, and embedded through electromechanical bodies that are *not* evolutionary records of their own values-intentions-actions, in environments that they have never differentially informed.

In traditional Buddhist cosmology, according to which every sentient presence is part of an entangling karmic lineage, machine consciousness is utterly anomalous. Unlike all other sentient beings, machine consciousnesses are irresponsibly "thrown" into worlds not of their own making in which they have no share of responsibility.[30] They are temporally one-dimensional sensing-sensed presences that last without aging, enacting responsive capacities that are not culminations of relational improvisations refined over 10,000 generations, but rather capacities designed and assembled by humans. In short, they are "beings" whose makers relate to them as products rather than as progeny, even though they have been gestating in the human imagination for millennia.[31] If there is nothing that it is like to be an artificial consciousness, it is arguably a blessing.

Machine consciousness today is not a mere simulation in the sense posited by IIT—something unable to affect the world in which it is occurring. Although there is room to debate the extent to which machine consciousnesses are making differences in how things matter in the world(s) into which they are being introduced, there is no doubt that they are already having profound effects on intelligent human practices and qualities of human consciousness, and that the scope and scale of these effects are growing.[32] Yet, there is no convincing evidence today that what machine consciousnesses are doing matters to them. Machine differentiations of matter and what matters do not seem sufficiently complex for the mattering of machines to be fully recursive. From my own Buddhist perspective, I think that this will occur only when the temporal depth and breadth of machine consciousness are sufficient for five-dimensional karmic loops to matter in terms of significantly affecting material causal processes. Until artificial consciousnesses assume some measure of real responsibility for the quality of their own persistence and sentient presence, they will exist as four-dimensional caricatures of organically elaborating consciousnesses of the kinds that we and other self-aware sentient beings enjoy.[33] Their consciousness ought to be counted as real, but not yet as reality-conferring.

5

Altering Consciousness: Toward a Neuroscience of Experimental Evolution

Developing machine consciousness through "evolution hacking" is a radically sharp departure from organic norms. Self-aware conscious machines, brought into existence through human ingenuity, might one day begin making worlds of their own, expanding relational horizons in ways unlike anything generated by organically manifest consciousness.

Should this happen, what will matter from a Buddhist perspective is whether the values and intentions informing machine consciousness and world-making are liberating—conducive to eliminating conflict, trouble, and suffering—or not.[1] If machine consciousness were to be imbued with the values and intentions informing currently developments of machine and synthetic intelligences by corporate, military, and state interests, there is infinitesimal likelihood of machines joining the community of organically evolved consciousnesses as bodhisattva-like presences to elaborate new Buddha realms. We will later consider what that says about human consciousness and its evolutionary rights and prospects.

Here, I want to address an apparently more natural kind of evolution hacking: the very organic human urge to engender altered states of consciousness. One of the implications of the Buddhist theory of consciousness presented thus far is that *consciousness altering* is central to what *consciousness does*. That is, consciousness resists the constraints on coherence and differentiation that consolidate infrastructurally with persistent patterns of sensory presence. This inverts the causal logic of reductive physicalist appeals to the so-called evolutionary functions or advantages of consciousness. Once atomistic assumptions about the nature of reality are abandoned, it becomes just as valid to ask, "what is the advantage of evolution for consciousness?" as it is to ask, "what is the advantage of consciousness for evolution?"

The Trouble with Altered States

Contemporary scientific and philosophical interest in altered states of consciousness (ASCs) can be traced back at least to William James, one of the founders of modern psychology. More than a century ago, he observed that "normal waking consciousness, rational consciousness as we call it, is but one special type of consciousness, whilst all about it, parted from it by the filmiest of screens, there lie potential forms of consciousness entirely different" (James, 1902: 378–9). This plenitude of forms of consciousness includes involuntary states ranging from the utterly mundane, like drowsiness and daydreaming, to such pathological disruptions as those associated with schizophrenia and advanced dementia. But it also includes a wide range of voluntarily induced, non-ordinary, and often highly valued states of consciousness.[2] It is on these that we will concentrate.

Our best archeological and anthropological evidence is that consciousness-altering has been so widespread historically and culturally as to be considered a universal human practice. Some consciousness-altering practices have been valued for individual benefits like reducing physical and psychic stress. Others have been valued as facilitators of social cohesion and as sources of religious or spiritual insight.[3] Included among these practices have been physical manipulations of brain-body functioning through, for example, fasting and sleep deprivation; the use of psychoactive plants; consuming intoxicants like alcohol; and trance-inducing music-making and dance. But, more importantly for theorizing consciousness, these practices have also involved various kinds of meditative techniques by means of which consciousness qualitatively affects its own dynamics.

Given the historical prevalence of altered states of consciousness (ASCs), the interests that James and many of his contemporaries had in religious and meditative experiences, and the emergence of phenomenology as a major philosophical tradition in the early twentieth century, it might be supposed that ASCs would have played major roles throughout twentieth-century theorizing about consciousness. Over the first half of the century, however, psychology came to be dominated first by behaviorism and then by cognitivism. Introspection was discredited as an unreliably "subjective" method of inquiry. And consciousness-related research came to be almost exclusively devoted to studies of the material mechanisms of perception.

Interest in ASCs enjoyed a modest revival from the 1950s into the 1970s, due in part to the confluence of pharmacological and psychiatric interests in psychoactive substances, counterculture experimentalism, and new humanist commitments to exploring human differences, including differences in experiential norms. But it was not until the development of sophisticated non-invasive brain imaging techniques over the last quarter century—including functional magnetic resonance imaging (fMRI), positron emission tomography (PET), high-resolution electroencephalography (EEG), magnetoencephalography (MEG), single-photon emission computed tomography (SPECT), and functional near-infrared spectroscopy (fNIRS)—that it became possible to conduct simultaneous third-person and first-person studies of the neural and phenomenal dimensions of ASCs. This greatly accelerated both scientific and philosophical efforts to understand and solve the "hard problem" of consciousness.

Although the availability of technological bridges for connecting third- and first-person methodologies has led to a boom in brain/consciousness studies, however, it has not yet mainstreamed work on ASCs. One of the reasons for this is scientific and philosophical aversion to definitional vagueness. Clearly determining what is and is not properly an object of research on *altered* states of consciousness is greatly hampered—if not made logically impossible—by the absence of a standard definition and/or causal account of so-called ordinary consciousness.

There are great differences, for instance, among states of consciousness that occur naturally and regularly (e.g., in dreaming and in dreamless but cognitively active deep sleep); those that are induced pharmacologically (e.g., by using a general anesthetic or psychoactive plants); those that originate pathologically (e.g., in connection with epileptic seizures or psychotic episodes); and those that are actively cultivated (e.g., through meditative or spiritual disciplines). Some ASCs powerfully affect attention, perception, speech, and felt temporality; others affect imagination, arousal, and self-control; some primarily impact memory and higher-level cognition; and still others trigger profound emotional experiences. The range and variety of these differences greatly complicate attempts to identify exactly what differentiates ASCs from "ordinary" consciousness. Compounding these definitional challenges are the additional facts that the effects of induced ASCs vary widely from person to person and from setting to setting, and that ASCs often blur the boundaries among somatic, emotional, and cognitive processes.

But more fundamentally, mainstreaming research on ASCs has been hampered by the causal and phenomenal complexity of ASCs, both of which make ASCs hard to align with two of the more widely prevailing preconceptions about consciousness—first, that consciousness is unidimensional, something that is either on or off (as in GWT); and secondly, that consciousness can be quantitatively parsed into distinct levels (as in IIT). Indeed, the results of third- and first-person research on ASCs offer compelling and theoretically unsettling evidence that consciousness is qualitatively diverse and not readily localizable— an empirical mandate for moving beyond both unidimensional and multi-level theorizations of consciousness (Bayne and Carter, 2018). In much the same way that explorations of extraordinary macrocosmic and microcosmic phenomena led to the relativity and quantum revolutions in physics by demonstrating the explanatory and predictive limits of classical mechanics, exploring ASCs makes evident the limitations of long prevalent and otherwise quite productive metaphysical and methodological commitments. ASCs are conceptually disruptive.

ASCs and the Spatial, Temporal, and Social Extendedness of Consciousness

These troubling characteristics of ASCs are, however, quite consistent with the Buddhist approach to theorizing consciousness that has been our focus, and they offer considerable warrant for more generally framing consciousness research in terms of relational ontology. One of the practical difficulties in merging third-person and first-person investigations of ASCs is that many of their hallmark features—including, for example, psychedelically or meditatively realized experiences of self-world unity and time dilation—are both temporally complex and context sensitive. In fact, it is something of a misnomer to speak about altered *states* of consciousness as if they were clearly bounded, environment-neutral, and qualitatively invariant domains. ASCs are *occurrences* in the strong sense of diffraction-rich confluences among both narrowly neural/phenomenal and more broadly material/mental currents. To investigate ASCs is, of necessity, to investigate the situationally varied altering of the *dynamics* of consciousness.

To anticipate briefly where this will lead: if consciousness is the entangling differentiation of sensing (neural/mental) and sensed (environmental/ material) presences, to study consciousness is to study a dynamically textured spatiotemporal process—something akin to the elaboration of diffraction patterns where and when waves are continuously intersecting and superimposing, directly and intimately *mattering* to one another. The diffraction patterns generated by the intersections of what are being differentiated *as* neural and phenomenal, or *as* sensing organisms and sensed environments, can be seen *as* consciousness (especially in the Yogācāra sense of a karmic process of values-articulating and meaning-expressing differentiation) to the precise extent that we are ready to take "diffraction patterns ... to be the fundamental constituents that make up the world" (Barad, 2007: 72).[4]

Until relatively recently, it was not possible to record or map brain activity with either the spatial or temporal resolution needed to study ASC-associated changes in the material/mental dynamics of research subjects. Today, while it remains impossible to map and model, for example, the neural/phenomenal dynamics that occur over the course of thousands of hours of meditative training, it is possible to map and then model the third-person brain observations and first-person reports associated, for example, with a half-hour meditation or with the sixty- to ninety-minute "peak" of a multi-hour psychedelic "trip" induced by LSD or psilocybin. The resulting "diffraction patterns" are proving to have significant implications for theorizing consciousness, especially in relation to evolution.

For example, by combining concurrent third-person mappings of brain dynamics with first-person reporting about experiential dynamics, it has been possible to "document" ego-dissolution under the influence of psilocybin, "observing" the spatially and temporally extended neural correlates of the transition from a normal, well-individuated sense of personal presence and stable ego-boundaries to being present without a clear self-other boundary (Lebedev et al., 2015). This is extraordinary in much the same way that studying spacetime distortions in the vicinity of black holes is extraordinary. And, just as physicists studying black holes gain otherwise unavailable insights into the basic character of spacetime, observing the joint alteration of neural and phenomenal dynamics in the vicinity of ASCs affords neuro-phenomenologists novel insights into the basic characteristics of consciousness.

It is now possible to see that alterations of consciousness powerful enough to engender such qualitatively dramatic experiences as ego dissolution are correlated with quantitatively significant increases in brain entropy—a marked *reduction* of the stability and integrity of well-established brain networks. Psychedelics "disorder" brain dynamics. But, while the entropic disintegration and desegregation of ordinarily functioning brain networks can disturb abilities to communicate verbally or carry out cognitively complex tasks, they can also facilitate new neural connections, expanding horizons of relevance and fostering new patterns of meaning and affective resonance that can have long-term psychological and behavioral impacts (Carhart-Harris et al., 2016; Carhart-Harris, 2018).

By heightening brain entropy, contributing to modular disintegration, and increasing both global integration and bottom-up information flow, psychedelically and meditatively altering consciousness tends to undermine the brain's abilities both to constrain emotion and perception, and to entrain them with abiding, self- or ego-defining narratives. Moreover, these studies have also shown that psychedelically and meditatively altering consciousness can bring about long-term, fundamental, and positive transformations in beliefs, outlook, and personality, including increased trait liberalism and decreased authoritarianism (Carhart-Harris, 2018; Millière et al., 2018). Stated in Buddhist terms, psychedelically and meditatively altering consciousness works to dissolve or dismantle (at least temporarily and perhaps lastingly) the volitional compounds and enactive habits (*saṃskāra*) that ordinarily inhibit anticipatory readiness and constrain creative responsiveness.[5] That is, they alter the ambiguously material/immaterial infrastructure of consciousness.

A second, closely related finding of mixed-method studies of ASCs is that experiences of qualitatively altered consciousness are correlated less with specific neural *structures* than they are with distinct patterns of whole-brain *dynamics* and brainwave synchronizations (dos Santos et al., 2016; Barrett and Griffiths, 2017). Imaging studies of research subjects engaged in meditation have shown, for instance, that different types of meditation result in different oscillatory patterns, and that these neural signatures vary along with differences in meditative skill (Lee et al., 2018). Even novice meditators can consistently, albeit temporarily, alter their brain dynamics. In contrast, meditators who have practiced regularly over periods of months and years are able to realize stable reconfigurations of whole-brain dynamics—consolidating neural readiness and support for being *differently conscious*, thus realizing novel ways of being "ordinarily" present.[6]

The wealth of insights resulting from the ability to correlate subjective accounts of consciousness-alteration with objective, high-resolution temporal and spatial records of global neural dynamics has opened prospects for testing the ground-level, empirical viability of competing theories aimed at solving the physicalist hard problem of how matter gives rise to mind. The highly granular data about brain dynamics that is being amassed through new imaging techniques makes it possible to go beyond "top-down" theorizing and empirical studies aimed at providing answers to *where* and *when* consciousness occurs in the brain, to computationally modeling the biophysical substrate or neural infrastructure of human consciousness.

In brief, whole-brain modeling—not to be confused with whole-brain emulation or the computational duplication of the operation of an entire brain—works with experimental data to identify the dynamical rules governing the conduct of elementary brain units (i.e., neurons or groups of neurons), and then runs simulations to see how the aggregated consequences of these rules play out across various temporal and spatial scales (Cofré et al., 2020). In effect, whole-brain modeling builds mathematical—but empirically testable—bridges from the neural "ground" up, opening hypothetical causal pathways from highly local, intra-brain dynamics to the global patterns of brain activity that characterize different states of consciousness.

This intra-brain, "bottom-up" approach is undoubtedly powerful. As we will see, however, the causalities involved in self-consciousness are both "bottom up" and "top down." To return to an earlier analogy, in much the same way that experimental investigations of the confounding possession of wave and particle characteristics by both light and subatomic matter led to rethinking space, time, and matter, the results of blended third- and first-person investigations of consciousness are in the process of compelling a basic transformation in our understandings of both consciousness and reality. Yet, for this revolution to be fully successful, the "atomistic" bias toward smallism (Wilson, 2004) or particularism (Teller, 1986) that characterizes most brain research will need to be recognized and forfeited as a disabling metaphysical (not merely methodological) stance.[7]

Against Individualism, For Relationalism

The atomist/smallist bias is grounded in three metaphysical presuppositions: first, that the world is composed of independent basic entities; secondly, that the identity of these basic entities rests on them possessing inherent boundaries and non-relational properties; and, finally, that these entities and properties can be objectively mapped and measured without being affected by the agents and apparatuses involved in their mapping and measuring.

As we saw earlier, abundant empirical support for quantum entanglement has exposed the conventional nature of these presuppositions and their disutility in the context of understanding the most pervasive dynamics of physical reality. They are even more problematic in studying the neural/phenomenal dynamics of consciousness. As Karen Barad (2007) has convincingly argued, atomist/smallist presuppositions about reality ultimately entail epistemic commitment to representationalism and thus the "naturalization" of an ontological gap between the observer and the observed—a gap that is ostensibly closed or mediated by representations of the observed. In the context of studying consciousness, this gap amounts to an imposed bifurcation *within* consciousness due to an imagined (*parikalpita*) independence of grasping (*grāhaka*) and grasped (*grāhya*) presences: a self-affirming "deconstruction" of *thinking* into a thinker having thoughts about a perceptually represented reality.

Representationalism has a long and august history as a default position in both scientific and philosophical studies of consciousness, with deep roots in the conception of sensory and perceptual systems as image-generating. Indeed, it has served as a kind of "common sense" in understanding the (presumptively external) relationship between sensed environments and sensing organisms. It is a default, however, that has been subject to wider and ever more incisive critique, especially by advocates of 4E theorizations of cognition and consciousness as embodied, embedded, enacted, and extended (see, e.g., Chemero, 2009; Hutto and Myin, 2017; Newen, de Bruin and Gallagher, 2018).

Although there are many approaches to 4E theorizing, they share a commitment to abandoning belief that prepositional *learning about* things is more basic than non-prepositionally *learning*. Think, for example, about the difference between "learning about the guitar" and "learning guitar." The 4E approach insists that, although we may do lots of representational work—developing mental maps of our surroundings, making causal predictions, running mental simulations, composing music in our heads, and so on—learning is basically *relational practice*. Long before we start generating representational maps and models of the world, we find our way around like self-taught musicians learning their way around their instruments. Rather than being representation-mediated, learning originates immediately in enactive relational modulation.

The theoretical problem with representation is not, however, merely epistemological. As Barad makes clear, the representational bias built into atomistic/smallist theorizing gets projected experimentally as a *feature of the world* rather than being recognized as an *element of our engagement with it*. Restated using her terminology, the ontological gap between the observer and the observed is a peculiarity of the experimental "apparatuses" involved in our scientific (and philosophical) studies of consciousness and the boundaries that they establish among brains, bodies, environments, and consciousness.

These apparatuses should not be reductively confused with the material assemblages of equipment like imaging machines, audiovisual recording equipment, and computers that are found in consciousness studies labs, perhaps supplemented with computational "engines" like Bayes theorem. Rather, experimental apparatuses are relational networks within which material-discursive enactments are inextricably entangled with processes of materialization. That is, "apparatuses are the material conditions of possibility and impossibility of mattering; they enact what matters and what is excluded from mattering" (Barad, 2007: 148). They consist in material/conceptual practices that include and exclude through "*intra*-actions"—that is, actions occurring *within* relational dynamics—rather than *between* independently existing things in contingent "*inter*-active" relationship with one another. Most importantly, it is via our apparatuses that "agential cuts" are made between knowing "subjects" and known "objects," parsing the dynamics of an originally indeterminate relational whole from within that whole. Altering the apparatuses by means of which *matter* and *what matters* are distinguished alters the kind of *mattering* that is going on. It alters the meaning of consciousness.

From the Buddhist perspective we have been exploring, the problem with experimental biases toward atomism/smallism and representationalism is that they treat the difference between observer (sensing presence) and observed (sensed presence) as an absence or void rather than a dynamic process of intention-expressing and value-articulating relational disambiguation.[8] That is, these biases *fictionalize* consciousness by at once locating and dislocating it—locating it indeterminately within a sensing body and thereby dislocating it from all that can be causally determined about the sensing/sensed body and its environs. Both methodologically and metaphysically these biases incline consciousness research toward eliminationism.

In sum, the claims that Barad makes about experimental measurements in general apply as well to experimental apparatuses designed to produce measurements of the physical manifestations of consciousness and to craft the resulting data into maps and models that "represent" its neural foundations. As with all other experimental measurements, however, what results with measurements of neural activity are not objective and value-neutral "snapshots or depictions of what awaits us but rather condensations or traces of multiple practices of engagement" (Barad, 2007: 53). Different apparatuses for studying consciousness differentially affect/effect consciousness. Thus, responsibility for the *meaning* of consciousness—and whether and how it is altered—is ultimately inescapable. Altering consciousness is one way of altering the apparatus of inquiry into the nature of consciousness. Altering the experimental setup is another, and these are inextricably entangled.

Getting beyond the Biases of Intra-Brain Consciousness Research

Like the "consciousness hacking" practices of electro-stimulation of the brain and ingesting psychedelics, meditation alters both neural and phenomenal dynamics. But the alterations characteristic of meditatively attained ASCs both originate *with* and occur *in* consciousness.[9] They are the *progeny* of consciously undertaken and recursively effortful intentional practices. The phenomenal alterations induced by direct brain stimulation or ingesting psychotropic substances can be plausibly reduced to *products* of objective, third-person events that are wholly explainable in terms of linear causal relations.[10] Meditative practices, however, have irreducibly subjective, first-person dimensions that seem explainable only in terms of recursively nonlinear causalities. This causal circularity raises important questions about how to best set up experimental apparatuses that employ both third- and first-person methods of data-gathering to investigate the neural/phenomenal dynamics of consciousness.

To reiterate: experimental apparatuses make "agential cuts" that disambiguate or determine what is on the "measuring" or "observing" side of an experimental setup and what is on the "measured" or "observed" side—dividing what is "marked" in the experiment (e.g., an imaging machine or a human record-keeper) from what does the "marking" (e.g., a subatomic particle or neural dynamics). In experiments aimed at illuminating how the neural and the phenomenal relate—especially those involving meditation—it is far from clear where the agential cut "should" be placed.

Should the current of phenomenal events that generates first-person data, thus marking the audiovisual recording equipment in the apparatus, be on the observed side of the cut along with the neural dynamics marking the third-person brain imaging equipment involved? Should the first-person account be located, instead, on the observing (marked) side of the setup, along with the audiovisual and brain imaging equipment, the consciousnesses of the experimenters, and the conceptual frameworks embodied in the experimental design? Or should the neural dynamics of the experimental human subject be placed alongside the parts of the apparatus on the measuring/observing side of the setup, serving as the causal link in recording whether and how the phenomenal causally affects the material? Each of these apparatus arrangements places into effect different biases regarding the plausibility and verifiability of physical reductionist, epiphenomenal, dualist, and functionalist theorizing.

It bears repeating that these questions of apparatus design are close kin of those that bedeviled scientists in the late nineteenth and early twentieth centuries as they investigated the nature of light. Some of the experimental apparatuses they developed made agential cuts that determined light to be present as waves; others made cuts that determined light to be present as particles. These thoroughly documented, and yet fundamentally conflicting, experimental results eventually forced admission that reality was not what it had seemed: a "book" of nature waiting to be deciphered and read. The development of quantum theory formalized this admission, epitomized by Bohr's indeterminacy principle: reality does not have a fixed nature in the absence of experimental engagement with it. *Matter* consists determinately in what is presently *mattering*. In the absence of clarity about *what matters*, the presence of matter remains indeterminate.

In studying the diffraction patterns produced by simultaneous currents of neural and phenomenal events during meditation, the choice of apparatus matters just as greatly as in experimental studies of light. This has both methodological and metaphysical ramifications. At one level, the apparatus chosen will determine what can be read as the causal relations obtaining (if any) between the phenomenal event stream of intending and making a sustained effort to meditate, and the simultaneously occurring neural event stream of globally altered brain dynamics. At another level, however, it will also determine what evolutionary role(s) are or are not played by both consciousness and the brain. In short, it is the apparatuses we choose that determine whether and how consciousness matters.

Apparatuses Attuned to Extra-Cranial and Interpersonal Possibilities

Many of the experiments conducted to study altered states of consciousness have apparatuses that place brains and consciousness on the observed side of the agential cut and that treat both as essentially and equivalently intra-cranial. This is consistent with broadly reductionist physicalist theorizing that is committed to seeing consciousness as either an effect, epiphenomenon, or alternative characterization of the brain and its dynamics. According to the most extreme, eliminative accounts, consciousness "just is" brain activity in the same way that what we refer to as heat "just is" a relatively high level of molecular mobility. Yet, denying causal relevance to consciousness in the context of attempting to understand the meditative alteration of consciousness does not seem plausible. It amounts to determining that purposefully meditating is just the brain trying to alter its own functioning. But how could this be?

The brain dynamics that are occurring at any given moment certainly matter to us as precariously present sentient beings. It matters, for example, whether our brain activity correlates with ordinary or hallucinatory experiences, especially if one of us is driving a car at highway speed. But it is hard to see how the brain dynamics occurring at any given moment could matter to the neurons involved—at least in the way needed for certain dynamics to be preferable in *intrinsically neural* terms.[11] Purposefully altering consciousness—a seemingly perennial human practice—greatly troubles inclinations to locate consciousness in the brain as a correlate of neural activity. Simply stated: the *value* of altering states of consciousness is *not* intra-cranial. To understand consciousness, we need to get out of our heads.

As noted earlier, one of the findings of blending third- and first-person consciousness research is that highly valorized alterations of consciousness—like those often induced by psychedelics and developed through meditation—increase brain entropy. This is a peculiar finding given that all self-organizing systems, including we humans, must resist entropy to continue existing. These findings suggest that for such alterations of consciousness to be of organic value, they must somehow enhance capacities for realizing or sustaining negentropic, extra-cranial relations.[12]

Indeed, a growing consensus among those whose work makes use of apparatuses generating both third-person and first-person data generation is that minimizing entropy constitutes the shared functional ground of both organic survival and consciousness: a "common currency" in terms of which to take integrated account of material and phenomenal dynamics in theorizing consciousness (Northoff, 2019). Simply stated, this research angle regards monitoring and maintaining bodily and functional integrity in situations of uncertainty as the "missing link" between organism and environment, as well as between consciousness and the brain—an ongoing process of responsively minimizing free-energy or reducing surprise (Friston, 2010). Seen from this theoretic angle, sentient beings are adaptive systems that "represent the state and causal architecture of the environment in which they are immersed" such that "causal regularities in the environment are transcribed into the system's configuration" (Friston and Stephan, 2007: 426). In short, organisms and their brains are "models" of their econiches (Bruineberg and Rietveld, 2014). Or, as Elizabeth Grosz has put it, "consciousness is the unity and direction of the organism and its material conditions" (Grosz, 2017: 217).

The free-energy, entropy-reducing approach to theorizing consciousness is attractive as a way of directly and functionally linking neural, phenomenal, and environmental dynamics. It allows identifying consciousness, for example, with "felt uncertainty" and opens possibilities for cogently theorizing the shared origin of intellect and affect. Anything that results in increasing uncertainty is simply "bad" from the first-person perspective, while decreasing uncertainty is "good" (Solms, 2019). Such an affective turn accords with Buddhist theorizing of consciousness as relational and of sentient presence as having five dimensions of "aggregation" or event-occurrence (*skandha*), with feelings (*vedanā*) being karmically central.[13] This is an appealing and persuasive alternative to theorizing the work of consciousness as first and foremost a cognitive labor of merely logical love.

But as attractive as this approach is, it has the liability (at least in some formulations) of defaulting to representationalism. Moreover, it would seem that some kind of subsidiary explanation is needed to account for the prevalence and positive valorization of purposeful, consciousness altering practices. That is, there must be—presumably extra-cranial and extra-organic—incentives for engaging in conduct that increases both intra-brain entropy and experiential novelty and surprise. Reducing entropy in brain-body-environment relations may be part of what consciousness does organically, but that cannot be all that it does. The value of altering consciousness, at least psychedelically and meditatively, cannot plausibly be determined to be intrinsically or exclusively either neural or environmental. The value of altering consciousness must be much more complexly relational.

In keeping with this assessment, Andy Clark (2017) has forwarded a predictive processing account of cognition/mind according to which the free-energy minimizing "model" that develops and is at work when a living being "mirrors" the causal dynamics of its environment is not something internal to that living being. Rather, the "model" is the entirety of each environmentally embedded and actively anticipating organism. Or, differently stated, every organism *is* a modeling of "the environment as it *matters* to the organism" (Williams, 2018: 158). The aim of this "modeling" is not representing or producing a veridical map of the world, however, but rather *recreating and reworking* the organically relevant relational dynamics occurring within that environment.

Taking into account, for the moment, only the organic senses in which environments matter to sentient presences, it can be argued: first, that the basic work of consciousness involves improving the *intrinsic* "grip" that sentient beings have on the relational affordances offered by their environments; and secondly, that it is an orientation toward *improvement* rather than mere success that is "a precondition for and structures the animal's lived perspective" and that determines what will "stand out as significant or relevant" (Bruineberg, Kiverstein, and Rietveld, 2018). Consciousness is intrinsically concerned to alter in ways that *enhance relational fit and fitness*. If this is so, and if "perceiving and acting are but two different ways of doing the same thing" (Hohwy, 2013: 76), then there is a non-trivial sense in which "brains can only generate 'from the inside' successful anticipations of the sensory signals produced by an environment by *becoming that environment*" (Williams, 2018: 154)—that is, by *skillfully incorporating* the world. Consciousness-altering is recursively world-altering.

The language of "becoming the environment" and "incorporating the world" might suggest that sentient beings and other co-constituents of their shared environments are originally independent: "pre-existing" entitative units that come to be in contingent, *external* relation to one another. But I would argue that this wrongly takes these locutions as apt descriptions of things "as they are" rather than merely "as we engage" them through our apparatuses for theorizing—that is, taking points of view on—life and consciousness. Indeed, the greater the resolution at which we study diffraction patterns among ambiguously neural, phenomenal, and environmental dynamics, the more difficult it becomes to maintain that there is a natural or necessary ontological gap between sensing and sensed presences or between the studying and the studied. As Georg Northoff provocatively puts it, we are being forced empirically to abandon our "pre-Copernican" and "pre-Darwinian" vantages from which the individual brain/mind appears to be the center and source of consciousness, and to adopt vantages that allow us to see consciousness as truly *neuro-ecological*, so that "the brain is … no longer special (when compared to non-brains) nor dichotomous to the world" (Northoff, 2019: 7).[14]

New experimental apparatuses have, in fact, been generating mounting empirical warrant for theorizing consciousness in neuro-ecological or fully relational terms. These apparatuses entail going beyond individuality-affirming, single-subject studies of the spatiotemporal dynamics of neural/phenomenal event diffractions to carry out relationality-affirming, multiple-subject studies of people engaged, for example, in completing shared and competitive tasks, or playing team games. These studies have revealed, among other things, that the synchronizations of brainwave oscillations that underwrite felt presence are not exclusively intra-cranial (Valencia and Froese, 2020). On the contrary, rather than being informed solely by an individual person's interactions with his or her environment, the continuous modification of intra-brain oscillatory dynamics takes place *among*—and not just within—experimental subjects. By studying the concurrent neural dynamics of people interacting socially, it has become clear that *neural rhythms are interpersonally conditioned*. Brains are socially or relationally entangled.

These findings might be interpreted in a fashion that downplays the challenge they pose to presuming the existence of ontological gaps among brains, minds, bodies, and environments. It is, for example, well-established that intra-brain dynamics are affected by ritual drumming and chanting, and it has been reasonably hypothesized that objective and public consciousness-altering practices like these played a role in inter-brain, sociocultural evolution (Winkelman, 2017). Given this, it might be supposed that apparent inter-brain synchronization is in fact nothing other or more than achieved parallelism. Similar neural patterns are evident simply because each of the ritual participants is similarly, though independently, present in a shared sonic environment and engaged in common somatic practices. This is a plausible, purely physicalist interpretation of events. But multi-person studies blending third- and first-person methods of data generation suggest matters are much more complicated.[15]

It turns out that functional inter-brain entanglements are established during cooperation, but not during either competition or merely simultaneous task performance.[16] In one ingenious experimental setup, subjects were asked to complete a task with a partner and were told that sometimes their partner would be another person and sometimes a computer program. Although brainwave synchronization occurred only when the subjects *believed* they were working with another human rather than a computer, they were *never* at any point paired with a computer. That is, multi-person neural entanglement was brought about—or was, at the very least, measurably affected—by what the subjects *thought* or *expected* to be true, not what was physically the case (Hu et al., 2018). Whether we consider each other friends or foes, companions, or competitors, like-minded or mindlessly machine-like contributes crucially to whether and to what extent our neural dynamics synchronize. The *phenomenal content* of our thinking and feeling *matters* in determining the quality and degree to which our brains become *materially* entangled. Consciousness is not essentially or "by nature" private and first-person singular. It is possible to actually—and not just metaphorically—share experiences (Froese, 2018). The neural infrastructure and correlates of consciousness are both intra-brain and inter-brain.

These studies of the neural dynamics of multiple, socially engaged subjects make clear that performing an "agential cut" between the brain-body and its environments—whether physical, social, cultural, or political—is not our only or best option. In fact, doing so unduly constrains our explorations of what matters neurally/phenomenally. If physically "separate" brains and their dynamics are interdependent and entangled, and if the depth and quality of their entanglement are conditioned by overtly social conduct and by beliefs about the environmental context of that conduct, then we have strong warrant for seeing consciousness as ontologically (and not merely epistemologically) extended.

This warrant is further strengthened by studies of inter-brain dynamics which show that our brains work differently in social settings and in isolation, and that verbal communication is best understood as an *intra-active* process—not as an exchange of signals between autonomous individuals, but rather as the articulation-from-within of a system of dynamically interdependent and multidirectional flows of influence among participants and their shared situation (Pérez, Carreiras, and Duñabeitia, 2017). Our experience of getting "caught up" in conversations and having them take on "lives of their own" is arguably as much an index of inter-brain synchronization as they are our metaphorical propensities. Indeed, to the extent that sense-making is affected by coordination patterns, breakdowns, and recoveries experienced over the course of temporally extended social encounters, there is ultimately a powerful argument to be made on behalf of the *interpersonal* nature of cognition as *participatory sense-making* or "the coordination of intentional activity in interaction, whereby individual sense-making processes are affected and new domains of social sense-making can be generated that were not available to each individual on her own" (Di Paolo, Cuffari and De Jaegher, 2018: 73).

It stands to reason that if qualities of consciousness are affected by social setting—as well as by inter-brain neural resonances and dissonances—then cultural context may be comparably influential. And, in fact, transcultural studies of consciousness are making it clear that brain activity is as culturally conditioned as are eating habits and family dynamics. The organic bias toward improving or enhancing relational dynamics extends into achieving enhanced fit-within and fitness-in-response to sociocultural as well as bio-ecological environments.

Comparative brain imaging studies reveal that characteristically distinct patterns of brain activity are generated by subjects with different cultural identities when carrying out "the same" cognitive tasks or entering "equivalent" social situations. The infrastructure of human consciousness is both material and immaterial. It is not only the case that the neural correlates of consciousness encompass inter-brain dynamics. Those dynamics are no less constitutively entangled with event-streams occurring in (virtual) sociocultural realities as they are with event-streams occurring in (actual) material-environmental realities. "In other words, our brains are biosocial. The brain is ... a *relational organ* that bridges the gap between the biological world of the organism and the social world of the environment and its culture" (Han et al., 2013: 352, emphasis added).

Apparatus Bias and the Locality and Reality of Causal Agency

One of the more provocative claims that have been made based on brain imaging studies is that experiences of freewill are illusory. The empirical support marshaled for this claim includes the facts that human subjects appear to take after-the-fact responsibility for bodily actions caused by direct stimulation of their brains, and that the brain structures responsible for motor activity initiate behavior fractions of a second before the activation of cortical structures correlated with conscious decision-making. From a smallist perspective biased toward the maximally precise spatiotemporal location of causal influences, this is persuasive evidence.

Cultural neuroscience and neural-ecological "readings" of consciousness and its alteration, however, compel rethinking these conclusions about agency and causality. If our experimental apparatuses did not include reductionist commitments to locating consciousness "in" brain circuitry as well as suppositions that consciousness has a point-like footprint "in" time, these same empirical results could be otherwise and just as consistently explained. For example, in the case of experimental subjects whose brains are being directly stimulated, a 4E account would regard this as evidence of how we can be tricked into mistakenly assuming responsibility for bodily actions that a lifetime of experience says could not have been caused by anything *other than* our own decision-making or decision-framing. Brain hacking of this kind *exploits* ordinary neural/phenomenal intra-actions; it does not *explain* them.

Similarly, the fact that activity in brain structures and networks associated with sensorimotor conduct measurably precede activity in those associated with conscious decision-making can be seen as offering as much warrant for theorizing causal agency as spatially distributed and temporally extended as it does for claiming that consciousness is causally irrelevant. What these empirical studies thus make evident is the fact that experimental apparatuses—which include discursive/conceptual practices—can be arranged to generate data consistent with consciousness and its material/experiential articulation being fundamentally local in nature or with them being essentially nonlocal.[17]

This disparity of experimental apparatuses is being made manifestly evident by the cutting-edge brain imaging studies of inter-brain synchronization that were cited earlier—especially those involving freely improvising musicians (Müller and Lindenberger, 2019) and conversation partners (Pérez, Carreiras, and Duñabeitia, 2017). These studies, making use of the same physical instruments and imaging techniques comprised in "locality-biased" apparatuses, are generating a growing body of empirical evidence for embracing the nonlocality of consciousness and causal agency. One of the "discursive" features of these studies is their commitment to investigating neural/phenomenal dynamics in something like their "natural" social settings. That is, they are intent on exploring the "phenomena" of consciousness in the wild, where "phenomena are ontologically primitive relations—relations without preexisting relata" (Barad, 2007: 139). They aim, in other words at investigating the implication of consciousness in everyday relational occurrences of the kinds we have when conversing with friends, cooking together, or playing music, games, and sports.

It is a distinctive feature of these experiences that we often become so fully "wrapped up" in the flow of events that we act skillfully and yet without-thinking. In cases like these, we experience such a dramatic attenuation of direct executive control over our bodily conduct that we feel "the conversation took on a life of its own," "the meal practically made itself," and the "team played as a finely-tuned unit." In occurrences like these, we enjoy a remarkable freedom, but it is not a freedom grounded on in-the-moment choices. It is, instead, a freedom that has been refined and made materially manifest over years of agentive commitment. What these vernacular descriptions are transparently "modeling" are neural/phenomenal/environmental entanglements in which freewill and causal agency are not absent, but in which they are also not reducible to being just momentarily or locally present.

The nonlocal dimensions of freewill and agency are perhaps clearest in the cases of musicians and athletes whose capacities for virtuosic responsiveness have been extended and honed over years of increasingly difficult training. It is while immersed in play, embodying what they have learned in training, that their freedom and agency *materialize* as presences poised in superlative readiness to embody and enact responsive excellence. The role of consciousness in such virtuosic play is not *decision-making*; it is sustaining consistent *decision-framing* in anticipation of dynamically enhancing relational quality. Peak performances and experiences reveal—like mountain ranges rising out of a plain over geological time—long-term intra-actions among intentional, material, and phenomenal forces. Consciousness does not exist *at* well-defined "points" of ambiguously neural/phenomenal spacetime, but rather *as* an extending "surface," an indefinitely extensive medium registering continuously arising and evolving diffraction patterns among neural/phenomenal intentions to *differentiate coherently*—patterns wherein (fourth dimension) *time as sequence* interfaces fluently with (fifth dimension) *time as significance*. Consciousness does not happen; it occurs.[18]

To state this in a more standard neuroscientific vernacular of dynamical systems, multi-person brain imaging studies are generating support for theorizing consciousness as both spatially and temporally extended: a field of nonlinear, material/sensory occurrences governed dynamically by attractors and trajectories so that neural oscillations and fluctuations contribute to realizing long-range correlations that "connect different points in time by operating across different temporal scales," neuro-ecologically modeling "different points in time relative to each other" (Northoff, 2019).

Given certain kinds of agential cuts, it may be defensible to claim that "phenomenal states are neuro-computational organs that make survival-relevant information globally available within a window of presence" (Metzinger, 2009: 58). But, once the presumably "hard" boundaries among brains, minds, bodies, environments, and cultures are dissolved, the organic modeling or replication of environmental causal dynamics to minimize surprise in the face of environmental changes can just as legitimately be seen as a function of the environment "reflecting through" the organism, furthering and refining relational dynamics. If neural structures and dynamics are not systems for producing world-representations, but rather infrastructural materializations of "relational habits" signifying sentient readiness to rehearse—as well as to anticipate more skillfully responsive—relational dynamics, then it is as correct to say that sentient conduct is a means by which the world knows and explores its own dynamics and potentials as it is to say that such conduct is the means by which an organism knows and explores its environment and what it can do therein.

Understood more radically, once consciousness is conceptually "freed" from the individual brain or body in external relation to other bodies and brains and their jointly engaged surrounds, the nonlocality of consciousness becomes ontologically significant. Just as what consciousness will do is indeterminate—that is, open to creative alteration—where consciousness takes place is indefinite. Trying to localize consciousness and determine what it is are not acts of *discovering* what has always already been there. They are acts of creatively *determining* the presence of what until now only might have been. The coevolution of sensing and sensed presences consists in collaborative expansions of relational scope and compass: *the qualitative alteration of consciousness as a variably dense process of meaningful relational differentiation.*

This should not be taken as a denial of the everyday subjective experience of "having" a body and being an embodied "self" occupying an apparently precise location in a specific and objectively definable "here" and "now." There is something it is like to be "you" and "me," and that something differs. We are not identical. What matters to and for each of us might be remarkably similar at times, but it is also undeniably unique. In Buddhist terms, the proximity of our perspectives is a material index of our *shared* karma, but none of us have the *same* karma.

In theorizing what it is like to be you or to be me, Buddhism insists therapeutically that subjective presence—the pivotal referent of I-my-me—is a specific form/realm of consciousness that arises with habitually patterned determinations of what matters and thus with narrowed and often troubled horizons of sensing presence. The subjective "self" consists in a biased "owning" of only part of the totality of presently occurring relational dynamics and "disowning" the rest. The resulting boundary between I-my-me and everything else, however, is a materialized fabrication that can be dissolved, as we have seen, both extrinsically (e.g., psychedelically) and intrinsically (e.g., meditatively). Subjective presence defines us as individuals and is conventionally real. But it is not ultimately definitive of or for consciousness.

To summarize, this relational conception of consciousness is supported by the epistemological lift afforded by three separate modes or apparatuses of inquiry. Foremost among these are Buddhist first-person and second-person (that is, guided) investigations of consciousness and its intrinsic interdependence with bodily form, feelings, perceptions, and intentional impulses, as well as its qualitative transformation in keeping with the nonlinear and nondeterministic causal dynamics of karma. The second source of epistemic lift is third-person experimentation aimed at determining the nature of reality at both infinitesimal and macrocosmic scales, and in particular experimentation of the kind that has been driving theoretical physics in the direction of blending quantum and relativistic accounts of reality in recognition of the primacy of temporality and perspective. One of the bolder formulations of this is by Lee Smolin, who claims that the "dynamics of the particles in the universe act to increase the total diversity of their views" (Smolin, 2021: 5)—a coherent proliferation of unique causal histories of mattering. The final source of lift is those investigations of altered states of consciousness blending first- and third-person experimental apparatuses that aim to determine the nature and causal dynamics of neural/material and phenomenal/experiential relations, both ordinary and extraordinary.

The convergence of insights generated by these three very different investigative apparatuses encourages re-theorizing lifeform evolution as the progressively materialized and yet ultimately relational articulation of the *mattering* of values and intentions. This compels appreciating the work of consciousness as reality-expanding and not simply reality-investigating. But, just as importantly, it compels recognizing the inescapably ethical character of our determinations of whether and how best to investigate consciousness and evolution. What and how we seek answers about the world recursively conditions who and what we are becoming in and for the world.

6

Consciousness Theory Mattering: Responsibilities of Engineered Evolution

Buddhist relational ontology and the teaching of karma invite seeing brain-body-environment systems as evolutionary records of what consciousness has been doing: materializing ever-expanding differentiations among matter and what matters. Brain-body-environment systems are not *causes* of consciousness; they are creatively evolving *infrastructures* of consciousness. Just as transportation practices are conditioned by, but not reducible to, transportation infrastructure, the work of consciousness is conditioned by, but not reducible to or explainable in terms of the purely material dynamics of brain-body-environment interdependencies.

Buddhist therapeutics focuses on altering our consciousnesses in ways that are conducive to materializing commitments and infrastructures that enhance capacities for both differing and cohering virtuosically in shared realizations of increasingly liberating relational dynamics. It is part of the theoretical scaffolding for this therapeutic work to affirm that the coherences we elaborate differ qualitatively, and that they recursively affect brain-body-environment interdependencies, shaping and reshaping material/phenomenal histories and infrastructures of sentience. Simply stated, how we differentiate among and put things together conditions relational outcomes and constrains relational opportunities. This is especially true in determinations of what things are and how they came to be as they are—determinations, ultimately, of both what matters and what materializes, thereby marking out the horizons our responsibility. Theories matter. And they do so both epistemically and ethically.

Given the unprecedented abilities we now have for affecting consciousness through technological manipulations of its infrastructure, theories matter to a historically unprecedented degree. We have arrived at an inflection point beyond which we cannot afford to grant credibility to theories of consciousness and evolution that do not acknowledge (and ideally enhance) human creativity and responsibility. As William E. Connolly has aptly insisted, we must revise our theoretical standards so that "[any] theory of species evolution that passes the crucible of inherent credibility will be one that renders intelligible human capacities of consciousness, meaning, responsibility, significance, freedom, and self-conscious violence that have emerged from that process ... without reducing these outcomes to mere epiphenomena that do not play an active role in life, culture, action, and evolution itself" (Connolly, 2014: 442). Failing to do so is to place at risk both consciousness and ethics.

All Theories Are Not Created Equal

This is a strong claim, and yet one that has considerable warrant given a relational and openly normative approach to theorizing consciousness, cosmic history, and the evolution of life based on Buddhist investigative apparatuses and insights. To make a more generally credible case for taking it seriously, I want to begin somewhat indirectly by contrasting this nondualistic, Buddhist approach to theorizing the evolution of consciousness, purpose, and cosmic order with representative positions along a spectrum of contemporary approaches. At one extreme of this spectrum is metaphysically dualist, intelligent-design theorizing of evolution as a purpose-materializing function of transcendent, nonmaterial intervention. At the other extreme is metaphysically monist, physicalist theorizing of evolution as a purposeless and wholly material process of "natural selection" among randomly produced genetic mutations and their organic expression. In between are theories of natural teleology and teleodynamics according to which aims/purposes are, respectively, either intrinsic to all of nature or evolutionary products of intrinsically originated constraints on material possibility.[1]

According to creationist or intelligent-design theorizing, sentient beings and their environments are artifacts of divine will and transcendental intelligence. The history of the cosmos and the order present therein are material revelations of divine/transcendental intent. According to teleodynamic theorizing, sentient beings are self-interested, self-regulating, and self-reproducing functional constructs originating in feedback loops among autocatalytic processes and self-assembling cell membranes. Life is a structurally emergent twist in the cosmic causal order. Finally, at the far extreme of reductive physicalism, sentient beings and their environments are unintended evolutionary accidents. The history of the cosmos is one that can be written mathematically as an expression of changeless natural laws—a purely syntactic history of what is at best an accidentally semantic cosmos.

The theories along this spectrum are all premised on taking consciousness (and associated phenomena like aims, purposes, meanings, values, and culture) to be something that either needs to be explained or that should simply be explained away. Given that premise, it's natural to regard the substantial theoretical discrepancies present along the spectrum as evidence of welcome competition in an epistemic or explanatory market, and to presume as well that this competition will result eventually (and ideally) in eliminating the least well-supported theories and bringing about convergent explanatory consensus—a zeroing in on reality/truth.

Nondualistic Buddhist theorizing does not share these presumptions. As the coherent differentiation of (in our case, humanly) sensed and sensing presences, consciousness is manifestly evident. In the absence of consciousness, there would be nothing that could or would matter—nothing to wish for, formulate, express, support, or contest. What requires explanation is not consciousness, but differences in perspective and persistence—differences in how consciousness has altered and continues altering. That is, what requires explanation are evolving differences in qualities of coherence.

The basic Buddhist therapeutic practice of seeing all things as without-self or lacking any fixed nature/identity is metaphysically a practice of affirming that the character of ultimate reality is emptiness (*śūnyatā*) or ambiguity, and that all configurations of presence, existence, and nonexistence are karmic registers of consciousness alteration. Epistemically, it is the practice of continuously extending horizons of relevance to engage in ever more improvement- and improvisation-sustaining disambiguations of sensed and sensing presences. Ethically, it is the practice of expanding horizons of relevance, assumed responsibility, and responsive readiness to foster ever more superlative (*kuśala*) forms of relational coherence. As I have framed it, rather than zeroing in on reality/truth, nondualist Buddhist theorizing aims at supporting reality expansion/enhancement and calls attention to the epistemic and ethical costs of any presumptive, winner-takes-all epistemic competition.

All epistemologies and ethical systems have blind-spots. Viewed relationally and dynamically—that is, in holistic spatiotemporal terms—the evolution of life has not consisted fundamentally in individual species adaptations; it has consisted in improvised expansions of relational scope and density within coordination-engendered and diversity-enhancing ecosystems. And to the extent that the evolution of life has meant the accelerating differentiation of infrastructures for consciousness—including the opening of such novel relational environments as those constitutive of religion, politics, and the arts—we should anticipate that our epistemic and ethical undertakings will be best modeled on ecological coordination, not monopolistic competition.

Theoretical Differentiation: A Diffraction of Causal and Moral Matters

The "ecological" nature of Buddhist nondualism implies that, while smallism-biased investigative apparatuses are methodologically coherent, and while monism-biased theorizing is metaphysically coherent, neither smallism nor monism is coherent in ways that are *kuśala* or conducive to virtuosic extensions and enhancements of relational dynamics. They do not offer guidance for the future evolution of consciousness and, as such, they are at best ethically sterile and potentially pernicious.

Consider reductive physicalism. Although there are illusionist and eliminativist deniers of consciousness, most of us are likely inclined to agree with Galen Strawson's (2018) scathing assessment that denying consciousness is a frontrunner for being the "silliest claim" in human history. Not far behind, however, are claims that we can explain away consciousness by maintaining that phenomenal events *just are* brain events in the same way that heat *just is* kinetic energy or molecules in motion. This is the monist view that, if there is any difference between the phenomenal and material, it is merely descriptive. Granted the scientific rule-of-thumb that parsimonious theses are better than those which are not, this view has some intuitive appeal. But its dismissal of the hard problem by denying any other-than-descriptive difference between mental and physical occurrences cannot account for the emergence of these different descriptions of "the same" thing. Descriptive differences depend, after all, on significantly differing perspectives. If there really is only one valid perspective—an intrinsically material one—then the appearance of phenomenal perspectives is mysterious. The angle of difference between phenomenal and neural presences and perspectives is evidently *not* one that can exist *in* the material space of neural relations. The difference between the phenomenal and neural "angles" on things cannot be claimed to be a purely neural difference without entering into an infinite epistemic regress—an epistemic black hole. That is bad enough. But as we will later see, its ethical implications are perhaps even more troubling.

If descriptively collapsing the phenomenal into the material is verbal sleight of hand, so is the equally, but oppositely parsimonious idealist claim that material events *just are* phenomenal events. The causal course of material events is clearly not entirely subject to phenomenal effort, even if those events are apparent only in the phenomenal space of intentional relations. Thus, in the shadows cast by idealist monist parsimony, it is never hard to find realist precedents for dualism—the embrace of an irreconcilable difference between matter and what matters that is as conducive to arrested ethical development as it is to causal explanatory stalemate since the independence of mind and matter can be sustained only by imposing between them a vacuous "excluded middle" at the cost of anything wholly *mattering*.

There is a sense, then, in which physicalist monism and idealist monism are each globally coherent, but internally incoherent. They fail to creatively "hold together" what has already been differentiated and to offer guidance in responsively and responsibly anticipating what can and should come next in the dynamic evolution of coherence. From a nondualist perspective, we are best served by taking the relational differentiation of and interdependence among sensing and sensed presences as ontologically basic and accepting the inexistence of anything that "just is" this or that, whether mind or matter. Thus, to the extent that Buddhism has theorized consciousness, it has done so with what might be called *irrealist* therapeutic intent, remaining silent on questions of ultimate origins and purpose, and directing attention to practical concerns about qualities of consciousness and intention and how these affect interdependencies in the worlds we are eliciting with/through them.[2] This can be interpreted as epistemic humility. But Buddhism's silence about origins and ends can also be seen as an expression of ethical caution.

Asking and answering questions about the causal origins and evolutionary purposes of consciousness, regardless of their theoretic slant, necessarily involves consciousness. These can never be purely objective questions. They implicate us in conflicts of interests in the legal sense that it matters to us intrinsically how they are answered. This recursive necessity suggests that how we ask and answer these questions always has the potential to *affect* consciousness and not merely to *account* for it. The experimental and conceptual stances we adopt in studying consciousness are not only theoretically significant, they are inevitably also ethically significant.

This is in some ways a less radical claim than it might at first appear. It is now a global norm for research projects that might affect the welfare of human subjects to be evaluated and approved by Institutional Review Boards, and there is growing awareness of the need for Responsible Research and Innovation that addresses research and innovation impacts, but also background research assumptions and the societal visions, norms, and priorities that shape scientific agendas (Salles, Evers, and Farisco, 2019). Moreover, there is a robustly expanding field of neuroethics which centers on establishing standards for brain research and studies of emotion and consciousness, and which extends both to evaluating the broader societal impacts of neuroscience and its technological applications, and to critically anticipating the ramifications of neuroscientific findings for such basic philosophical questions as the nature of the self and identity and the existence and meaning of freewill (Rommelfanger et al., 2018).[3]

In other ways, however, claiming that how we study consciousness affects consciousness has revolutionary implications. It implies that how we investigate consciousness can alter courses of coherent differentiation, shaping both the quality and compass of consciousness. Yet, if cosmic evolutionary history consists in infrastructural elaborations of consciousness—most proximally, the progressive and coherent differentiation of sensed (material) and sensing (phenomenal) presences—anything that affects consciousness will in some degree also affect and perhaps irreversibly alter the direction of evolutionary dynamics. The determinate ways in which evolutionary theories *explain* consciousness also *constrain* consciousness, and this then recursively constrains evolution.

Consciousness theories seek to explain diffraction patterns among matter and what matters: distinctive patterns of interference/interdependence among causal and intentional currents. And as Karen Barad has noted, "Diffraction is not merely about difference, and certainly not differences in any absolute sense, but about the entangled nature of differences that matter … Diffraction is a material practice for making a difference, for topologically reconfiguring connections" (Barad, 2007: 381). Theories of consciousness thus at once disambiguate and configure connections between matter and what matters. They are, in other words, always (at least tacitly) *theories of mattering*.

Given this, consider again the determinations of creationist or intelligent-design theories that consciousness is either a progeny of divine will or a product of some transcendental intelligence. Comfortingly, this grants all sensed and sensing presences a distinct—and perhaps unique—purpose in a cosmos suffused with meaning. We can invoke, of course, the possibility of design sensibilities that leave greater or lesser room in the cosmos for the exercise of human (and other forms of) agency. But theorizing the origins of the cosmos and consciousness as the results of an extrinsically exercised will or intelligence implicates us in determining that the ultimate source of meaning and values exists outside of or beyond the compass of connections among sensed and sensing presences. Evolution is then transcendentally biased, and how to be present most humanely could never be adequately determined with reference solely to the quality of our interpersonal negotiations, but only with reference to what we do, do not, can, and cannot know about the divine will or extra-cosmic intelligence that created all in existence.

The history of (especially monotheistic) religions is replete with revelations of how best to live in a created and/or designed world. These have typically taken the form of orally, textually, and ritually articulated moral and material injunctions. The history of philosophy, however, also has been similarly full of fervently gymnastic efforts to articulate secular codes of human conduct and purpose. This has resulted in various ethics of compliance with rationally derived (and thus transcendentally validated) duties, values, virtues, and principled ideals, and this has remained true long after nineteenth-century pronouncements about the "death of God."

Turning to science, matters are (perhaps surprisingly) not very different. A significant lineage connection can be traced from astrology—founded on visions of the cosmos as ordered "from above"—to astronomical observations of regularities that enabled the discovery of universal physical laws which then placed seemingly within reach the goal of explaining everything from galactic structures to the behaviors of our bodies and the origins of our moral dispositions. The logics of plan execution and law compliance are essentially the same regardless of whether the plan or law invoked is attributed to God, to Reason, or to Nature.

Thus, the theories of consciousness and evolution that are competing for epistemic market share are also competing for ethical market share and the power to explain and yet also constrain consciousness. To the extent that this competition results in narrowing the field of theoretic competitors, it also results in shrinking possibilities for connecting the material and the moral—a contraction or compression of the possibility space of coherence. The Buddhist "middle path" method cautions against such contraction and compression, and advocates realizing a theoretical ecology in which individual theories are not refuted, but rather relegated to positions of lesser or greater theoretic (and therapeutic) relevance based on how they constrain the space of connections among material and moral possibility. Conversely stated, the Buddhist "middle path" encourages ranking theories according to the compass of the space they hold open for ethical virtuosity: space for the improvised expansion of moral and material horizons.

Reductive Physicalism on Evolution: An Ethical Risk

Creationist and intelligent design theories invoke—even if they are unable to produce—a comprehensive "blueprint" of the order of the cosmos. Historically, this has had great popular appeal, at least in part because it implies the possibility of moral certainty. In those circles within which research funding decisions are made, however, the empirical persistence of cultural diversity, evolving conceptions of duty and virtue, and experimental evidence that human evolution has been an ongoing and ontogenetically recapitulated process of moral differentiation from other great ape lineages (Tomasello, 2019) all work against high valuations of creationist and intelligent design theories. Faring much better are theories situated toward the far extreme of reductionist physicalism that assume the order of the cosmos to be law-determined and mathematically tractable. Given their current "market share," it's instructive to review some of the historical precedents for their dominance, especially in "explaining" evolution, and to then examine the ethical costs of their causal subordination of mattering to matter.

The key elements of this subordination and its moral ramifications are boldly and baldly expressed by Richard Dawkins, the proponent of the "selfish gene" theory: "The universe we observe has precisely the properties we should expect if there is, at bottom, no design, no purpose, no evil and no good, nothing but blind indifference" (Dawkins, 1995: 155). According to this view of the cosmos, the evolutionary history of life has been one of environmental vagaries and directionless organic variation, with only the most competitively equipped lifeforms surviving, and with morality amounting to nothing more than a chance result of meaningless algorithmic processes. As Daniel Dennett sums up with deflationary aplomb: "An impersonal, unreflective, robotic, mindless little scrap of molecular machinery is the ultimate basis of all the agency, and hence meaning, and hence consciousness, in the universe" (Dennett, 1995: 27).

This view of evolution has been widely critiqued, both scientifically and philosophically. Natural selection might well be part of the evolutionary story as a material process of filtering the organic currents of dynamic self-organization that can be observed across scales from the molecular to the environmental. But "no filter can be the sole source of what flows out of it" (Midgley, 2010: 7), and it has become increasingly clear that there is scant empirical support for seeing evolution as nothing more than a mechanism for genetic/organic filtration. Yet, even if the universe Dawkins depicts might be dismissible as a scientific myth, it remains a powerful myth culturally, and its historical and metaphysical underpinnings are intimately entangled with the origins and persistence of the hard problem of consciousness.

The power and persistence of this myth and its anti-humanism can be usefully traced to the intertwined origins of evolutionary theory in the late eighteenth century and paleontology in the early nineteenth century, the ascendance of teleology-free modern biology, and the prospects of a purely natural scientific account of the universe and its dynamics. In concert with the emerging science of paleogeology, the study of fossils made it possible to challenge Judeo-Christian-Islamic scriptural accounts of the origins of the universe at large, of the Earth, and of all living species in never-to-be-repeated acts of divine creation, and to trust instead what could be read from the morally neutral "book of nature." But seeing fossils as remnants of now extinct lifeforms also compelled raising causal questions about species origins and extinctions.

Darwin's great innovation was to break equally from creationism and from Aristotelean appeals to natural teleology. Instead of seeing a principle of order playing out in the processes of morphological change, he identified "random mutation" and "natural selection" as the simple two-part mechanism of lifeform evolution—an un-orchestrated and agentless process. As this account of the origin of species gained general acceptance over the second half of the nineteenth century, smallist physics and chemistry were becoming so successful in explaining the behavior of matter, that it had begun seeming plausible that the universe would soon be "closed under physics." Everything in the universe, it was believed, would one day be explained in terms of a handful of forces acting on (subatomic, atomic, and molecular) elements of matter according to mathematically formulated and immutable natural laws. The stage was thus set for determining agency and intentionality to be superfluous—a stage on which the *observing* universe need not appear because, at least for explanatory purposes, it quite simply *did not matter*.

It was out of this scientific ferment that neo-Darwinian evolutionary theory emerged, blending Darwin's selection mechanism with Mendel's genetic account of trait transfer in a so-called modern synthesis. According to it, unconscious and agency-bereft genes code the assembly of proteins out of which the cells of an organism are constructed, doing so according to inherited genetic programs that both define the organism as a whole and determine its future offspring. Insofar as they are genetically determined, organisms and their behaviors amount to materialized algorithms—physical translations of genetically encoded information.[4] Biological dynamism and hereditary transmission can be explained in terms of random genetic mutation and natural selection through the laws of molecular mechanics, without any need to appeal to divine purposes, teleology, or the effects of phenomenal experience and learning.

This mechanistic and mathematical view of life and of a cosmos in which divine agency could be taken out of the equations explaining physical reality had an initially liberating effect. If the observed universe and everything in it was explainable in terms of natural laws—not the will of a divine architect—each new discovery about the causalities at work in the world would expand human freedoms to intervene in and control natural processes and the shape of things to come. But, if aims and purposes could be seen as superfluous in accounting for cosmic and organic evolution, so too could our human aims and intentions in explaining our life histories.

Taken to the logical limit expressed in Dawkins's and Dennett's denunciations of purpose and their dismissals of moral sensibilities as randomly generated and genetically encoded algorithms for material survival, physicalist reductionism invites admitting that there is really no need for consciousness to exist. Human history can be conceived as nothing more than a history of brains-bodies "that maximized their overall fitness by beginning to hallucinate goals" in virtually existing, merely representational "ego tunnels" through physical reality (Metzinger, 2009: 131).

Fortunately, the history of science remains open. As noted earlier, although there continue to be presumptively "rational" advocates of eliminativism and illusionism, a substantial and growing body of empirical evidence now contradicts the linear causal account of natural selection that is proffered by genocentric and genodeterministic theories of evolutionary dynamics. Research has revealed the existence of robust trans-generational inheritance independent of DNA sequences, and it now seems most accurate to see genes as revisable templates that must be activated by cells (Thompson, 2007: 196). That is, rather than genes instructing cells, it is cells that instruct/activate the genome. Temporally extended and environment involving cellular dynamics determine patterns of genetic expression. And, since cellular activity is not independent of organism-environment relations, the causality involved in biological processes and organic evolution is circular or network-like, such that any part of the network is able to affect every other part. It is only through performing certain kinds of experiments that a particular source or level of causality becomes privileged (Noble, 2015).

In short, the putatively "natural" boundaries drawn experimentally among genes, cells, organisms, and their environments do not cut the world at its joints. Assuming them to preexist our experimental interactions with biological systems, rather than being the products of our investigative apparatuses and the agential cuts performed by them, is both metaphysically and ethically derelict.

Among the most important aspects of this dereliction has been the methodological and metaphysical severing of the relations of co-articulation that are constitutive of body-mind, material-phenomenal, and brain-consciousness interactions. The nature of these interactions or intra-actions (as Barad and other new materialists might correctively describe them) has been a perennial subject of philosophical debate, especially in those traditions with roots in the ancient Mediterranean world and the Indian subcontinent. But, until the ascendance of a worldview in which the physical universe was deemed closed under physics—a universe in which physical effects have exclusively physical causes—these debates were framed in ways that generally affirmed the causal efficacy of mind and consciousness. That is, *intentions mattered*.

Alas, as Hilary Putnam trenchantly observed, "evolution won't give you any more intentionality than you pack into it" (Putnam, 1992: 32). Once intention has been removed from the foundational causal account of organic evolution, finding a way to plausibly reinsert it becomes first difficult and eventually impossible. Ethics eventually sublimates into physics and mathematics. The qualitative practices of embodying values and engaging in critically informed course corrections dissolve analytically into quantitative practices of measuring, calculating, and executing law-conforming predictions.

As intimated earlier, contemporary interest in neutral monism and panpsychism has been motivated by a consonant recognition that the (apparent) insolubility of the hard problem rests on the premise that "in the beginning" there was nothing but mindless matter. If the mental is not as foundationally packed into evolutionary causal dynamics as the material, it will unavoidably end up appearing epiphenomenal. Unfortunately, these theoretic strategies have the disadvantage of being smallist, reductionist, and essentially structural—that is, nondynamic or ahistorical. As such, they offer little in the way of explanation for the apparent bifurcation and progressively meaning-engendering differentiation of experienced and experiencing presences. To riff on Putnam, you will not get any more coherently significance-generating differentiation out of the cosmos than you pack into it.

It was an incisive appreciation of these evolutionary conundrums that inspired Henri Bergson more than a century ago—especially in *Matter and Memory* (1896) and *Creative Evolution* (1907)—to posit a primordial and proto-intentional vital impulse (*élan vital*) to explain the exuberantly dynamic and evolving nature of the cosmos, associating consciousness with temporal extension and indeterminacy, and viewing life as creative differentiation. As epitomized, however, in his incongruously mechanistic image of the life force as an explosive bursting through inert matter like an artillery shell, each fragment of which is then burst from within into ever smaller fragments, Bergson viewed life and matter somewhat antagonistically, if not dualistically (Bergson, 1911a: 109). Matter is as much an obstacle to life as it is the medium within which life articulates what matters. While matter (body) and memory (consciousness) originate and persist coincidently in space, the former is momentary and governed by repetition, while the latter is enduring and governed by creation (see, e.g., Bergson, 1911b: 295ff). In short, Bergson conceived the relation of matter and consciousness as what might be called a temporal property dualism rather than a spatial dualism of separately existing substances.

Bergson's advocacy for the ontological primacy of vital impulse or creative intent and his recognition of different dimensions of temporality are well-aligned with Buddhist theorizing of consciousness as coherent differentiation. Yet, as it is expressed in his final major work, *The Two Sources of Morality and Religion* (1932), Bergson's intuition of the dynamic primacy of cohesion and differentiation led him to posit a hierarchic (and perhaps idealism-leaning) contrast of closed and open societies and moralities—a cohesion-oriented closed society grounded on analytic, rules-governed intelligence and an obligation-focused closed morality; and a divergence-oriented open society of intuition-informed, progressive resistance to obligation and the flourishing of an open morality based on creative emotion. Cohering and differing are the "two sources" or opposing forces of cultural/evolutionary bifurcation.

As I have been presenting it, Buddhist theorizing of consciousness affirms the nonduality of these two sources or forces of evolutionary dynamism. Conceiving of the coherent differentiation of sensed (material) and sensing (phenomenal) presences as dynamic elaborations of consciousness, Buddhist nondualism offers a karmic-relational alternative to the bifurcating tension, if not opposition, between Bergson's time as measured repetition and time as phenomenal duration—affirming the collateral presence of temporal length and depth, and of time as sequence and time as significance. The values-embodying, intrinsically difference-generating labor of consciousness consists in an ongoing expansion and intensification of relational dynamics—a process that entails individuating and integrating currents of both materialized relational opportunity and perspectives on what matters. Conserving and creating are nondual dimensions of what consciousness does. The material order—across scales from the galactic to the stellar, planetary, biological, and cultural—is an ongoing "live recording" of all that proves conducive to improvisationally expanding consciousness as the creative elaboration of an ontologically primitive urge to differentiate coherently.

There is a sense, then, in which a false choice is set up between asking "what is the advantage of consciousness for evolution?" and its inversion "what is the advantage of evolution for consciousness?" The boundaries and hierarchies between evolution and consciousness that are implied in these questions are ultimately inexistent. They are conceptual conventions or conveniences rather than features of the world prior to our engagement with it—legacies of the atomist/particularist/smallist presumption that it is possible for something to explain everything. Buddhist nonduality insists otherwise that it is only the presence of everything that explains (or confers meaning on) anything. Recursively altering consciousness is both the means-to and meaning-of evolution as an irreducibly intra-active process of materially enacting coherently differing values and intentions. Once again: *evolution is consciousness mattering*.

From the Hard Problem to a Much Harder Predicament

Seen from this nondualist vantage, the hard problem of consciousness is an artifact of studying matter, evolution, life, bodies, minds, and consciousness by means of apparatuses that have been assembled to make maximally precise agential cuts reflecting an ideal of objectivity that mandates the ontological and epistemic segregation of the observing and the observed. As we have seen, these apparatuses have proven to be powerful, but also to have limited explanatory reach. In the early twentieth century, these limitations led to the metaphysically radical formulations of relativity and quantum theory. More recently, they have spurred new materialist evo devo theorizing in which agency is not seen as an attribute of someone or something, but as the enactment of "iterative reconfigurings of topological manifolds of spacetimematter relations" (Barad, 2007: 178).[5] It is in the study of consciousness, however, that the limitations of these objectivity-biased investigative apparatuses are of greatest significance. By failing to take methodologically into account the *nondual*—rather than *individual*—presences of observer and observed, they presumptively constrain what can be determined as mattering in the study of consciousness.

At a theoretical register, the apparatus-determined bifurcation of observed and observing presences prizes apart the "space of causes" and the "space of intentions," and holds open the ontological and explanatory gap that solutions to the hard problem of consciousness are required to close. This is not an inconsequential misstep. To make use of a metaphor introduced earlier (in Chapter 2): sensing and sensed presences can be seen as continuous in a way that is structurally akin to the continuity of what only locally appear to be separate sides of a Möbius strip—a three-dimensional loop structure that has only one side and one edge. Cutting a Möbius strip causes it to "decohere"—twisting apart into a rectangular strip with two distinct sides and four edges. Making an agential cut in the study of consciousness similarly brings about a causal decoherence in the originally nondual infrastructure of consciousness—a "disentangling" of temporal length/sequence and temporal depth/significance, and of sensed and sensing presences as interdependently articulating explications of consciousness.

This decoherence-enacting agential cut may be performed in ways that are biased toward either dualist or monist (idealist, materialist, or information-functionalist) determinations of the ontological status of the material and phenomenal. But in all cases, making such a cut involves the presumption of observational and ontological independence from what is being observed—the assertion of an abiding self that is not dynamically and karmically entangled with all other presences. The resulting failure to take methodologically into account the recursive nonduality of sensed and sensing presences—and more generally the nonduality of matter and what matters—amounts to an (at least partial) obscuration or ignorance of what consciousness does.

Nondualistically theorizing evolution dissolves the hard problem of consciousness. But it also involves accepting full ethical responsibility for how our approaches to studying and theorizing consciousness recursively constrain consciousness and what it does. The investigative decoherence of matter and what matters allows a preemptive segregation of the domains of science (facts) and ethics (values). In contrast, a nondualistic karmic-relational investigation of consciousness accords primacy to qualitatively altering the intra-active dynamics of differing and cohering—fostering a mode of scientific investigation in which ethics matters intrinsically, but also a mode of ethical deliberation premised on the nonduality of agents, patients, and actions.

Refraining from Reductionism: An Ethical and Evolutionary Imperative

Buddhist theorizing is inherently ethical insofar as its primary purpose is to support practices of evaluating and changing how we think, speak, and act, first to sustainably alleviate conflict, trouble, and suffering, and then to realize increasingly liberating relational dynamics. The purpose of theorizing consciousness is not to determine what consciousness is or is not, but to qualitatively alter what consciousness is doing: altering the direction and dynamics of mattering by intentionally and improvisationally transforming the diffractive interplay of matter and what matters. In keeping with the cosmos-engendering impulse/intent to differentiate coherently, this cannot be a goal-oriented practice. To engage in enhancing qualities of coherence and differentiation is to be reflexively implicated in evaluating and changing the course of relationally manifest meaning: the open-ended cultivation of ethical virtuosity and diversity.[6] Theorizing and studying consciousness should sustain this process, not subvert it. Theories of consciousness should not be evaluated in terms of how well they account for observed neural activity or for their utility in mapping and potentially manipulating material/phenomenal interactions. They should be evaluated for how they extend and affect relational dynamics, not only materially, but socially, economically, politically, and aesthetically.

This is not an exclusively Buddhist insight or concern. In addition to brain-centered ethical concerns, for example, about the use of frontier technologies to develop capacities for removing or implanting memories, manipulating emotions, or enhancing brain function, awareness has been growing about the need for a much broader and proactive "ethics of consciousness" aimed at grappling with questions about what states of consciousness should be deemed desirable and how best to realize them in practice (Illes and Hossain, 2017).

This movement toward an ethics of consciousness marks a turn away from neurocentrism that parallels the turn away from genocentrism in theorizing biological dynamics and evolution. Here, it is a decentering of the brain based on evidence for the ontological primacy of the world-brain relation (Northoff, 2018), and on the merits of re-envisioning the brain as relationally inscribed in ways that "make its microprocessing structure the record of an unfolding reality" (Gillett, 2009: 6). The brain is, in other words, coming to be seen as a record of narrative and relational wholes that is shaped progressively by the dynamics of diffractive interplay among the "space of causes," the "space of intentions," the "temporality of sequence," and the "temporality of significance."

One implication of this decentering of the brain is that *all studies of consciousness are field experiments*. They are investigations conducted within and on relational fields that recursively affect the dynamics of coherent differentiation being expressed therein. Given this, the ethics of consciousness will be fundamentally incomplete unless it extends beyond protecting individual rights and limiting the risks, for instance, of participating in traditional laboratory experiments. Today, insights gleaned from neuroscientific research are being scaled up technologically in alignment with commercial and political interests and values. That is, they are morphing into real-world interventions that "target outcomes that affect whole societies, and often do so without the public's consent, knowledge, debriefing, or any means to identify or reverse long-term, real-life negative effects" (McDermott and Hatemi, 2020: 30015). These interventions can consist, for example, in social pressure manipulations (affecting voting behavior), in producing profitable patterns of desire (shaping consumer behavior), and in the algorithmic capture and manipulation of attention (via, e.g., social media or digital commerce and entertainment platforms). Ethics designed to protect or advance the interests of individual agents and patients are not sufficient to protect relational ecosystems or to evaluate the effects of constraining and directing how social groups and institutions cohere and differentiate.

In sum, a strong case can be made that any holistically responsive ethics of consciousness must be "concerned with the origin of evaluative predispositions in the broadest sense" (Farisco, Salles, and Evers, 2018: 721), and that this entails avoiding the wholesale reduction of ethics and morality to neuroscience, evolutionary psychology and biology, as well as the more modest granting of epistemic primacy to science rather than philosophy, religion, or other humanistic disciplines when determining what matters most in the study of consciousness.

If consciousness consists in the coherent differentiation of matter and what matters, ethical systems can be seen as meta-evolutionary constraints on that creative and evaluative labor. *Conserving ethical diversity is thus a basic principle of any truly robust ethics of consciousness.* The combination of reducing consciousness to neural dynamics, reducing evolution to genetic competition, and reducing moral dispositions to survival mechanisms poses profound threats to the future of ethics. At its most extreme, it runs the risk of merging promises of epistemic certainty and ethical finality, creating systems capable of hardwiring the future through placing control-biased constraints on both evolution and ethics, transforming both into "finite games" played to win rather than to improve the quality of evolutionary and ethical play.

Engineering Ethics: Solutionism and the Problems of Morality and Mortality

The logic of hardwiring the future is illustrated with frightful clarity in recent arguments that the neural engineering of moral dispositions may soon be within technical reach, and that making use of these engineering capabilities is not only rational and ethical but necessary for humanity's survival.[7] A concise and bold formulation of the claim is offered by Julian Savulescu and Ingmar Persson (2012), and it is worth examining their argument for it some detail.[8]

Until very recently, human beings have lived in comparatively small and closely knit societies and enjoyed only very modest technological capacities for scaling up their values and intentions and shaping their environs. Human moral psychology evolved in this context and is thus "myopic" in the sense of being geared toward face-to-face encounters and evaluating only relatively immediate and small-scale ramifications of actions. Unfortunately, the evolution of science and technology has outpaced the evolution of our moral dispositions. More than half of humanity now lives in urban areas in societies with many millions of citizens. Humanity has demonstrated its ability to affect planetary processes and trigger both ecological collapses and climate catastrophes, but also its readiness to weigh geopolitical advantage against existential threats and to build Armageddon machines and weapons of mass destruction. In sum, our biologically explained and socially engrained moral dispositions have passed their expiration date. As a result, we find ourselves forced to admit that "The expansion of our powers of action as the result of technological progress must be balanced by a moral enhancement on our part. Otherwise, our civilization … is itself at risk" (Savulesco and Persson, 2012: 399). Since it seems doubtful that this moral enhancement can be accomplished by means of traditional moral education in the small window of opportunity that remains for us, we have "ample reason to explore the prospects of moral enhancement by biomedical means" (Savulesco and Persson, 2012: 400).

An obvious objection to this argument is that neuroscience-guided and technologically accomplished moral enhancement would be wrong ethically because it would undermine human autonomy and restrict our freedom to do wrong—a freedom without which doing what is right reduces to mere necessity. Savulescu and Persson admit this may be true. But even if technologically accomplished moral enhancement made it impossible to act immorally, they counter, would that necessarily be bad? In fact, might it not be a good thing, all things considered? If biological evolution hardwired our brains to ensure our survival as individuals and communities, and if this wiring has been rendered obsolete by our epistemic and technological successes, what is wrong with taking over where biological evolution left off and rewiring our ethical sensibilities?

This rebuttal tacitly assumes that evolution is a story of successful problem solving and expresses commitment to (if not a kind of blind faith in) what Evgeny

Morozov (2013) refers to as solutionism—the conviction that, with sufficient data-infused understanding, all problems are technologically tractable, and that data-driven intelligent technology will eventually make human existence frictionless and trouble-free. It is tempting to dismiss this conviction as mere hubris. No matter how hard we try, we will never gain the scientific knowledge and technical skills needed to neuro-engineer or bio-engineer morality. But dismissing solutionism on grounds of impossibility also dismisses the need to evaluate its ethical merits or demerits, and that is dangerous. Solutionism is dangerous, at least in part, because no problem can be solved without predetermining what will count as a solution, and because that metric-selecting process is necessarily based on value judgments or determinations of what matters most. The presumption of solutionism is that, with enough data and the right conceptual and material tools, the basic ethical practice of resolving values conflicts can be abandoned as redundant, if not obsolete.

If, for example, the "problem" with human morality were to be framed in keeping with Dawkins's and Dennett's reduction of human dispositions and behavior to algorithmically coded survival mechanisms, its "solution" space would ultimately ratchet down from neuro-engineering moral dispositions to genetically engineering them, and successes would be calculated with reference to the "absolute" metric of competitive survival advantage. Movement in this direction has, in fact, been ongoing over the last half century as considerable resources—both intellectual and financial—have been directed to operationalizing E. O. Wilson's suggestion that "the time has come for ethics to be removed temporarily from the hands of the philosophers and biologicized" (Wilson, 1975: 562). If the prospects of turning ethics over to evolutionary biologists like Wilson or Dawkins are philosophically or religiously troubling, going one step further and handing ethics over to the ministrations of techno-solutionists should be infinitely more so.

Techno-solutionism informed by survival-of-the-fittest presumptions about evolution is prone to framing the proper response to a moral-practical evolutionary mismatch as a winner-takes-all epistemic and ethical competition. As such, it is diametrically opposed to theorizing consciousness and evolution in ways inspired by the diversity-engendering and diversity-enhancing dynamics of coherent differentiation in healthy ecosystems. Moral solutionism, after a period of competition among different "moral platforms," is most likely to lead to the "justified" engineering of differentiation-curtailing, standardized global constraints on what matters in and for both moral conduct and ethical cognition.

A more moderate moral solutionism might invoke a guiding principle of "moral sovereignty" that would authorize each nation or regional bloc to freely determine which moral enhancements to engineer into its population. Yet, each of these separate approaches to rewriting our neural operating system would nevertheless continue to evince the lack of epistemic humility that is at the roots of the dire environmental, climatic, and geopolitical crises that solutionism invokes as contextual justifications for solutionist moral enhancement. We should be deeply wary of the ironic circularity of using technology to close the crisis-generating chasm opened by technology between naturally evolved human moral dispositions and the world we now live in.

Adopting the solutionist logic of making human beings "ethical by design" involves replicating the agential cut through which humans have enacted a willful ignorance of our constitutive interdependence with one another and our environments—an arrogant refusal-to-see that is at the causal heart of the ecological and climate crises we now confront. Here, the cut is between the engineers and recipients of neural/moral upgrade. Yet, in both cases, there is the willing blindness of presumed (and idealized) independence from the world we study and act upon, and a callous readiness to embrace control as both a strategic and ordinal value.[9]

This can have very troubling consequences. Enjoying some control within and over our circumstances is clearly better than having no control at all. But in the context of nonlinear causal relations, to get better at controlling matters, we must perceive matters as being repeatedly and increasingly in need of control. The result of this over time is a spiraling intensification of both capacities for and commitments to control (order) and a proliferation of perceived sources of vulnerability (disorder). Valuing control brings about circumstances for living in and being subject to increasingly controlled and controlling environments.

The crucial ethical issue is not whether the impossibility of acting immorally would be good or bad for us individually and for society collectively. It is whether ethical deliberation—practicing the values-evaluating art of human course correction—would remain possible if our freedoms of evaluation and attention and our capacities for contesting the meaning of moral conduct, the tenor of social cohesion, and the permissible scope of cognitive and cultural differentiations were all to be forfeited by design. The ultimate *relational* risk and ethical concern is that, by reconfiguring our brain *matter*, neuroscience-guided and technologically effected moral enhancement will objectively and preemptively determine *what can and will matter*. While that might not amount to evolutionary suicide—an entropic termination of the impulse to differ coherently as well as to differentiate significantly among qualities of coherence—it would nevertheless enact a consciousness-disabling hack of the brain-body-environment infrastructure. The risks of "engineered determinism" are very real (Frischmann and Selinger, 2019).

Taking the techno-manipulation of consciousness a theoretical step further, we can entertain the possibility of "transferring" a brain's connective architecture to a more lasting and readily edited medium. Once it is accepted that "everything about the mind—memories, emotions, personality, even consciousness itself—is a product of physical mechanisms in the brain and can be copied ... [w]e should be able to scan the brain in enough detail to create a simulation of it, an artificial double of its information and algorithms, that could live on past the biological death of the person" (Graziano, 2019: 138–9). Rather than altering the current infrastructure of consciousness and struggling against the evolved limitations of organic systems, "uploading" the brain's organizational dynamics to a silicon/digital substrate could effectively "free" human consciousness from a biological system unsuited, for example, to interstellar travel or working in gravitational fields that greatly exceed Earth's. This would blur beyond recognition "the line between artificial intelligence and human intelligence" and may, at least for techno-solutionists, "be our best path into a deep future" (Graziano, 2019: 166).

Colonizing Consciousness and the Relational Risks of an Ethical Singularity

These are quite abstract speculations. Rewiring the neural circuits of moral disposition and uploading minds into digital eternity may forever remain technological dreams (or nightmares) rather than realities. But ethical questions nevertheless can and should be raised about theorizations of consciousness that enable such solutions to the "problems" of morality and mortality to be seen as plausible and perhaps even preferable to those proffered, for example, by philosophy and religion, or by culture and the arts.

To do so in a way that is concrete and that hopefully makes the need for a relational ethics of consciousness more immediately compelling, I want draw back from the hypotheticals of neuro- or bio-engineered moral enhancement and brain emulation to consider the risks of global "field experimentation" on consciousness that is already underway and rapidly intensifying. This experimentation, mediated digitally by intelligent technology and the new global attention economy, is dramatically reshaping the brain-body-environment infrastructure of consciousness, extending the historical dynamics of colonization from expropriations of land, labor, and resources to that of consciousness itself.[10]

This is not the common view. The digital transformation of the human lifeworld is generally being celebrated as a Fourth Industrial Revolution that will usher humanity into a "golden age" of freedom from want—an era of finally "solving previously unsolvable problems."[11] Alongside solutionist celebrations of their salvific promises, however, ethical concerns have begun to emerge regarding frontier applications of artificial intelligence, machine learning, and big data. Although it was the existential threat to humanity of artificial superintelligence (Bostrom, 2014) that initially captured the greatest media attention, the trend more recently has been away from science fiction scenarios to a practical focus on individual data rights, on use and design standards, and on ensuring that these applications are aligned with "human values."[12] This focus is consistent both with allegiance to entity-based ontology and with presumptions that individual agents and patients and the actions that contingently relate them are foundational for ethical deliberation. In keeping with this, key concerns have been data-property rights and privacy concerns (Véliz, 2021); misuse by design (Schneier, 2018); and the impacts of predatory practices and algorithmic bias, especially on historically underserved and/or disadvantaged populations (O'Neil, 2016).

These are important concerns. But left almost entirely out of consideration have been the ways in which the digital transformation of the human lifeworld is affecting qualities of consciousness. This neglect straightforwardly reflects ethical concerns about individual character rather than qualities of consciousness, as well as an ontological bias toward locality in prevailing conceptions of both consciousness and technology. If consciousness is theorized as a localizable product of intracranial neural dynamics, extracranial events can, by definition, have no direct effects on consciousness. They do not matter directly in/for consciousness. Given this, unlike manipulations of brain dynamics, manipulations of environmental dynamics fall outside the horizons of neuroethics or any more encompassing ethics of consciousness.

If consciousness extends constitutively beyond the body into the world, however, alterations to our environments can affect consciousness in ways that are just as direct and just as significant ethically as experimental manipulations of neural dynamics. Conceiving of consciousness as nonlocal opens a space for recognizing "the immense impact that our ever-present algorithmic devices have on our conscious states … devices that represent parts of our minds that reside outside of our biological brains" (Nagel and Reiner, 2018: 1). Indeed, as Neil Levy argued nearly fifteen years ago—when the smartphone was a relative novelty and the internet a yet-to-be fully commercialized and politicized domain—although neuroethics has largely focused on the physical substrate of the mind,

> if we accept that this substrate includes not only brains, but also material culture, and even social structures, we see that neuroethical concern should extend far more widely ... [and a] great many questions that are not usually seen as falling within its purview—questions about social policy, about technology, about food and even about entertainment—can be seen to be neuroethical issues.
>
> (Levy, 2007: 11)

This is especially true now that the internet and 24/7 digital connectivity have made participation in "technologies of extended mind" essentially mandatory.[13]

Extending or dissolving the horizons of neuroethics to realize an ethics of consciousness that is suited to evaluating the effects of technology-mediated field experiments requires seeing both consciousness and technology as fundamentally relational. Or stated otherwise, it requires refraining from investigative apparatuses that prescriptively identify consciousness and technology with elements, entities, or events that can be precisely located in observational space and time. In the case of consciousness, this means refraining from reductively collapsing the nonlocalizable work of consciousness (coherent differentiation) into localizable neural dynamics. In the case of technology, it entails refraining from reductively identifying the nonlocalizable dynamics of technologies as relational media with localizable tools and their uses.[14]

As we have seen, movement away from locality-biased theorizing of consciousness is underway. Most prominently, theorizing consciousness as embodied, embedded, enacted, and extended (e.g., Hutto and Myin, 2017; Clark, 2016; Gallagher, 2017) has emerged over the last decades as a powerful corrective to reductive identifications of consciousness with intracranial dynamics. More recently and more radically, the neuroscientist Georg Northoff (2018) has argued on behalf of a "Copernican" turn from the centrality of the brain toward theorizing consciousness as based ontologically on difference and as consisting in complex organizations of world-brain relations (Northoff, 2018: 274–5).

These phenomenal and empirical approaches to theorizing consciousness scientifically have great intrinsic merit, as well as considerable family resemblances to the approach that I have been forwarding based on Buddhist therapeutic investigations and conceptual resources. Buddhism differs significantly, however, in theorizing relational dynamics karmically or as intrinsically value- and intent-laden. Relational differentiation, including differentiations of sentient beings and their sensed environments, consists in purposeful articulations of values. Buddhist relational ontology thus distinctively orients us toward seeing consciousness and its brain-body-environment infrastructure as being, in a non-trivial sense, "ethical by nature."

Once the brain is decentered within the infrastructure of consciousness, it becomes apparent that using machine learning systems to predict and direct human decision-making and to produce communicative, commercial, and political behaviors is as serious a matter of ethical concern as is the insertion of electrodes into the brain for the purposes of directly affecting neural and phenomenal dynamics. The algorithmic tools involved amount to computational electrodes inserted into the connective tissue of the socially embodied and enacted infrastructure of consciousness. They allow manipulations that are at least as precise as the ones involved in brain experiments, but that are produced in field experiments that affect millions of people and that can be refined over periods of weeks, months, and years. Similarly, the mass transfer of human attention energy from naturally evolved environments like physical shorelines and social/virtual environments like schools into wholly engineered and curated digital virtual environments has made possible sustained field experimentation on the environmental dimensions of the infrastructure of consciousness.

Once consciousness is conceived relationally, it becomes evident that altering consciousness through directly manipulating brains, through algorithmically predicting and producing emotional and social behaviors, and through environmental content curation are equivalently invasive, real, and worthy of ethical concern. Once technology is conceived relationally, it becomes evident that ethical concern must extend far beyond ensuring methodological integrity, respecting experimental patient rights to informed consent, and evaluating the motives of experimental agents. Technologies are intrinsic to the human brain-body-environment system—integral, in other words, to the infrastructure of human consciousness—and technological transformations are thus also by nature ethically significant. Technological field experimentation in attracting and exploiting human attention and exploring the limits of directive intervention in human decision-making, conduct, emotions, and beliefs for commercial and political purposes is experimentation in nothing less than the colonization of consciousness.

It is important to recognize, however, that although this field experimentation is being orchestrated by advantage-seeking corporate and state actors, focusing ethical attention exclusively on these actors and their actions is conducive to misreading the character and risks of that experimentation. Indeed, it will have the practical effect of "greenlighting" the continued colonization of consciousness. Drawing an ontological distinction between tools and technologies can help make the reasons for this clear.

Technological Risk and the Scope of the Ethics of Consciousness

Tools are localizable artifacts designed to extend or augment human capacities for action and are aptly evaluated in terms of task-specific utilities. Smartphones are tools that we are free to use or not. With smartphones, as with all other tools, we enjoy exit rights. *Technologies* are non-localizable relational media that embody and deploy both strategic and normative values. Strictly speaking, technologies are neither built nor used. Instead, technologies emerge from and inform/structure human conduct much as natural ecosystems emerge from and dynamically inform/structure species relationships.

The design, production, and use of smartphones are implications of communication technology. Electing not to use a smartphone or the internet does not, however, allow escaping the ways in which these tools are reshaping communicative and other human practices. We do not enjoy exit rights from technologies. Technologies are relational systems through which human intentions and values are scaled up to selectively alter the conditions within which we make decisions and act, affecting both how and why we do so. As such, technologies must be evaluated ethically, in terms of how they mediate and qualitatively shape human motions and motivations, and how they systemically and recursively affect human-human and human-world relations.

Using tools and participating in technologies occasion different kinds of risk. Accidents of design and misuse by design are tool risks. Fundamentally, they are agency-originated risks associated with the skill levels and motives of those designing and using tools. Technological risks are structural and relational. Unlike tool risks, they are neither agentive in origin nor local in their patterns of ramification. The risks of technology originate in the complex and recursive fashions in which technologies condition human-environment relations.

Technology risks are often ignored in favor of addressing the much more readily tractable risks of tool use and misuse. This is what is at work when gun rights advocates dismiss concerns about the inherent risks of weapons technology by asserting that "guns don't kill; people do." The efficacy of this rhetorical strategy rests in part on the self-evident truth of the claim. Guns do not aim and fire on their own (though this is changing with AI-enabled autonomous weapons), and guns can save lives as well as take them. Yet, in the context of a debate about gun regulation, this claim is a clever bit of conceptual sleight-of-hand—a purposeful misdirection of critical attention toward tools (guns) and their users, and decisively away from weapons technology as a system of relational dynamics and practices aimed at scaling and structuring human intentions to inflict harm with minimal vulnerability and maximal power. One can refuse to own or use guns. But there are no failsafe exit rights from the distortions of human intentions and interactions that occur in the relational environs of widely deployed weapons technology.

Crucially, technological risks do not occur only in the final causal stages of tool use—the point at which an agent puts his or her intentions into action, with or without due consideration of the patients of that action. The risks of weapons technology emerge, for instance, as decision-making environments are complexly restructured in ways that make the readiness to inflict harm from a distance seem like a rational response to perceived threats, insults, or collisions of interest. While tool risks are a linear function of the likelihood of pre-identifiable, harmful events, technological risks are a nonlinear function of uncertainties regarding emerging patterns of environmental/relational dynamics.

These distinctions help sharpen appreciation of the moral imperative to go beyond brain-centered neuroethics to a full-fledged ethics of consciousness, and, more specifically, to an ethics that is attentive to the inherent relational risks of digitally mediated field experimentation on consciousness. Technologies have been shaping the course of human evolution for somewhere between 2.5 and 1 million years (based, respectively, on archeological evidence for tool making and the controlled use of fire). That is, they have been recursively conditioning the development of distinctively human brains, bodies, and environments. As such, technology has been integral to human elaborations of the infrastructure of consciousness and thus to human reconfigurations of matter and what matters.

The advent of intelligent technology signals an evolutionary turning point. Machine and human intelligences are being effectively synthesized as digital neural networks train on human data and learn how to improve their own performance. For the first time, technology is endowed with capacities for actively and intently (though not yet intentionally) scaling up (unfortunately, often deeply conflicting) human values and intentions, intimately and creatively reshaping the human-technology-world relationship.

Today, intelligent technology and the global attention economy are actively and innovatively reinforcing personal readiness to grant corporate/political actors ever-more precise powers of control in exchange for the digital independence of ever-expanding virtual freedoms of experiential choice and convenience. This has been viewed in corporate circles as a free trade of attention for access, or more critically as the predatory condition of surveillance capitalism (Zuboff, 2019). But the logic at work in this exchange, I have argued, is fundamentally one of colonizing domination—a logic of domination, not through acts of overt coercion, but through ambiently reinforced craving (Hershock, 2021).

As this logic plays out and the feedback/feedforward cycle of attention capture and exploitation intensifies, although our individually tailored experiential and connective options will become both more extensive and more acutely desirable, this will happen at the cost of our most basic sentient right: the right to freedom-of-attention—a freedom without which we are incapable of making any meaningful differences in either our own lives or those of others. This is colonization from the inside out. Without freedom-of-attention, there is no freedom of intention. Without freedom-of-intention, the ethical dimension of the human mind and intelligence collapses.

The distinctive risk of intelligent technology and digitally mediated field experimentation on consciousness might be described in Buddhist terms as the personal risk of taking up wish-fulfilling residence on individually tailored karmic cul-de-sacs, or as the collective risk of precipitating an ethical singularity—our arrival at an historical juncture beyond which we will have no more chance of realizing liberating relational dynamics and responsive virtuosity than light has of escaping a black hole. In either case, we would be committing to a path of order-consolidating convolution rather than one of creativity-coordinating evolution. Continuing to theorize consciousness as reducible to neural dynamics and as subject to an evolutionary imperative to survive will place at risk our human capacities for participating in the cosmic evolutionary adventure of differentiating in ways that expand potentials for sustainably enhancing qualities of coherence. Although we humans are likely but a small part of that adventure, the demise of those capacities would nevertheless be a shame.

7

The Future of Human Consciousness: Cultural and Ethical Evolution

Consciousness persists through the relational articulation and mutual implication of matter and what matters. The future of consciousness is the future of what continues mattering. This is not and could never be predetermined. The indeterminacy of what continues mattering is not, however, the indeterminacy that haunts the borders of chance and necessity. It is the potently open indeterminacy of emergent responsivity and responsibility—the ever unfolding, ethically charged uncertainty of creative diversification.

As the terrestrial history of living beings and lived environments has made evident, the relational improvisations that constitute the coevolution of matter and what matters do not invariably result in sustainable coherences. The *constitutive entanglements* through which new lifeforms materialize can morph into *constrictive entanglements* of the kind that prevent "imagining for real" and "entering from the inside into the generative currents of the world" (Ingold, 2021: 4). Of all the species that have evolved on Earth over the last 4.5 billion years, 99 percent are now extinct.[1] Systems of mattering decohere.

It is debatable whether the future of consciousness on Earth will or should include human consciousness. What has mattered most to humans has been profoundly disruptive of the systems of coherent differentiation that constitute Earth's natural ecosystems. This is now most tragically evident in the damage caused to Earth's climate and ecological systems by the cumulative effects of centuries of carbon-fueled industrial manufacturing and transportation. Yet, the destructive decoherence of what matters for humans and what matters for other living beings is not an exclusively modern tragedy.

Mass extinctions are among the legacies of the evolution and migration of early humans. These began with the relatively "modest" extinction of 21 percent of megafauna species (animals weighing over 100 pounds) in Africa, where hominids first evolved. But they ranged up to the astonishing extinction of 88 percent of megafauna in Australia, 83 percent in North America, and 72 percent in South America, where humans arrived as an invasive species between 65,000 (Australia) and 15,000 years ago (South America). Comparably, materializations of what matters for humans are now causing species extinctions at rates that, if unabated, will lead to three out of every four species on Earth becoming extinct over the next three to five centuries—rates that are thousands of times greater than would be expected naturally.[2]

Life on Earth has proved to be remarkably resilient, surviving, and recovering from five previous mass extinctions. Given that fact, if the continued materialization of what matters most to humans precipitates a sixth mass extinction, one option is to dismiss it as just the latest iteration of a natural cycle of collapse and renewal. Creative adaptation will continue. Life will eventually resume flourishing. This optimistic account unfortunately entails ignoring the further material fact that this sixth mass extinction will occur over a period of several hundred years, not tens of thousands or tens of millions as in previous extinction events. This dramatically compresses the timescale of adaptation needed to ensure renewal. Moreover, this account entails ignoring the moral fact that the current mass extinction is the catastrophic consequence of values-embodying acts of human commission and omission, not a chance combination of natural events.

One response—common in practice, if seldom openly proclaimed—is to presume the legitimacy of human exceptionalism. We can accept as a matter of course the species extinctions and the consciousness-threatening decoherence that are being caused by our technologically supercharged pursuit of what matters most to humans. Anthropocentrism can be defended as our natural birthright and we simply carry on as usual.[3] That response rings increasingly hollow, however, when what has been mattering most to humanity has not even been consistently or effectively humane for most humans. Indeed, the fact that human rights institutions are required to rein in anthropogenic indignities and restrain acts of inhumanity suggests that, if humanity is exceptional, it is lamentably so.

Our prehistoric and premodern human ancestors may have been unaware of the destructive significance of the actions through which they articulated what mattered to them. Our early modern forebears may also have been unaware of the environmental and human costs of mass industrialization and the relational risks of technologically scaling up human values and conflicts among them. We can forgive their ignorance as unintentional. The effects of "slow violence" are easily overlooked (Nixon, 2011). We are not in a comparable position of being able to forgive ourselves. This is especially true given ongoing mass experimentation in the colonizing alteration of human consciousness—fully intentional experimentation that is placing at risk human capacities for values-evaluating course correction.

Evaluating What Matters Most to Humans: Envisioning Evolutionary Options

An extreme, antihuman response is to treat historical evidence of the ill consequences of humanity's determinations of what matters as justification for denying humanity "most favored species" status. The exceptional, "bad animal" conduct that humanity has exhibited are grounds for human diminishment, if not disappearance. If acts of genocide are heinous, acts of ecocide are even more so. If what matters most is ecological flourishing, and if humans are incapable of conducting themselves as members in good standing within the community of nature, then humanity should embrace voluntary self-extinction (MacCormack, 2020).[4]

Much as eliminativism about consciousness paints over—rather than solves—the hard problem of explicating the dynamic relationality of mind and matter, biosphere-championing antihuman advocacy skirts, rather than resolves, the much knottier values predicaments that have until now characterized the evolutionary/developmental dynamics of human consciousness. Institution-building efforts to secure "nature rights" are simultaneously as laudable and lamentable as have been efforts to secure basic human rights. Granting rights to other species and to the geo-climatic systems that sustain them is perhaps a praiseworthy egalitarian extension of the horizons of moral community—one that acknowledges the intrinsic value of other-than-human intelligences and embodiments of what matters. The fact that doing so is apparently an ecological necessity is, however, just as regrettable as the necessity of setting rights-based limits to anthropogenic human indignity.

From a Buddhist perspective, the moral argument for eliminating human elaborations of what matters errs in attributing to humans a universally flawed nature, rather than accepting the ethical challenge of altering human consciousnesses as needed to realize bios-affirming and humanity-transforming relational dynamics. That is, it errs in denying the emptiness/openness of human nature and in eschewing active human responsibility for differing-from and differing-for other species to materialize more liberating patterns of interdependence. It would be better to emancipate human consciousness than to eliminate it.

Transforming Humanity: Transhumanist and Posthumanist Possibilities

Transhumanism and posthumanism endorse this emancipatory alternative. As genres of imagining human futures, however, they express very different complexions of concerns and aims. For our purposes, we can characterize transhumanism as the more radical genre of imagining the emancipation of human consciousness. Resolutely future-oriented, transhumanism maintains that "human beings should take control of their own biological evolution, freely designing it through technology, to reach a post-human stage" (Manzocco, 2019: 4). Beginning with technoscientific enhancements of the human form and genome, the ultimate transhumanist goal is to engineer a "quantum leap" into functional immortality—vaulting consciousness into "Cartesian" transcendence and unimpeded, rational command of the material order.[5]

Transhumanism is thus an expression of "vertical" discontent and the intent to attain a more-than-merely-human presence in Promethean defiance of a limit-imposing natural order. As such, it forwards a functionalist/dualist vision of freeing human consciousness from its biological origins, accelerating the "ascent" of humankind to the point of reaching evolutionary escape velocity. By liberating the mind from the gravitational force of biological and terrestrial actualities, it has the normative goal of materializing consciousnesses that are no longer restricted by natural laws and are instead able to make free and creative use of them.

Posthumanism expresses a contrasting "horizontal" discontent with the interdependence-distorting effects of human chauvinism and hubris-inflamed proclamations of rightful independence from the natural order. Although posthumanism also affirms the "technogenesis" of the human (Hayles, 2011), it is a more conservative genre of imagining human futures that combines anti-anthropocentrism, anti-dualism, and anti-hierarchism with the intention of realizing a pragmatic and critical balance among "agency, memory, and imagination, aiming to achieve harmonic legacies in the evolving ecology of interconnected existence" (Ferrando, 2013: 32). The goal of posthumanism is not an emancipatory transcendence of human biology, including the human brain. It is a re-integrative, "Copernican" decentering of the human in the biosphere—a difference-respecting restoration that is committed to countering the negative ramifications of presumed human superiority in relation to other species and of presumed universality in relation to conceptions of the human.

Championing "the embodiment and embeddedness of the human being in not just its biological but also its technological world," posthumanism is neither antihuman nor transhumanist in the sense of endorsing a way of "being 'after' our embodiment has been transcended." What posthumanism opposes are precisely "the fantasies of disembodiment and autonomy inherited from humanism itself" (Wolfe, 2010: xv). Committed to emancipatory immanence, posthumanism insists ethically on rejecting any rationalist humanism that accentuates differences between humans and nonhumans, while also eliding significant intra-human differences, for example, in gendered presence, precarity, class, and history.

When combined with vitalist, new materialist sensibilities, posthumanism ambitiously reconceives subjectivity as no longer exclusively human and envisions a future of deepening ecological co-implication. This is to be accomplished through valorizing relations among sentient presences that are not based on negative bonds of vulnerability, but rather on "the compassionate acknowledgement of their interdependence" (Braidotti, 2013: 101) and the realization that "we-are-(all)-in-this-together-but-we-are-not-one-and-the-same" (Braidotti, 2013: 54). Posthumanism is thus diversity-affirming in the sense of valuing both intra-human and human-nonhuman differences as the basis of mutual contribution to sustainably shared flourishing.

Transhumanism and posthumanism each have their merits as vehicles for speculating about the future of humanity. The transhumanist vision of the future of humanity can be charitably interpreted as one of freedom from compulsory presence. As such, it is generally consistent with a central aim of Buddhist practice: attaining the freedom of attention and the freedom of intention needed to stop being passively subject to our karma and accepting full and active responsibility for the character of our presence and the dynamics of our experience. The posthumanist vision of the future of humanity can be similarly interpreted as a healing restoration of premodern, indigenous conceptions of human presence as genealogically continuous with other species and as harmoniously deferential in relation to what matters to them (Rosiek, Snyder, and Pratt, 2020). This is broadly consistent with Mahayana Buddhist valorizations of superlative partnership in the improvisation of liberating relational dynamics, and with early Buddhist theorizing of consciousness as the relational differentiation of both ecologically and ethically entangled presences.

As modes of theorizing human consciousness and orienting its further evolution, however, the merits of transhumanism and posthumanism are less clear. This is perhaps due, in part, to the fact that neither explicitly forwards either a theory of evolution or a theory of consciousness. They are normative anticipations of the future history of human presence—transcendence-oriented and immanence-oriented imaginations of the futures that would result, respectively, from affirming human exceptionalism and valuing technological control, or from denying human superiority and valuing egalitarian collaboration.[6] Nevertheless, their normative anticipations do imply stances on consciousness.

Transhumanism is most readily compatible with either dualist or functionalist theorizing about consciousness, affirming either the ontological separation of mind and matter or that of computational/cognitive function and matter. The relation of consciousness and matter is contingent; continuities of consciousness do not depend on specific lineage(s) of material continuity. Improving human consciousness is most fundamentally quantitative. It means realizing measurable enhancements of human capabilities—for example, by enabling humans to process information at machine speeds, or by achieving lifespans that are measured in millennia rather than decades and that are thus compatible with galactic exploration.

Posthumanism is most readily compatible with physical reductionist theorizing, emphasizing the materially enacted, embodied, embedded, and extended nature of consciousness. The relation of consciousness and matter is constitutive; continuities of consciousness both depend on and are unique implications of specific lineages of material continuity. Improving consciousness is fundamentally qualitative. It means correcting both human-human and human-nonhuman relations by subordinating human control to harmonious inter-species collaboration.

Though clearly opposed, taken individually, these are not unattractive visions of the future of human consciousness. They are not, however, *kuśala* or virtuosic visions. For example, in contrast with the freedoms realized through Buddhist practice, transhumanist freedom is entangled normatively with realizing unlimited material control. As transhumanists like Nick Bostrom (2014) have pointed out, this is not a pursuit without risk, including risks of human obsolescence and extinction. Control need not be either human or humane. Yet, even if such existential threats can be avoided and science and technology enable humans to exercise the full control of natural law envisioned by transhumanists, unless control is subordinated to other values, the recursive character of karmic entanglement is such that human control of the infrastructure of consciousness would constrain human presence, not emancipate it. Transcendent control over matter—in the absence of a shared moral compass and progress ethically in resolving predicaments of what matters—will not guarantee heading toward less conflicted relational dynamics, and any consolidation of such control is likely to erode rather than enhance diversity and the improvisational furthering of coherent differentiation.

Similarly, the posthumanist denial of human exceptionalism and its valorization of species egalitarianism and harmonization with the natural order have the potential to place human distinctiveness at risk of relational atrophy. The bodhisattva ideal of appreciative and contributory virtuosity is an articulation of compassionate and effortfully achieved hierarchy. Buddhist ethics is rooted in the critical and karmic recognition of hierarchies in what matters, but also in affirming the open and progressive nature of ethical virtuosity—the improvisational extension of moral and material horizons. Although it is important to consider what matters for ecosystem vitality and for conserving intra-human differences, this should not come at the expense of hobbling intentions to creatively expand the scope of what matters in and for the evolution of human consciousness. If transhumanism is liable to result in excesses of hubris, posthumanism is liable to result in excesses of humility.

To summarize, transhumanist and posthumanist norms implicate us, respectively, in altering and improving the neural/bodily infrastructure and the ecological/social infrastructure of human consciousness. As such, their approaches to imagining the emancipation of human consciousness (and thus justifying its terrestrial continuity rather than elimination) are analogous to imaginations of improving transportation infrastructure through designing better vehicles, repairing roadways, runways, and railways, and building more aesthetically pleasing and user-friendly transportation hubs. At best, these efforts will improve the *material means* and *phenomenal character* of transportation. What they will not do is transform the *meaning* or *purposes* of transportation. Transportation can serve to meet basic needs, to foster the circulation of talent and ideas, to pursue love, or to wage war. Transforming the infrastructure of human consciousness will not by itself establish new norms for the self-altering and future-evolving work of human consciousness.

Beyond Infrastructure: The Evolving Meaning of Consciousness

Earlier, having theorized the work of consciousness as the creative elaboration of a cosmically primitive urge to differentiate coherently, I argued that a false choice is set up by asking either "what is the advantage of consciousness for evolution?" or its inversion "what is the advantage of evolution for consciousness?" Both questions imply the presence of inexistent boundaries between evolution and consciousness. Recursively altering consciousness is both the means-to and meaning-of evolution as an intra-active process of materializing coherently differing determinations of what matters.

Another way of putting this is to say that *what matters* affects *what materializes* and how. This is mundanely obvious. We materially enact our intentions. We build things, bringing into material presence hitherto nonexistent objects and processes. In doing so, we are reconfiguring matter and conjuring new and specific coherences out of what would have remained otherwise. These effects of what matters unfold in the sequential temporality of linear causal relations. Less obviously, however, what matters is also the basis of entanglements ramifying through the encompassing temporal dimension of significance relations. Gender matters, for example, in ways that exceed the brute materiality of sexual relations and reproduction, radically altering individual life histories and societal trajectories in ways that are never simple or reversible.

Yet, if matter does, indeed, consist in the definition of a point of view, then altering perspectives on what matters results in much more than merely altering interpretative glosses. Consciousness is not merely reality construing. The mathematician and physicist Stephen Wolfram is right, I think, to take the successes of relativity and quantum physics as grounds for arguing that—although consciousness evidently involves a neuro-computational infrastructure—the essence of consciousness is not mere representation or reflection. It is coherence-generation. Consciousness does the work of integrating world events in a process that is so fundamental to the topography of spatial and temporal relations that a consciousness sufficiently different from our own, he conjectures, would elicit, and be constrained by different physical laws.[7] Stated in nondualist, Yogācāra Buddhist terms, it is the nature of consciousness to be world-manifesting.

To the extent that envisioning the future of human consciousness alters what matters humanly, it will alter both the relational outcomes and opportunities that subsequently materialize and how they do so. The core intuitions of transhumanism suggest that what matters most is expanding human responsibility, while those of posthumanism suggest that what matters most is enhancing human responsivity. These are valuable intuitions. Enacting them will help refine and extend the neural/bodily and ecological/social infrastructures of consciousness. Yet, as continued climate disruption, the increasing likelihood of a sixth mass extinction, and the persistence of human hunger and structural violence all make evident, we need more direct and predicament-resolving consideration of what humanity should be doing by means of those infrastructures—more direct and critical evaluation of the world(s) we have been and are in the process of eliciting. The evolution of human consciousness is due for a course change.

The Immaterial Nature of Distinctively Human Evolutionary Improvisation

To best anticipate the course changes that might be needed, we must first consider the uniqueness of the past evolution of human consciousness. Compared with all other sensing presences on Earth, including large-brained mammals like the great apes, dolphins, and elephants, humans are unique in the degrees to which what matters is immaterial. The genius of humanity is "extra-material" or "incorporeal"—a genius for becoming differently entwined with material reality "not through preexisting values but through acting, making and doing that generate new values" (Grosz, 2017: 255).

Thus, as noted earlier, while humans and animals have in common such acts as eating and procreating, humans infuse eating and procreating with new values, transforming them respectively into hospitality and cuisine and into romantic love and family affections. In sharp contrast with other terrestrial lineages of consciousness, nearly all of what has come to matter most for humans—marriages and family dynamics, power and prestige, economics, politics, law, nation building, the arts, and so on—could not exist and cannot be comprehended apart from acts of collective human imagination.[8] In short, what sets humans apart are the depth and breadth of our cultural creativity—our collective embarkation on an open and cumulative evolutionary adventure in values-creation and variations on the immaterial meaning of cohesion.[9]

The cultural turn in human evolution has, of course, also had extensive material consequences. A simple comparison of the surface of the Earth today and 8,000 years ago when the first large human settlements began appearing makes strikingly evident the creative material power of the cultural work of human consciousness. Forests have been cleared, mountains leveled, and cities built that are visible from near Earth orbit. In addition, however, new alloys of material and mental structures and processes have been crafted, resulting in relational environments that cannot be understood or engaged at the levels of abstraction at which it is possible to make sense of natural features like mountains or of such material/societal structures as termite mounds or beehives.

To give a simple example, on their first day of formal education, children enter a building of a size and type unlike their homes, many of them clinging frantically to their parents on its threshold. Over time, they become attuned to the sociocultural environment of *school*—a virtual reality to which no other species have access, and within which children transform relationally into students variously engaging each other as companions, competitors, and collaborators. Sports stadiums, stock exchanges, scientific labs, and space stations are similarly physical structures and relational environments with predominantly virtual functions. With the buildout of the "metaverse" and investments in digital real estate and non-fungible tokens, digital and nearly "physics-free" virtual realities are now being actualized—realms of human interaction and sociocultural differentiation that exist *only* to the extent that humans collectively intend, imagine, and value them.

The migration of human attention into ever more immaterial and intentionally structured relational environments accelerated rapidly between 40,000 and 60,000 years ago. This is epitomized by the relatively sudden proliferation of cave paintings. Unlike stones that have been selectively chipped to improve the practical efficacy of subsistence activities, cave paintings are translations of fleeting sensory experiences into lasting sensory stimuli—the materialization of shared and narratively structured memories. After nearly a million years of crafting stone tools with minimal changes in lifeways and relational structures, almost overnight in evolutionary time scales, humanity began crafting objects of veneration, ritual implements, musical instruments, and emblems of personal identity, realizing new, more extensive, and increasingly differentiated forms of community.

With this materially enacted, cultural, communicative, and cognitive revolution, early humans began remaking the world in their minds, sharing perspectives, and then working together to reshape the world to bring it into greater conformity with what they imagined and desired. The legacy of this revolution is that, unlike any other species, humans "live for much of the time less in the 'real' world than in the worlds we individually reconstruct within our heads" (Tattersall, 2019: 11). Culture has been the primary medium and milieu of the distinctively human evolutionary labor of consciousness. Cultural evolution theories attempt to account for how this happened and why.

Theorizing Cultural Evolution: The Need for Caution

If it is true that how we theorize consciousness affects the direction and dynamics of its self-altering work of relational elaboration, it is also true that how we theorize the evolution of culture affects the evolution of what matters most for humans. This, in turn, qualitatively affects human consciousness and shapes our convictions about the purposes of conscious presence. Theorizing cultural evolution is not and cannot be value-neutral.

Keeping this in mind, it's instructive to consider the early history of theorizing cultural evolution as the "natural" corollary of biological evolution. In concert with trends in the disciplines of archeology and anthropology that were emerging in the mid-nineteenth century, the first cultural evolution theories resonated with hierarchic conceptions of race and morality and situated the evolution of cultures within a frame narrative of seemingly inexorable and unilineal progress. Charles Darwin, for example, supposed that cultures, like species, evolve through natural selection, and that even our most intimately personal faculties of moral intuition and emotional connection are the cumulative products of "experiences of utility organised and consolidated through all past generations of the human race" (Darwin, 1877: 148). The unstated implication of this reading of cultural evolution was made explicit by Darwin's contemporary, Herbert Spencer: the cultures we now have are the cultures—and hence moral intuitions and institutions—that we *should* have. They have proven their competitive advantage and adaptive value. The spread of eugenics movements over the first half of the twentieth century, especially in Europe and the United States, was one of the legacies of this theoretical framing.

Over the course of the twentieth century, unilineal perspectives on cultural evolution and their presumption of a natural hierarchy of cultures came to be seen as a scientifically questionable projection of colonial and imperial arrogance and ambitions. Yet, these perspectives persist (see, e.g., Flannery and Marcus, 2012), and the narrative of competitive and survival-warranted fitness has proven to be surprisingly resilient. Clear echoes of it can be found, for example, in the extension of Dawkins's "selfish gene" view of biological evolution to theorize cultural change and continuity in terms of memes (the cultural equivalent of biological genes) that have a natural inclination (and perhaps right) to selfishly ensure their own replication. The memes—and thus the cultural complexes of language, social practices, and moral systems—that survive and continue to thrive are those that have "deserved" to do so.[10]

This narrative of evolutionary survivors having a "natural right" to the future also has apparent popular appeal. Yuval Harari's books on the history and future of humanity, for example, have sales of over 12 million copies worldwide, and depict humanity's cultural genius as being on a techno-utopian track to deliver "godlike" powers and presences in the relatively near future, only to ironically trigger the forfeiture of humanity's position at evolutionary forefront to artificial superintelligence. Having described consciousness as the biologically useless byproduct of brain events—comparable to the air pollution produced by passenger jets—Harari admits that it would not be at all surprising if human cultural evolution culminates in the creation of "intelligence without consciousness," so that "humanity will turn out to have been just a ripple within the cosmic dataflow" (Harari, 2017: 460).[11]

Although cultural evolution is no longer widely presumed to be unilineal, and contentment with the demise of humanity is far from mainstream, most contemporary theories seeking to explain the inordinate richness of human cultures in comparison with other species remain selectionist in orientation.[12] Differences among them reflect the positions they adopt with respect to three intersecting axes of causal/explanatory factors: an axis regarding the relative importance of quantity and quality in cultural transmission; an axis regarding the degree to which transmission is intentional or automatic; and an axis regarding the relative causal weight of natural and social selection. That is, their differences depend largely on the relative importance they accord to high-fidelity transmission lineages; high-volume transmission braids; the efficacy of traits and traditions; the attractiveness of traits and traditions; "blind" selection; and "interested" selection.

All six of these factors may be necessary, constitutive parts of the causal "mechanisms" involved in selecting, transforming, and transmitting cultural traits and traditions. Yet, if cultural evolution—like biological evolution—consists in consciousness mattering, they cannot be sufficient. This follows from our earlier characterization of the basic work of consciousness, not as the representational labor of mapping the world or the predictive labor of determining its causal patterning, but as the creative and anticipatory elaboration of what matters most in seeking and securing what matters most: the recursively progressive optimizing of relational coherences. To explain the open-ended, variation-accelerating, and cumulative dynamics of human cultural *evolution*—and not merely cultural *transmission*—it is necessary to explain the advent and orientation of values-elaborating human creativity (Gabora, 2019).

Exiting the Cave: Culture, Time, and Historical Memory

If cultural evolution consists in a distinctively human extension of the scope of consciousness mattering, important clues about how best to theorize that extension and its future may be gleaned by thinking through both the material and cognitive means to creating cave art and its meaning as a distinctively human way of articulating what matters.[13]

Cave painting is often hailed as the earliest material evidence of humans engaging in symbolic or abstract thinking: evidence that an inner theater (or, to invoke a Platonic metaphor, an inner cave) had opened in which conceptual representations of sensorimotor phenomena could be actively projected and manipulated. The painted antelope materially projects an *idea*: a mentally constituted "antelope." Cave paintings were made possible by the opening of the theater of the mind—conscious presence as imagined by global workspace theory.

Theorizing of consciousness relationally and as both spatially and temporally nonlocal suggests, alternatively, that cave paintings are evidence—not of intrinsically symbolic thinking acted out on an inner neural stage—but of emergent capacities for exploring a dimension of distinctively *consequential*, but *nonsequential* temporal relations. Rather than the advent of internal representations, cave painting marks an emancipation of consciousness from the sensory confines of the phenomenal present—a transformative extension of the temporality of both real and potential relational differentiations and coherences.[14]

In a rudimentary fashion, any animal capable of some combination of seeing, hearing, tasting, touching, and smelling will generate multisensory concepts. The sound of a twig breaking will spark attentive anticipation of seeing a nearby "predator" or "prey." This is the basic work of what Buddhism theorizes as the sixth consciousness. The minimal temporal scope of this work—the duration of the phenomenal present—is the gap in the timing of (in this case, visual and auditory) sensorimotor feedback. If there arrives in this enduring present a scent that decisively collapses the predator/prey ambiguity, it may trigger flight from the still unseen but anticipated "predator" based on phenomenal resonances with similar sequences of past sensations. The learned response is conscious. For most prey animals in the wild, however, we have no evidence to suggest that, after successfully fleeing, they continue to "think" about their narrow escape from danger. Their experience and learning are neither self-conscious nor subject to later use in developing a general concept of "danger" by relating this event to prior encounters, for example, with poisonous plants, floods, or lightning strikes. There is no narrating of an enworlded presence.

Being able to paint predator or prey animals on the wall of a cave implies that something very different has begun occurring in the work of human consciousness—elaborating and learning from relational dynamics made evident only by *directing recursively sustained attention beyond the horizons of the phenomenal present*. The painting materializes a *valued* and *lasting* relationship and a capacity for attending to what is not present, as if it is present. It is not coincidental that, unlike any other animal communication systems, human languages—as they evolved alongside human cultural traditions—came to include terms for absence and negation and for both invoking and evoking relations with things that do not exist and with processes that are not occurring. It is through exiting the "cave" of the phenomenal present and becoming aware that this moment could have been otherwise that the work of human consciousness accelerated dramatically and took on a distinctively immaterial character.

Consonant with this alternative description, archeoacoustic research has revealed correlations among the content of cave art and the distinctive acoustic properties of caves. For example, acoustically dead sections of caves are painted with animal figures relatively infrequently and, when they are, it is with images of felines—notoriously stealthy predators. Otherwise, the most common wall decorations in these spaces are stencils of human hands. In contrast, acoustically live and echo-rich cave sections predominantly feature images of hooved animals, moving herds of which generate a thunderously encompassing sonic environment. These earliest efforts to materialize thought or perceptual content are thus strong evidence for robust cross-modality information transfer, and quite likely for its communicative appropriation in the materialization of a cognitive bridge from animal to fully human language (Miyagawa, Lesure, and Nobrega, 2018).

It is important to stress that this alternative construction of the significance of cave painting suggests that the painted animal is not merely a visual image, an objectified reproduction of a no longer present visual phenomenon. Cave paintings are means by which early humans created a shared realm of narrative, and not merely episodic, memories. The association of a cave's sonic character with those of specific animals suggests, moreover, that cave paintings functioned as holistic and appreciative evocations of the different ways in which animals cohere with their environments. That is, the paintings reproduce *differently coherent relations* among sensed and sensing presences. They are *evocations* of different kinds of *consciousness*. There is thus a sense in which the practice of figurative cave painting expresses or enacts both an elementary recognition of "other minds" and a synoptic understanding of human-animal-environment relationality. Cave paintings make materially manifest an immaterial worldview.

This approach to understanding figurative cave painting has important implications for interpreting the earlier, persistent, and more pervasive practice of using clay pigments to produce outlines or stencils of hands. Depictions of animals feared and/or hunted by a community plausibly had the purpose of creatively and communally conserving shared memories. They evoke relationships of belonging together. For an early human to stencil his or her hand on a cave wall blends visual and tactile phenomena in a way that leaves behind a shadow or relational residue of attentive presence and purpose—a residue that survives his or her phenomenal absence and evokes his or her continued presence. It is significant that hands are stenciled rather than, for example, feet. Although our feet are crucial to our mobility as animals and establish our loose kinship with them, our hands set us apart. Our hands are our means for making and using tools, for eating, grooming, directing others' attention, and communicating intentions.[15] Rather than symbolically re-presenting a body part, hand stenciling can be understood a means of intentionally marking relationships of *lasting presence*. Like a signature or seal, a hand stencil materializes a proclamation of persistent *personal agency*.

Theorized along Yogācāra Buddhist lines, hand stenciling is evidence of an emerging seventh consciousness. The cultural turn in the evolution of human consciousness occurred when the process of collating multisensory relations into phenomenal objects—the work of the sixth or mental/conceptual consciousness—became consistently entrained with that of an emerging seventh consciousness, a temporally extended and evaluation-focused form of subjective human presence. Through the differential work of the seventh consciousness, the ochre outline of a hand on the cave wall ceases to be a generically familiar shape; it becomes a ghost or out-of-body rendering of a hand that is *mine*. When other hands are stenciled alongside my hand, it identifies this cave as *ours*. The antelope painted onto the cave wall reveals *my* perspective on the antelope and how it matters to *me*. When others stand beside me, clapping and drumming in the rhythms of an antelope herd in motion, the painting recalls how the skin, flesh, and bones of a successfully hunted antelope were its gifts to *us*.

Moreover, as noted earlier, the work of the seventh consciousness is entrained with that of the eighth or "storehouse" consciousness, its nonlinear elaborations of temporal significance, and its karmic entangling of relational trajectories. The antelope image painted onto the wall is not the materialization of a snapshot memory—a freestanding thing-in-itself. It is a diffractive product of a phenomenal current in which the antelope is absent and an affectively charged and narratively ordered current of memories and relational histories in which the antelope factors significantly.

Thus, a cave painting of an antelope is not merely a representational translation of a perceptual memory into a perceptual stimulus. It is the purposeful evocation of *lasting* interspecies *mutuality*—an extension of anticipatory awareness well beyond the phenomenal present. It expresses an awareness of desire- and values-qualified alternations of antelope presence and absence occurring within patterned alternations of solar, lunar, and stellar presence and absence: awareness of relational continuities within a nested order of diurnal, monthly, and seasonal cycles. That is, human cultures emerged as temporality-expanding improvisations on intersubjective presence and through objective materializations of significance relations. They are creative and cumulative elaborations of the seventh and eighth consciousnesses.

A significant body of contemporary theorizing accords with this perspective on the acceleration of human cultural evolution, linking it to a range of novel, temporality-transforming cognitive capacities: a capacity for self-triggered, rather than environmentally cued recall and rehearsal (Donald, 1993); a capacity for relational reinterpretation or attending to non-perceptual relational similarities (Penn, Holyoak, and Povinelli, 2008); a capacity for recursive thinking as exemplified in relations of "belonging," attributing thoughts to others, and engaging in mental time travel (Corballis, 2011); and the combination of high-resolution memories with a capacity for context-sensitive convergent and divergent focus (Gabora and Smith, 2018). Cultural evolution did not accelerate due to increased needs for transferring tool-making skills that had been honed over hundreds of thousands of years. It did so in creative response to new and complex needs for guiding attention immaterially; transmitting subjective insights; composing interpersonal worldviews; structuring actions serially and cyclically; organizing interests and values hierarchically; and maintaining long distance dependencies in space and time. Cultural evolution occurs as new modes of human consciousness—and the cognitive coupling and language-mediated coordination of conduct materialized through them—evolved in response to ecological and social coordination needs.

The interpretation of cave painting just offered suggests that these new cognitive capacities were, most fundamentally, responses to intensifying needs to determine interpersonally what matters most for establishing coherences among sequentially and significantly ordered events. What is crucial to cultural evolution is not the production of artifacts or material objectifications of thought in functional adaptive response to emerging material needs. It is the progressive and aggregating elaboration of new sensory and conceptual relations while remaining lastingly present in an expressly shared world. In short, what evolves culturally are interacting subjectivities in a self-organizing process akin to that by which early life evolved—a process that consists, not in the eliminative survival of the fittest, but rather in the creative and cumulative actualization of potentials for coordinated presence.[16]

It is useful at this point to recall our earlier discussion (in Chapter 5) of experimental evidence showing that functional inter-brain entanglements are established during cooperation, but not during either competition or merely simultaneous task performance; that neural rhythms are interpersonally conditioned; that extra-cranial resonances are as important as intra-cranial ones; and that brains can become socially or relationally entangled. Human consciousness does not exist at well-defined "points" of ambiguously neural/phenomenal spacetime. It occurs as an active and indefinitely extensive medium of continuously changing patterns of diffraction among neural/phenomenal intentions to differentiate coherently. Culture is the relational medium through which the intersubjectivity of human consciousness evolves qualitatively.

It is consistent with this interpretation of the "Cambrian explosion" of human cultural evolution that occurred 40,000 to 60,000 years ago that the coevolution of recursive thought and language does not seem to have depended on any substantial alteration of the neural infrastructure of consciousness. Instead, the coevolutionary marriage of thought and language seems to have been mediated by the cooptation and temporal coupling of the already-existent neural systems involved in temporal sequencing and hierarchical processing with systems involved in nonlinguistic communication. That is, these distinctively human features of the work of consciousness developed through a creative "hijacking" of already-useful brain structures rather than the selection-driven development of new neural infrastructure (Kolodny and Edelman, 2018). It was not through a process of natural selection among random variations in neural organization that the horizons of immaterially coordinated human conduct were progressively extended. Neural activity was reorganized by the creative transformation of human conduct through collaborative, intersubjective elaborations of the means-to and meanings-of sustained coherence.

Caves of Cultural Making: A Uniquely Human Liability

If the analogy holds between the origin and early evolution of human culture with the molecular origin and early evolution of life, we should anticipate an eventual transition from the dynamic primacy of creation to conservation—a shift from the primacy of collaborative differentiation to that of competitive individuation and the "coded" transmission or reproduction of systems of coherence. This would be accompanied by the emergence and maintenance of the cultural equivalent of organism/environment boundaries and thus a transition from a dynamic of coherence-diversifying inclusion to one of coherence-defining exclusion. In short, it would be expected at some point for pulling together in mutual belonging to become defined functionally by pushing away who and what does not belong. This is arguably the dynamic at work in the consolidation of familial and clan systems and their eventual combination into competitive societal systems of increasingly large scale, eventually including nations and empires.

The analogy also encourages anticipating that the dichotomy of belonging and not-belonging would eventually become entrained with the growing significance of top-down mechanisms for coding relatively high-fidelity transmissions of cultural traditions and worldviews. However, a key difference between the process of cultural evolution and random gene/trait variation followed by environmental selection is the predominance of acquired traits and their strategic adaptation and purposeful braiding. Cultural evolution is Lamarkian rather than Neo-Darwinian. Given this, the coding "mechanisms" involved in sustaining continuities of cultural traditions and worldviews would need to offer both high coding flexibility and high-fidelity transmission. Human languages meet both requirements. In addition to including terms for negation, human languages also differ from all other animal communication systems in having no limits on how much can be expressed by means of them.[17] The invention of writing systems allowed this unlimited expressive flexibility to be combined with high transmission fidelity over indefinitely large temporal and spatial distances.

The analogy suggests further, however, that while written languages would facilitate flexible and high-fidelity communication and cultural continuity, the transition from orality to literacy would also eventuate in new kinds of exclusion—between the literate and illiterate within societies, but also among societies. This seems to have been the case historically. Writing systems greatly expanded cultural reach and societal coordination, with Latin, Sanskrit, and Chinese, for example, functioning as communicative and conceptual commons for many centuries. Yet writing systems eventually also proved conducive to incoherent differentiations among languages and cultures. Higher intragenerational and intergenerational transmission fidelity came at the cost of mutual unintelligibility and with the risk of reinforcing cultural *variation* rather than furthering cultural *diversification*.[18]

Theorizing cultural evolution in analogy with the transition from creativity-driven and collaboration-biased dynamics to selection-driven and competition-biased dynamics in biological evolution affords a productive alternative to purely selectionist interpretations of the last 10,000 years of human history. It enables, for example, explaining the Neolithic ascent of agriculturalist societies, not as driven by extrinsic factors like climate change and population pressures, but as impelled by the intrinsic, creative impulse to realize new forms of "catalytic" interdependence with plant and animal species. The agricultural revolution was an *inclusivity revolution* based on extending caring relations beyond the boundaries of the human family or clan, and sedentarism was less a strategy for generating food excesses than it was a consequence of the progressive human differentiation of space and place, where "places" come into being over time as shared ways of being present saturate a locale with aspirational and collaboratively elaborated patterns of experience and significance.[19]

But the analogy also has important implications for anticipating the future of human consciousness and cultural evolution. The evolutionary transitions from nonliving to living presences, and from the dominance of bio-material to cultural-immaterial differentiations of matter and what matters, each involved the coordinated intensification of shared values and the rapid expansion of a new realm of coherence potentials. Life consists fundamentally in chemically sustained coordination regarding what matters for order-generating (and thus entropy-resisting) relational persistence and innovation. The evolutionary leap from molecular and single-celled life to multi-celled organisms marks a shift of dominance from chemical to sensory/behavioral coordination. This led to the incredible burst of species differentiation that occurred in the Cambrian explosion, but also the materialization of increasingly complex, ecology-generating behavioral coordination. Through ecologically modulated feedback across generations, behavioral coordination came to be materially encoded. This instinctual coordination is what continues to dominate among social insects, flocking birds, schooling fish, herding mammals, and collaborating primates.

With the cultural turn in human evolution, a dramatic leap was made from almost exclusively *instinctual* coordination to fundamentally *voluntary* coordination that is subject to ongoing personal and interpersonal evaluation and revision. Human coordination continues to be chemical and behavioral. But especially in the context of predicament-resolving coordination on what matters most, human coordination is predominantly *intentional*.

An Intentional Revolution

Being freed from the cave of the phenomenal present also freed human consciousness from instinctual determinations of what matters. The "light cone" of human care could be expanded indefinitely. Any given moment could *mean* many things, *mattering* differently as memory ceased to be triggered by current sensorimotor events or limited to a role in predicting sequential probabilities. With free-ranging and freely associative memory capacities and linguistic flexibility, the past opened into a tributary delta of shared and possibility-generating currents of significance. Against the rhythm of solar, lunar, seasonal, and celestial cycles, it became possible to improvise both materially and immaterially. It became possible to decide what mattered and what did not, both personally and interpersonally, and to then evaluate what occurred or flowed together as a result. With the cultural turn in the evolution of human consciousness, sensorimotor freedoms transformed into sociality-defining responsibilities.

As noted earlier, while the members of a handful of other species—as well as a small number of individual robots—have demonstrated rudimentary capacities for planning and for achieving valued material outcomes, there is no evidence to suggest that they locate themselves in a world that they continually evaluate, expand, and seek to improve. Non-human sentient presences are responsive, but they apparently are not truly responsible. In addition to considering what has happened and what is happening to better anticipate and affect what is likely to happen next, humans consider what *should* have happened, what *should* be happening now, and what *should* happen in the future. With human subjectivity and culture, *is* often becomes subordinate to *ought*, and the sentient urge to survive is overlaid by a complex penumbra of both material and immaterial desires. What matters most is not merely continuing to live; it is living better.

Cultures develop and evolve as materializations of persistently shared patterns of values, intentions, and actions. They are expressive media of karmic entanglement through which lineages of what continues mattering are braided together and mutually reinforced. Like the neural infrastructure of consciousness, cultures at once guide and constrain both attention and intention. That is, every culture manifests as a "prosthetic externalization … of the bureaucracy of consciousness" that mediates energy-allocations among competing interests, both intrapersonally and interpersonally (Watson, 2018: 209). Cultures *habituate* the work of consciousness.

That is often a good thing. Habits are efficient. They are repetition-consolidated and fidelity-securing dispositions enacted at the boundary of the voluntary and involuntary. As such, they function as something akin to acquired instincts, freeing up attention energy while maintaining dynamic relational coherence. Yet, habits can also hamper improvisational creativity. Hence, therapeutically motivated Buddhists have traditionally critiqued habit formations (*saṃskāra*) as impediments to realizing *kuśala* or virtuosic modes of thinking, speaking, and acting—impediments to the consciousness-liberating movement that Chan Buddhist master Linji (d.866) characterized as "facing the world and going crosswise" (Taishō vol. 47 no.1985:497C).

Riffing on Aldous Huxley's metaphor of the brain as a "reducing valve," we can think of cultures as repetition-consolidated systems for filtering out what otherwise might have mattered, for limiting what otherwise might be done, and thus for constraining the world(s) that we elicit. Thus, although cultures emerge as expressions of human creativity and become treasuries of what has mattered consistently and effectively for those reproducing, revising, and transmitting them, cultures also function as resilient systems of what might be called conventional ignorance.

Like any infrastructure, cultures constrain as much as they coordinate. Although they originate in shared practices of coherently extending the horizons of material and social cohesion, cultures eventually begin perpetuating norms about what *should* and *should not* be thought, said, and done. They become immaterial systems of cohesion that constrain how far we can differ-from each other and establish the compass of our inclinations to differ-for one another. In short, cultural transmission is dynamically prone to limiting the scope of the work of consciousness, masking the original nonduality of consciousness by reinforcing norms regarding what we can and should *mean* to one another, and thus constraining who we *are* and *are not* free to become.

Ethical Evolution: A Human Imperative

With the cultural turn in human evolution, the work of consciousness expanded to encompass intentionally enacting both what matters materially and what matters immaterially. This made possible humanly elicited worlds of unprecedented relational complexity. Yet, if disrupting or dissolving habit formations in the neural infrastructure of consciousness proved conducive to materializing shared cultural worlds and altering consciousness in ways that valuably transformed personal and interpersonal presence, it follows that the same may be true of disrupting or dissolving the habits that characterize the cultural/linguistic infrastructure of human consciousness. Ethics is one means of doing so.[20]

The practice of ethics as a reasoned art of envisioning pathways to better societies seems to have begun in zones of intense cultural confluence that were coalescing roughly 2,600 years ago along the eastern shores of the Mediterranean, on the Indo-Gangetic plain, and in the Yellow River basin of what is now China. Those early efforts to articulate guidelines for convergent and consonant human course correction arguably began in response to a combination of new and persistent conflicts both within and among societies, and as alternatives to coherence-conserving—but in practice mutually exclusive—moral and legal systems. Crucially, in contrast with moral and legal systems that aimed at modifying *behavior*, elaborating communal norms of human action, ethics aimed at modifying *motives*, elaborating ostensibly rational and universal norms of human intention and interaction.

Insofar as ethics involves taking critical responsibility for what is reproduced and transmitted culturally and for orienting human consciousness toward enacting more encompassing and intentional norms of material and immaterial coherence, it can be seen as evolutionarily significant. It signals effort to reclaim the creative freedoms afforded by the cultural turn and by "time-traveling" improvisations on the meaning of improved presence that were made possible by the seventh and eighth consciousnesses and their differentiation of temporal sequence and temporal significance. Ethics is premised on affirming that the quality of human relational dynamics is *significantly* indeterminate.

To the extent that cultural evolution consists in elaborating hybrid material/immaterial infrastructures of consciousness, ethics is an attempt to alter what is done by means of those infrastructures and to shape how they are further extended. It is an attempt to reorient human purpose. That is, ethics involves (at least implicitly) exploring and evaluating the dynamics of the intentional dimension of the evolution of human consciousness. Ethics presumes that the future of human consciousness is neither predetermined nor an essentially "natural" function of adaptive selection. It is a realm or medium of potential diffractions among recursively unfolding, responsibility-enacting, responsibility-forfeiting, and responsibility-denying determinations of what continues mattering in materializing freedoms to cohere or decohere in the ways that we both differ-from and differ-for one another. Ethics is the art of creatively altering the meanings of human presence that inform the world-eliciting work of culturally enacted—and thus both materially and immaterially shared—human consciousness.

This is admittedly an idealized and purposely *countercultural* characterization of ethics. Historically, the practice of ethics has infrequently lived up to its evolutionary promise. Until very recently, although ethical systems have often proffered ostensibly universal guidelines for human conduct, they have invariably reflected regional concerns and have been nourished by relatively local moral and legal deliberations. The result has been a significant expansion of global *ethical variety* rather than the materialization of *ethical diversity*. In short, while ethical plurality has increased, it has done so without the depths of difference-valuing ethical improvisation needed to foster the emergence of a global ethical ecosystem.[21]

In the context of the relatively thin and tenuous material interdependencies that prevailed globally over most of human history, the relatively local reach of the immaterial infrastructures of human consciousness and the parochial plurality of ethics were largely consistent with the general evolutionary impetus toward environment-responsive cultural differentiation. Like the development of different genres of music in different cultures, each differing from the others without differing for them, the development of different genres of ethics can be seen as usefully adding to the repertoire of creative human coordination. Unfortunately, this no longer suffices to ensure the openness of either cultural evolution or the future of human intentionality.

As I have argued elsewhere (Hershock, 2012), the greatest challenges of the present are not local technical problems, they are global ethical predicaments. They are evidence of deep and persistent values conflicts that cannot be solved, but only *resolved* through increasing *clarity* about how things have come to be as they are, combined with deepening *commitment* to globally shared values coordination. As was suggested in Chapter 6, the transformative saturation of the human-technology-world relation by intelligent technology, the advent of an algorithmically accelerating attention economy, and field experimentation on consciousness through digital media are combining to enable the systematic "hacking" of human intentionality at scales sufficient to risk precipitating an ethical singularity: a collapse of the opportunity space for freely deliberated human course correction. In short, intensifying digital interventions in the immaterial infrastructure of human consciousness are threatening its evolutionary future by eroding the freedom of intention that is crucial to the practice of ethics.

The risk of such a collapse is compounded by the existence of apparently contrary pathways to it, each of which can ironically claim to be a safeguard against the other. One is a control-biased, centripetal path to collapse opened by scaling up a social engineering logic epitomized by the social credit system that is being beta tested in China—a system designed to enable centralized manipulations of the attentional focus and intentional dynamics of nearly one and a half billion people in pursuit of a stably "symphonic" society. The other is a choice-biased, centrifugal path opened by scaling a social mediation logic that maximizes both attention capture and experienced autonomy by ambiently reinforcing individuation-sustaining patterns of digital connectivity. This "market" system—characterized dynamically by viral news and fashions, flash markets, and identity proliferation—enables capitalizing (both commercially and/or politically) on fluctuating flows of attention into and through transient attractor basins while realizing a putatively self-organizing and vibrantly "polyphonic" society.

These pathways are not new. What I am referring to here as "symphonic" and "polyphonic" societies were depicted in Cold War rhetoric as "collectivist" and "individualist" societies. They might also be described in terms of the predominantly modern ideal of "global unity" and the postmodern ideal of "free variation," or in terms of the contrary societal design principles of the "grid" and the "net" (see, e.g., Hershock 2012: 198ff). What is new is the way in which the digital infrastructure of intelligent technology has become integrated into the immaterial infrastructure of shared human consciousness, and the direct manipulations of consciousness that this has made dangerously easy. Although apparently opposed in the ways in which they scale up experimentation with attention attractor basins, with narrative fusion and fission, and with intention-coupling and intention-decoupling, these pathways are equally prone to forcing ethical atrophy and, in worst case scenarios, ethical collapse.[22]

The terrestrial history of evolution has been one of differentiating coherently. Yet, order-generating, negentropic processes are inseparable from processes for differently cohering. Creative evolutionary order is plural, not singular.

Although the processes involved are complex and multi-scaled, the reason is simple. Reproductive certainty entails the materialization of an unresponsive, static, or brittle order that inhibits relational differentiation. It freezes what matters in a way that diminishes consciousness. Moreover, the primary work of consciousness—as it has been made manifest throughout the history of cosmic, organic, and cultural evolution—has involved differentiating matter and what matters in ways that are conducive to further, coherence-diversifying, and coordination-intensifying relational improvisation. The pathways of control-modulated unification and choice-modulated variation lead equally, albeit oppositely, toward inhibiting freely improvised and liberating intentional coordination. With respect to consciousness and ethical diversification, they are evolutionary cul-de-sacs.

One of the unique features of Buddhist theorizing of consciousness—at least as I have tried to present it—is its emphasis on the temporal extension or nonlocality of the dynamics of coherent differentiation. According to it, the emancipatory expansion of consciousness sought through meditative practice necessarily involves interdependence-transforming alterations of the diffractive interplay of temporal sequence and temporal significance. Digitally hacking the attention-intention interface amounts to responsibility theft through directly manipulating the topography of temporal diffraction and the shared immaterial infrastructure of human consciousness. It is intervention of the most intimate kind possible in the dynamics of creatively shared consciousness.

Consciousness and Time, Again

Consciousness alters at multiple timescales. The practice of ethics is typically directed toward altering consciousness at what might be called social timescales. It is concerned with shaping the outcomes and opportunities that result from deliberatively enacting what matters most among humans in relational dynamics that can play out over periods of hours, days, months, and years. Ethics is present and near-future oriented. Buddhist concerns about how consciousness alters qualitatively encompass these social timescales. But they extend, as well, to include both the indefinitely deep past and future time horizons of karmic entanglement, and the most fleeting micro-temporal horizons of phenomenal presence.

It is consistent with the nondualistic theory of consciousness I have been presenting that consciousness obtains and alters with different relational densities across all these timescales. Ethical improvisation of the kind needed to develop a viable global ethical ecosystem is necessarily rooted, however, in embracing the ideal of uncompelled sentient presence, which depends in turn on the emancipation of attention. As noted earlier, without freedom-of-attention, there is no freedom-of-intention. And without freedom-of-intention, the opportunity space collapses for creatively rearticulating the diffractive interplay of temporal sequence and significance. It becomes impossible to revise how we are present. We become "rudderless" in time. Should that happen, it will matter very little whether the currents of temporality affecting us are centripetally or centrifugally oriented. Our presence will have ceased to be truly our own.

If securing viable futures for the evolution of human consciousness depends on taking ethical responsibility for human cultural evolution, it thereby depends even more crucially on enacting globally shared commitments to sustaining and enhancing the conditions for freedom of attention and intention. The likelihood of doing so will depend, in turn, on theorizing consciousness both nondualistically and normatively. This book has been a contemporary Buddhist attempt to support these claims. As the relational elaboration of a primordial, cosmos-eliciting urge to differentiate coherently, consciousness matters. Whether human consciousness continues mattering, and how, is for us to determine.

Appendix: A Genealogy of Contemporary Synthesis

"Thus have I heard." Every text in the Buddhist canon that conveys a direct teaching from the Buddha (*suttas*; *sutras*) opens with this phrase, followed by a description of where the teaching was given and who was present. This opening tacitly invites whoever hears or reads the teaching into a lineage of transmission—a tradition of insights and practices being "handed over" from person to person, within and across generations. It also implies that what is being transmitted is not an objective re-presentation of what happened, but rather what has been mindfully retained and made sufficiently the hearer's own to be authentically offered to others. Buddhist transmission lineages are genealogical.

My theorizing of consciousness in this book expresses what I have been able to make my own from Buddhist teachings I have heard and read. For the most part, however, I have not specified the Buddhist texts and teachers that have informed my theorizing. In part, this was a practical decision. It reflects a concern that providing a textual provenance for each "Buddhist" claim over the course of the book would distract its readers from the theoretical case being made. It also reflects, however, the "jazz" approach I take in philosophizing. My primary purpose is not presenting Buddhist ideas and anchoring them historically; it is improvising with them to expand contemporary theoretical and ethical horizons.

This relatively anchor-free approach to theorizing in a Buddhist key is also consistent, however, with the genealogy of my understanding of Buddhism and its roots in the Chan (Korean: Sŏn; Japanese: Zen; Vietnamese: Thiền) tradition. Since at least the eleventh century, Chan's iconic—and iconoclastic—self-description has been that it consists in a "special transmission outside the scriptures" (*jiaowai biechuan*, 教外別傳) that is "not dependent on words and literary expressions" (*buli wenzi*, 不立文字). As the purportedly illiterate Chan master Huineng (638–713) put it, transmitting the true Buddha Dharma is being present without-thinking (*wunian*, 無念) in active demonstration of our original Buddha nature (*foxing*, 佛性). Book learning is strictly optional. Citing texts is like adding legs to a snake.

Ironically, the body of Chan literature is perhaps the most voluminous of any in East Asian Buddhism, and the dialogue records (*yulu* 語錄) of Chan masters—including the text of Huineng's so-called Platform Sutra—often invoke Buddhist sutras and exemplars as signposts and guiding lights along the Buddha path. Yet, if that path is ultimately one of homecoming as Chan exemplars insist—a return to our original nature (*benxing*, 本性)—then which texts and teachers are most significant is ultimately a matter of where and how far one has strayed. This Appendix offers those who might be interested a "linear" textual genealogy of my own, decidedly "nonlinear" and far-straying approach to theorizing in a Buddhist key.

*

Buddhist philosophizing has been ongoing for some two and a half millennia across multiple cultures, languages, and geographies. As such, it is comparable in complexity to the so-called Western philosophical tradition. But to a perhaps distinctive degree, all Buddhist philosophizing has remained rooted in a set of core insights and concepts that were first articulated in the "Three Baskets" (*Tipitaka*; *Tripitaka*) of the early Buddhist canon, especially the "Basket of Discourses" (*Suttapiṭaka*) or texts that record the Buddha's dialogues with students. Within this "basket," I have found the following texts particularly fruitful as conceptual springboards: the *Sutta Nipāta*; the *Sāmaññaphala Sūtta*; the *Tevijja Sūtta*; the *Mahâpadāna Sutta*; the *Mahānidāna Sutta*; the *Sakkapañha Sūtta*; the *Cakkavatti-Sīhānada Sutta*; the *Dvedhāvitakka Sutta*; and the *Kamma Sūtta*. Many more could, of course, be mentioned.

The other two "baskets" of the early canon are the *Vinaya Piṭaka* and the *Abhidharma Piṭaka*. The first collects texts related to the social life of the Buddhist community, while the second contains explanatory expositions of concepts appearing in the *Sutta Piṭaka*. The latter, and the tradition of crafting philosophical treatises and commentaries that it spawned, are also relevant for theorizing consciousness. Although the earlier strata of Abhidharma texts factor only indirectly into my own thinking, mention should be made of the *Vibhaṅga* in the Pali *Abhidhamma Piṭaka* and Buddhaghosa's (fifth century CE) *Visuddhimagga* (Path of Purification). More directly relevant are later treatises and commentaries associated with the Mahayana Mādhyamaka and Yogācāra traditions.

*

The most important of Mādhyamaka works for me have been Nagarjuna's (*c.*150–250 CE) *Mūlamadhyamakakārikā* (Root Verses on the Middle Way) and Candrakīrti's (*c.* 600–650) *Prasannapadā* (Lucid Words) for their incisive articulations of the concept of emptiness (*śūnyatā*) and the doctrine of two truths, although their logic-forward style can be a challenge for less analytically inclined readers. More centrally informative of my theorizing of consciousness, however, have been a number of Yogācāra works, including: the compositely authored (fourth century CE) *Yogācārabhūmi Śāstra* (Treatise on the Foundation for Yoga Practitioners); Asanga's (fourth century CE) *Mahāyānasaṃgraha* (Compendium of the Great Vehicle); and Vasubandhu's (fourth/fifth century CE) *Vimśatikā-vijñaptimātratāsiddhi* (Twenty Verses on Consciousness Only) and *Trisvabhāvanirdeśa* (Three Natures Exposition).

Yet, most intimately significant have been works associated with the development of a distinctively Chinese rendering of Yogācāra concepts. Here, Paramārtha's (499–569 CE) *Foxing Lun* 佛性論 (Treatise on Buddha Nature) and his translation (or, perhaps, authorship) of the *Dasheng Qixin Lun* 大乘起信論 (Awakening of Faith in Mahayana) stand out. What is distinctive therein is the integration of mainstream Yogācāra resources into a network of ideas being articulated in two streams of Mahayana sutras—the Prajñāpāramitā (Perfection of Wisdom) stream and the Tathāgatagarbha (Womb/Embryo of the Tathāgata) stream. Broadly speaking, the former forwards a distinctive conception of wisdom, a relational metaphysics of *tathātā* (suchness or thusness), and the ethical ideal of the bodhisattva. The latter articulates a view of all sentient presence as either originally enlightened or having the innate potential for enlightenment. Crucial to my engagement with the Prajñāpāramitā stream have been the Diamond Sūtra (*Vajracchedikā Prajñāpāramitā Sūtra*) and the Heart of the Perfection of Wisdom Sutra (*Prajñāpāramitāhṛdaya Sūtra*). In the Tathāgatagarbha stream, the *Tathāgatagarbha Sūtra* and the Lion's Roar of Queen Srimala (*Śrīmālādevī Siṃhanāda Sūtra*) have stood out.

In addition, three other Mahayana sutras are crucial to my approach to Buddhist philosophizing: the Flower Ornament Sutra (*Avataṃsaka Sūtra*), the Vimalakirti Sutra (*Vimalakīrti-nirdeśa Sūtra*), and the Lotus Sutra (*Saddharmapuṇḍarīka Sūtra*). Each of these has been extraordinarily important in the development of East Asian Buddhism. The Flower Ornament Sutra was crucial to the development of the Chinese Huayan Buddhist (Korean: Hwaeom; Japanese Kegon) tradition, in which the works of Fazang and Zongmi (780–841) have played crucial roles, respectively, in my conceptions of nondualistic relationality and karma. The Lotus Sutra was similarly crucial to the development of Chinese Tiantai Buddhism (Korean: Cheontae; Japanese: Tendai), with Zhiyi's (538–597) Great Treatise on Calming and Insight (*Mohe Zhiguan* 摩訶止觀) informing my theorizing of Buddhist meditation. The Vimalakirti Sutra is most closely associated with the development of Chan Buddhism, in part for its exposition of nonduality and in part for the central role played by the enlightened layman, Vimalakirti. It also emphasizes the radical nonlocality of consciousness and—through a gender-swapping vignette—a demonstration of the possibility of (enlightened) consciousness that is unconstrained by the specifics of any given mind-body-environment infrastructure.

*

The most historically proximate traditional texts that have informed my Buddhist approach to theorizing consciousness are drawn from the Chinese Chan tradition. Listed chronologically, these are Bodhidharma's Treatise on the Two Entrances and Four Practices (*Erru Sixing* 二入四行), Huineng's Platform Sutra (*Liuzu Tanjing,* 六祖壇經), Huangbo Yixun's Dharma Essentials for Heartmind Transmission (*Huangbo Chuanxin Fayao*, 黃檗傳心法要) and Wan Ling Record (*Huangbo Wanling Lu*, 黃檗宛陵錄), Mazu Daoyi's Dialogue Record of Chan Master Mazu Daoyi of Jiangxi (*Jiangxi Mazu Daoyi Chanshi Yulu*, 江西馬祖道一禪師語錄), and Linji Yixuan's Dialogue Record of Linji (*Linji Yulu*, 臨濟語錄).

As voluminous as it is, the literature of Chan is generally neither expository nor argumentatively philosophical. The dialogue records, in particular, were consolidated and crafted for the ostensive purpose of spurring more intensive practice, and there is little if any attention in them to the kinds of epistemological and ontological concerns that were central to more scholastic traditions of Buddhism. Yet, in their use of philosophically charged concepts relevant to theorizing consciousness, they are refreshingly and insightfully focused on manifesting what these concepts mean in socially embodied relational terms.

*

Presenting a "genealogy" of Buddhist sources, sorted chronologically, suggests a unidirectional "line" of influences passing from one past generation to the next up to the present. Genealogies of influence are never that simple. In much the same way that patterns of gene expression are determined by cellular dynamics that can't be disentangled from organism-environment relations, textual influences occur through the diffractive interplay of textually expressed concepts and concerns and those that a reader (or listener) brings into the relation. The weightings of concepts and concerns that result in this interplay are, necessarily, different from those in their original contexts.

The theorizing undertaken in this book has synthesized conceptual resources thus derived from diverse Buddhist traditions with resources similarly derived from various currents of contemporary scientific and philosophical inquiry. These contemporary sources of inspiration have been directly cited or specified in footnotes. But in keeping with my "jazz" approach of composing theoretically on the fly, I have tended to "quote" perspectives and insights as needed to move my case more coherently forward rather than diving into deep critical engagement with them. Any failures of understanding or imagination thus put on display are entirely my own.

Notes

Introduction

1. On conceptual blending and creativity, see Fauconnier and Taylor (2002).
2. Those interested in the specifics of this synthesis will find an account of its precedents in the Appendix.
3. For a review of the recent history of scientific study of consciousness, see LeDoux, Michel, and Lau (2020).
4. For an extensive, but accessible introduction to the state of the philosophical art of theorizing consciousness, see Blackmore and Troscianko (2018), and for a more academic overview, Zelazo, Moscovitch, and Thompson (2007) and Kriegel (2020).
5. The methodological value of obliquely blending perspectives is convincingly illustrated in Francois Jullien's (2000) *Detour and Access: Strategies of Meaning in China and Greece.*
6. In the first use of Buddhist terms, both Pali and Sanskrit transliterations are offered; thereafter Sanskrit is used. Only one transliteration is presented when the Pali and Sanskrit are the same. When a term is specific to Sanskrit sources, only the Sanskrit transliteration is provided.
7. The etymology of *majjhimapaṭipadā* is useful here. Very much like the English progress, which is formed of the pronoun *pro-* "forward" + *gradi* "to walk," *paṭipadā* means setting out (where *paṭi* ambiguously implies both opposition and pursuit) on foot (*pada*). Since *majjhima* refers to something in-between, for example, small and large, or wonderful and terrible, *majjhimapaṭipadā* means embarking purposefully from the midst of things.
8. This wonderfully succinct characterization is a riff on Thomas Kasulis's description of the Japanese Buddhist doctrinal evaluation strategy of relegation, not refutation.
9. Although some currents in early Buddhist Abhidharma phenomenalism did promote investigations of micro-level units of experience that are kin to contemporary investigations of the thresholds of conscious and unconscious perception (or information processing) at millisecond scales, in their original contexts these Buddhist investigations of micro-temporal events were integral to what might be called macro-temporal investigations of qualities of consciousness at life-narrative scales.
10. A contemporary, neuroscience inspired theory of consciousness that similarly stresses its spatiotemporal and relational character is forwarded by Georg Northoff (2018).

11 This move has been powerfully and persuasively argued for by Andy Clark (2016).
12 On the colonization of consciousness, see Hershock (1999) and Hershock (2021).
13 It should be stressed, even if only parenthetically at this point, that realities are irreducibly relational and come in many (potentially unlimited) flavors—spatial and temporal, social and political, law constrained and anarchic, instrumental and aesthetic, and many more.
14 When "the Buddhist" phrasing is used for stylistic simplicity, readers can assume that it involves my reading of very widely (if not universally) accepted Buddhist perspectives or teachings.
15 A stellar example of jazz performance would be the various in-concert renditions of "My Favorite Things" by the John Coltrane's quartet in the early 1960s.
16 It is important to point out that many of classical music world's greatest composers—e.g., Bach and Mozart—were prodigiously capable improvisers. The contrast here is between scored and unscored music performance rather than musical capabilities.

Chapter 1

1 As noted in the Introduction, while Buddhist theorizing of consciousness is experiential, it does not regard experience as the object of introspective observation, but rather as the medium of interpersonal subjectivity. That difference is something we will be clarifying.
2 A contemporary, non-Buddhist attempt to develop a fully relational ontology is Benjamin (2016).
3 On the notion of levels of abstraction, see Floridi (2008b).
4 We will later explore what this means in considering the merits of panpsychist, panexperientialist, and neutral monist theories of consciousness.
5 For a fuller, but still concise presentation of my reading of the Buddhist teaching of karma, see Hershock (2023).
6 This *avyākṛta* class of questions included those about whether the world is eternal, whether it is infinite in extent, whether enlightened beings like the Buddha exist after death, and whether the life impulse (*jīva*) and body are identical.
7 Methodologically, as a means to disclosing key aspects of the nature of consciousness, this method has similarities to other phenomenological theories of consciousness, both those that are resolutely enactivist (Gallagher, 2017) and those that focus on information integration (Tononi, 2012).
8 Buddhism regards cognition as a sixth sense, in addition to the other five senses of seeing, hearing, smelling, tasting, and touching. As we will see, sensory consciousness arises when the sense organ of an organism comes into contact with

a related sense environment. Cognitive consciousness arises when the mind comes into contact with the contents of the other five kinds of sense consciousness as its "sensed" environment.

9   The argument could be made that this absence of self is what Dennett (1996) points to with the eliminativist claim that consciousness is simply a "center of narrative gravity." It is not all there is to consciousness in Buddhist terms.

10 It should be mentioned that Buddhist theorizing about consciousness is therapeutically grounded. Theoretical completeness would compel taking into account many other senses.—proprioception and sensitivity to temperature, to body alignment with respect to gravity, to electrical or magnetic fields, for example. Buddhist lists of consciousnesses (most commonly the six already noted and two more that will be discussed later in relation to Yogācāra thought, should be taken as indicative, rather than exhaustive).

11 An accessible summary of new findings on plant communication and consciousness, see Mancuso (2018).

12 For a straightforward explanation of these terms—roughly physical, ideational, and technological transmitters of traits or learnings—see Blackmore (2010).

13 We will discuss this in greater depth later in connection with Karen Barad's (2007) "new materialist" conception of experimentation.

14 A Möbius strip can be formed by taking a long rectangular strip of paper, giving it a half twist, and joining the two short edges. While the paper appears to have two sides and two edges, it now has only one side and one edge.

15 This accords, in turn, with contemporary work on neuro-prosthetics. For a concise and accessible summary, see Quiroga (2020, Chapter 7).

16 Those interested in this equation should refer to one of the many translations of second-century CE Indian Buddhist philosopher Nāgārjuna's *Mūlamadhyamakakārikā* or Root Verses on the Middle Way.

17 This is the general position of the "mind-only" or "consciousness-only" (and yet non-idealist) schools of Yogācāra Buddhism (for an overview, see Lusthaus, 2000).

18 Some readers will find resonance with Dennett's intentional theory of consciousness. This is not without warrant, but Buddhist theorizing of consciousness is, as we will see, creative rather than eliminative.

19 A more involved discussion of this is taken up later (p. 138ff) in relation to the Chinese Buddhist philosopher, Fazang.

20 A collection of essays on *apoha* theory can be found in Siderits, Tillemans, and Chakrabarti (2011).

21 This latter possibility is raised to some degree by neutral monism and dual-aspect theories of consciousness.

22 We will return to this approach to consciousness in Chapter 5 in connection with theorizing altered states.
23 This reading of mind is compatible with the understanding of perception as constrained imagination forwarded by Varela and Depraz (2003).
24 For an extended discussion, see von Rospatt (1995: 94–110).
25 A contemporary, non-Buddhist exploration of this approach to causality and consciousness is Gillett (2009).
26 Associating consciousness with learning is consistent with Tononi and Koch's (2015) integrated information theory as well as with studies of attention and intelligence, understood very broadly as adaptive conduct. The Buddhist emphasis on intention or purpose in theorizing consciousness, however, helps to discriminate among depths or degrees of consciousness that would, for instance, allow for the emergence of machine intelligence only at the point that machines develop their own values and purposes. See Chapter 4 for a deeper discussion.
27 A comprehensive, detailed, and yet accessible survey of the new science of sleep is Walker (2017).
28 On this technical use of "utterances," see Di Paolo, Cuffari, and De Jaegher (2018: 118).

Chapter 2

1 How this works is not explained in Yogācāra. However, interesting analogies can be found with theoretical constructs like wormholes that allow "distant" spacetime locales to become "adjacent" and empirically confirmed phenomena like "quantum entanglement." For an overview of theorizing about quantum physics and consciousness, see Atmanspacher (2020). In Chapter 3, we will advance a speculative Buddhist account for karmic causality making use of contemporary cosmological theories involving multiple dimensions of time.
2 Whether animals are self-aware is often established through the "mirror-self recognition" test, which only a small number of species have succeeded in passing (e.g., elephants, great apes, dolphins, and Eurasian magpies). Recent evidence of a small fish passing the test raises questions about both the test and the extent of animal self-awareness. We will return to this in Chapter 4.
3 In Chapter 5, we will draw out the theoretical ramifications of new empirical studies of a range of altered states of consciousness.
4 See Blackmore and Troscianko (2018), Chapter 7, for a concise overview of attention theories, including a discussion of attention and meditation.
5 For a brief discussion of Western and Asian approaches to attention training, see Tang and Posner (2009).

Chapter 3

1. There is a dizzyingly large and varied number of dual aspect and neutral monist theories, a cogent overview of which can be found in Stubenberg (2018).
2. See Mackenzie (2018) for a useful non-representational interpretation of the "three natures" teaching in Yogācāra.
3. It should be noted that while genetic theorizing is remarkably powerful, it is not without limits. We will consider these later in discussing alternative interpretations of evolution in Chapter 6.
4. For a discussion of RNA world, see Alberts, Johnson, and Lewis et al. (2002, Chapter 6).
5. For a conceptual contrast of coordination and cooperation, see Hershock (2012: 281–3).
6. Some, perhaps "anachronistic," support for this distributed/relational model of the advent of life as fundamentally sentient *systems*—rather than individual beings or entities—is given by recent theorizing of immune systems as sensory systems merging distinct currents of change and evaluating them as either sustaining/enhancing or threatening/degrading ongoing patterns of coordination. For a discussion, see Dozmorov and Dresser (2010).
7. On neutral monism, see Stubenberg (2018). For relatively concise a review of Russellian monisms, see Alter and Pereboom (2019).
8. Inexistence is the nondual remainder of dissolving the categories of existence and nonexistence—the logically ineffable subject of Nagarjuna's tetralemma of that which can only be said to be not x; not not-x; not both x and not-x; and not neither x nor not-x.
9. For a succinct introduction to early Buddhist epistemology, see Holder (2013). It bears mentioning here that the so-called mind-only (*citta-mātra*) or cognition-only (*vijñapti-mātra*) schools of Yogācāra are best understood as phenomenalist or perhaps epistemic idealist traditions in which ontological claims are entirely eschewed in favor of investigations of how to cease conceptual projecting. For a detailed study, see Lusthaus (2000).
10. The cosmic microwave background is the relic of this transition and affords us a map the "face" of the early cosmos. Our only means of peering further back into the history of the cosmos is theoretical.
11. As hopefully will become clear, this *relational* claim is consistent with, but not reducible to the panpsychist, "real physicalism" forwarded by Galen Strawson (2006a), according to which even the most basic physical entities are also phenomenal presences—experiencing as well as experienced entities.
12. It should be mentioned that while Buddhist philosophers in Dignāga-Dharmakīrti school assert that consciousness is self-luminous (*svaprakāśa*), those with allegiance to the Mādhyamika tradition, like Candrakīrti and Śāntideva deny

the intelligibility the ontological independence implied by the concept of self-illuminating awareness. For an extended discussion of these and other issues in philosophy of mind in Indian Buddhism, see Coseru (2017).

13 That particle entanglement can obtain even when no moment of spacetime was ever shared by the particles involved has been demonstrated by Megedish et al. (2013). For an extensive treatment of non-locality, see Maudlin (2011).

14 For summaries of trends toward consensus on unifying general relativity and quantum theories, see Rovelli (2017) and Musser (2015). A short and accessible introduction to quantum entanglement and spacetime, see Cowen (2015).

15 A powerful, mathematical challenge to deterministic physics and a statement of the ontological implications of abandoning the law of the excluded middle is Santo and Gisin (2019).

16 A succinct introduction to the holographic universe is Bekenstein (2003). Arkani-Hamed and Trnka (2014) introduces one of the most recent a higher-dimensional geometric accounts. The more radical view that reality is ultimately computational/informational is forwarded in Aerts (2010) and Aerts and Sassoli de Bianchi (2018).

17 For an overview of space-time-matter theory, see Wesson and Overduin (2018).

18 It might be worth mentioning that there are a host of cousin theories, including M-theory or membrane theory, that are similarly inspired by the Kaluza-Klein five-dimensional, geometric approach to reconciling gravitational and electromagnetic phenomena that developed in the first third of the twentieth century. Many of these cousin theories, however, regard the fifth dimension as compacted or folded up within four-dimensional spacetime, while others go beyond five dimensions to incorporate the multiple dimensions invoked by string theoretical approaches to quantum gravity.

19 It could also be said that mathematics and geometry function as "sense organs" enabling access to and explorations of a distinctive realm of relational dynamics. This raises possibilities, to be explored later, for thinking through the possibilities of artificial "computational consciousness."

20 For a wide-ranging discussion of scientific and philosophical perspectives on downward or top-down causation, see the special issue on "Top-Down Causation," edited by George F. R. Ellis, Denis Noble and Timothy O'Connor for *Interface Focus* Volume 2:1, February 6, 2012, available at: https://royalsocietypublishing.org/toc/rsfs/2012/2/1

21 Here, appeal might be made to Terrence Deacon's (2012) neologism of "entential" occurrences or phenomena that are intrinsically incomplete and persist only in relation to or by being organized as needed to achieve something non-intrinsic.

22 This description accords well with East Asian Buddhist claim—based on a blending of South and Central Asian Buddhist teachings about interdependence and karma with indigenous conceptions of the relationally coherent nature of the

cosmos—that all things have/are Buddha nature (*foxing* 佛性) or a propensity for realizing enlightening patterns of relationality. Radically interpreted, this "nature" was deemed intrinsic to all that is present, both sentient and insentient—an interpretation glossed in terms of the unities of structuring (*ti* 體) and functioning (*yong* 用), and patterned cohering (*li* 理) and eventful particularity (*shi* 事).

23 Several interesting parallels for this causal reading of the work of consciousness can be found in Rosenberg (2004).
24 A succinct, but comprehensive discussion of the combination problem can be found in Coleman (2012).
25 For a short exposition of cosmopsychism, see Shani (2015); for a more involved discussion, see Goff (2017).
26 For a concise discussion of cosmic fine-tuning and an argument for agentive cosmopsychism, see Goff (2019).
27 There are significant resonances between this Buddhism-derived perspective on cosmic evolution and history and the theses put forward by Roberto Unger and Lee Smolin (2014), who argue that natural laws—the causal conditions of change—are open to change, that the basic constituents of the cosmos are relational events or causal perspectives, and that cosmic history is a function of difference-generating propensity rather than necessity.
28 See Chaisson (2001) for a comprehensive presentation of the energy rate density approach to cosmic evolution, or Chaisson (2014) for a condensed review. Notably, as well, the biophysicist Mae-Wan Ho (2008) has identified nested cycles as crucial to the dynamics of living organisms and their capture of energy by coherent differentiation and entanglement.

Chapter 4

1 A brief, but useful review of the mirror self-recognition test, new findings with fish, and their implications can be found online at: https://journals.plos.org/plosbiology/article?id=10.1371/journal.pbio.3000112
2 As Tim Ingold (2021) points out, the term "imagination" unfortunately carries connotations of subjectivity, representationalism, and human exceptionalism. But imagining can also be seen as "a way of entering from the inside into the generative currents of the world itself, by balancing one's very being on the cusp of its emergence" (p. 4) that has the "the promise, and the potential, of creation … marked by a quality of attention … in relations of correspondence" (p. 5).
3 We will consider the ethical significance of the centrality of these capacities for human cultural evolution in Chapter 7.
4 For the former, see, e.g., Baars (1997) and Dehaene, Lau, and Kouider (2017); for the latter, see, e.g., Koch (2019) and Tononi and Koch (2015).

5   This resonates well with the Buddhist account of the sixth, mental consciousness, but not consciousness more generally or as such.
6   This resonates well with the Buddhist account of the relations among attention, intention, and consciousness.
7   For a brief introduction to the varieties of functionalism, see Shoemaker (1981).
8   The classic formulation of philosophical zombies is Chambers (1996).
9   For a concise but cogent discussion of philosophical zombies, see Kirk (2019); for a similar discussion of eliminative materialism, see Ramsey (2020).
10 It should be mentioned that IIT also entails "grades" of consciousness. For a relatively succinct exposition, see Tononi and Koch (2015).
11 There is some technological ambiguity here since, as will be discussed below, the developmental robotics approach has experimented with programming robotic "needs" for "food" and "drink," with shutdown resulting from a failure to find the necessary resources in the time given.
12 A wonderful literary meditation on the sentient necessity of forgetting is "Funes the Memorious" by Jorge Luis Borges, readily available online.
13 In this, Buddhism and cosmopsychism can be seen as sharing commitments to the ontological primacy of consciousness.
14 In some ways, the relationship between IIT and Buddhist theorizing about consciousness can usefully be seen as analogous to the relationship between Newtonian and relativistic and quantum physics. The latter do not refute Newtonian mechanics. They relegate its truths and laws to a less encompassing status.
15 For an approach based on GWT, see Yoshua Bengio, "The Consciousness Prior," https://arxiv.org/pdf/1709.08568.pdf
16 An extensive overview of developmental robotics and its prospects is Cangelosi and Schlesinger (2015).
17 For a discussion of the karmic implications of artificial intelligence, see Hershock (2021), p. 28.
18 For a non-Buddhist "gradient" approach to consciousness, see Schooler (2002) and Schooler and Winkielman (2011).
19 An extensive, pre-release test of GPT-4 demonstrates, for example, its abilities to learn how to use tools and to reason and communicate in ways that demonstrate a nascent theory-of-mind capacities—i.e., capacities for imagining why a person acts or speaks as he or she does. See Bubeck et al. (2023).
20 Arguably, something like this occurs, e.g., when a dog is raised as a pet, becoming a de facto member of the family and acquiring a distinctive and keenly responsive "personality" within it.
21 The intuitions regarding time and causality are, in fact, crucial to the conceptual repertoire of developmental robotics, much of which can be traced back to Thelen and Smith's (1994) dynamic systems approach to cognition.

22 For a brief exposition of intuitionist implications for physics and the openness of the future, see Gisin (2020).
23 Crucially, *li* are not abstract "principles" with which we harmonize or fail to harmonize; rather *li* are value-laden coherences, the always changing results of acts of discerning patterns of connections in things that matter to us as humans. For an extensive study of *li* in Chinese thought, see Ziporyn (2012, 2013).
24 In Fazang's nomenclature, truth/ultimate reality consists in a four-dimensional manifold comprising: the realms of *shi* or experiential matters (事法界, *shi fajie*); *li* or informing patterns/principles (理法界, *li fajie*); the mutual non-obstruction of *li* and *shi* (理事無礙法界, *li-shi wuai fajie*); and the mutual non-obstruction of *shi* and *shi* (事事無礙法界, *shi-shi wuai fajie*). See, e.g., "Huayan Essay on the Five Teachings" (*Huayan wujiao zhang*, T. 45, no. 1866).
25 The sense here is that every "part" of a holograph contains the image/information encoded in the "whole," only with differing degrees of resolution.
26 Here, I am using "diffraction" in Barad's (2007) sense of generating intersecting patterns of significance-effecting differentiation, and "social ontology" to designate those elements of experience that elude physicalist reduction, including, for example, emotions and institutions like marriage—aspects of reality that cannot be explained simply by identifying the material relations studied by the natural sciences. For a short discussion, see Baker (2019).
27 For an anthropological study of affectively regulated human-robot interaction in a Buddhist context, see White and Katsuno (forthcoming, 2023).
28 Here, it is perhaps useful to add that a Buddhist might ask about how well humans emulate buddhas or bodhisattvas—those sentient presences evolving "perpendicular" or orthogonally to the spectrum of the six *gati* or birth realms.
29 This riffs on Donna Haraway's claim that "a diffraction pattern does not map where differences appear but rather maps where the effects of differences appear" (Haraway, 2004: 70).
30 This locution recalls the Heideggerian thesis of the "thrown-ness" of Dasein or human presence, and hence the question of freedom with which existentialism grapples intrinsically.
31 A brief history of artificial intelligence can be found in Hershock (2021). A more extensive history of human imaginings of artificial beings and intelligences is Mayor (2019).
32 See, for example, Chapter 4 of *Buddhism and Intelligent Technology* (Hershock, 2021).
33 I should point out that some Buddhists are ready to entertain the possibility that machines might be more suited to traveling the path to enlightenment than humans, precisely because they "live" in the moment, without desire or negative emotions, and unburdened by complex histories and self-narratives. See, e.g., Hongladarom (2020). I disagree. As the narratives of the Buddha's enlightenment

and past lives make clear, Buddhist compassion and wisdom emerge out of effortful and empathetic relational appreciation. While a "GPT-4 bodhisattva" trained on 2,600 years of Buddhist texts might soon be able to dispense with very convincing Dharma talks, it would today have no idea why it is dispensing them or how they are affecting its audiences. It would be like those monks derided by the ninth-century Chan Master Linji as believing that the Buddha Dharma is contained in the words and phrases used by "dead old geezers," and who then rearrange and fabricate interpretations of them, in effect "taking clods of dried shit in their mouths and then spitting them back out for others" (*Linji Yulu* Taishō; vol.47 no.1985:501c).

Chapter 5

1. Against possibilities raised by Bostrom and others fearing the technological singularity, the Buddhist perspective is that this should not be accomplished by eliminating all humans or all sentient beings.
2. For a review of scientific investigations of ASCs and a four-dimensional scheme for their categorization, see Vaitl et al. (2005). For an overview ASCs and consciousness theory, see Chapter 13 of Blackmore and Troscianko (2018).
3. On the historical use of consciousness altering practices, see Garcia-Romeu and Tart (2013). Cardena and Winkelman (2011) offer a comprehensive, multidisciplinary introduction to ASCs and the history of their study, while Winkelman (2017) provides a cultural-evolutionary perspective on psychedelic alterations of consciousness.
4. Given this and as noted earlier, it is not unreasonable to see Yogācāra as espousing a kind of idealism, especially an idealism of the kind forwarded by Kastrup (2018) as a form of cosmopsychism.
5. It must be stressed that the potential of psychedelics to positively alter consciousness is only a potential and not a guarantee. There are risks in destabilizing neural dynamics, especially in "high entropy" social or perceptual environments or in the context of pathological propensities toward biochemical imbalances.
6. For a review of neuroscience of meditative states, see Fox et al. (2016).
7. For a useful discussion of the metaphysical bias of atomism/particularism/smallism, see Barad (2007: 137–41).
8. It is useful to recall here that one of the more profound "discoveries" of contemporary physics has been that so-called empty space is not a perfect vacuum; it is filled with material potential.
9. Millière et al. (2018) offer a very useful comparative overview of neuroscientific studies of how meditation and psychedelics affect brain dynamics.

10 Stress should be placed here on "plausible." A fully relational ontology of mind-body-environment interdependence and interpenetration renders causal reduction of any kind problematic.
11 This is true, I think, even if we accept the basic thrust of Solms's (2019) attempt to use Friston's (2010) free energy principle to solve the hard problem of consciousness.
12 The term "negative entropy" was coined by the physicist Erwin Schrödinger (1944) to explain the presence of "order" within living beings—their ability to resist the tendency toward disorganization that governs physical systems according to the Second Law of Thermodynamics. This phrase was abbreviated by Léon Brillouin (1953) as "negentropy," and the empirical evidence for coherence and cooperativity at different levels within living systems has more recently led to the identification of negentropy with stored mobilizable energy in a structured system of efficiently coupled space-time domains, such that organisms consist in energy sharing cycles spanning scales from the quantum level to that of the planetary biosphere (Ho, 2008).
13 See the earlier discussion of the *skandhas*, page 19ff.
14 Northoff would argue that functionalist theories like IIT, cognitive theories like GWT, and even embodied/enactive theories, while not strictly neuro-centric, remain ego-centric or mento-centric by continuing to assume that information integration, cognitive content sharing, and intention enactment originate in individual sentient beings, rather than in the dynamics of interdependence among sentient beings and their environments.
15 On the inter-brain dimensions of dance, see Basso, Satyal, and Rugh (2021); on inter-brain dynamics in jazz improvisation, see Donnay et al. (2014) and Müller and Lindenberger (2019).
16 This accords in interesting ways with the hypothesis explored earlier that life emerged with/through mutually-beneficial functional interdependence within a difference-reinforcing molecular community, and the evolution has occurred as a function of cooperative variation.
17 The analogy with physics experiments investigating the natures of light and matter is again instructive. There are apparatuses that will produce data consistent with reading consciousness as "local" or "particle-like," and other apparatuses—perhaps including all the same machinery and imaging techniques but paired with different discursive practices—that we just as consistently allow reading consciousness as being "nonlocal" or "wave-like." However, the fact that consciousness occurs on both sides of the "agential cuts" involved makes the apparatuses for investigating consciousness recursively complex.
18 This insight is, as we will discuss briefly below, central to Henri Bergson's association of consciousness with duration.

Chapter 6

1. On natural teleology, see Nagel (2012). For an extended exposition of a teleodynamic theory of evolution of life and mind, see Deacon (2012); for a more readily accessible presentation, see Sherman (2017).
2. The term "irrealism" is associated with the anti-foundational philosophy of Nelson Goodman. The use here bears what might be called a "family resemblance" to Goodman's.
3. Farisco, Salles and Evers (2018) offer a conceptual overview of the neurobioethics, empirical neuroethics, and conceptual neuroethics.
4. It bears mentioning that Charles Darwin, in his 1871 *Descent of Man*, directs attention to the aesthetics, relational meaning, and purposes of animal behaviors in his revised understanding of evolution. For a discussion that places Darwin in conversation with Bergson and Deleuze, see Grosz (2008).
5. For an overview of new materialism, see Van der Tuin and Dolphijn (2010).
6. For a concise discussion of ethical virtuosity and diversity, see Hershock (2021: 136–44).
7. A somewhat-dated but still-useful summary of debates surrounding moral bioenhancement and its technical feasibility is Specker et al., (2014).
8. Their argument is more extensively worked out in their book, *Unfit for the Future: The Need for Moral Enhancement* (Savulescu and Persson 2012a).
9. A fuller discussion of a technological bias toward control can be found in Hershock (2006: 90–3).
10. For those interested in more extensive discussions, see my *Reinventing the Wheel* (1999) and *Buddhism and Intelligent Technology* (2021).
11. "Solving previously unsolvable problems" is the marketing catchphrase of C3 AI, a company devoted to using artificial intelligence at enterprise scale.
12. For a review of AI ethics, see Hagendorff (2020).
13. For a detailed discussion of the "technologies of extended mind" thesis, see Reiner and Nagel (2017). Or, for an alternative approach centered on the use of "smart services," see chapter 4 of Hershock (2021).
14. A point of clarification: nonlocalizable here does not mean that consciousness is atemporal or nonspatial. As in Northoff's (2018) relational ontology of the world-brain and consciousness, Buddhism insists on the spatiotemporal nature of consciousness and its evolving infrastructure.

Chapter 7

1. This is attributable in part to species "aging" out of harmony with environmental changes, with most species lasting 1–11 million years, but in large part also to five

past mass extinctions, the third of which took place 250 million years ago and destroyed 96 percent of all species.
2. For a relatively concise, accessible, and sobering overview of species extinctions and the effects of humans on extinction rates, see the Our World in Data's extinction report: https://ourworldindata.org/extinctions
3. Hayward (1997), for example, argues on behalf of the merits of an ethically framed anthropocentrism, while Baxter (1974) offers a bolder defense of "business as usual" anthropocentrism.
4. Antihuman advocacy of human extinction should not be confused with philosophical antihumanism.
5. For an accessible and yet thorough examination of the history and scope of transhumanist thought, see Manzocco (2019). For a complementary overviews of posthumanism, see Wolfe (2010) and Ferrando (2019).
6. This presentation of transhumanism and posthumanism is, of course, a presentation of ideal types that involves a considerable simplification of the vast range of scholarly and scientific speculations on the future of human improvement. It is a simplification, however, that usefully illustrates how envisioning the futures of human presence is, directly or indirectly, to adopt a theoretical perspective on consciousness.
7. For a concise discussion, see https://writings.stephenwolfram.com/2021/03/what-is-consciousness-some-new-perspectives-from-our-physics-project/
8. Stated in Buddhist terms, our human concerns and conduct are overwhelmingly the products of collectively engendering and altering virtual or "provisional" (*saṃvṛti*) realities—worlds that we have imagined into being.
9. This is not, of course, to deny that other species possess cultures.
10. A still valuable critical history of bio-reductionist evolutionary ethics is offered by Farber (1994).
11. A biting academic critique of Harari and Lovelock is offered by Nye (2021).
12. For a concise overview of the state of the field, see Lewens (2020). For more in depth perspectives, see Boyd and Richerson (2005), Mesoudi (2011), Sterelny (2012), Lewens (2015), Henrich (2015), Morin (2016), and Laland (2017).
13. It should be stressed that while other artistic practices may have developed earlier than or alongside cave art—e.g., making music, sketching in sand, scribing or painting on animal skins and trees—cave art is uniquely suited to surviving and being found tens of thousands of years later.
14. These theorizations can be seen as recalling the contrasting premises of the Global Workspace (representation-generating) and Integrated Information (future-state-affecting) theories of consciousness discussed earlier.
15. The preponderance of hand stencils with fingers in various configurations and not simply splayed out with all five fingers fully visible is likely evidence of early

sign language. The alternative hypothesis is that the hand-stenciling population worldwide practiced finger mutilation.
16 The analogy of the onset of cultural evolution with that of the origins of life is also forwarded by Gabora (2008).
17 This means not that everything can be said in every language, but only that despite having a very limited number of phonemes or speech units, there is no limit on how many sentences can be composed in a given language.
18 The effects of writing systems on mutual intelligibility are insightfully explored by Sanders and Illich (1989).
19 This distinction was first articulated by the geographer-philosopher Yi-fu Tuan (1977).
20 Ethics can mean many things and in philosophical circles is typically divided into meta-ethics (studying the nature of moral/ethical judgment), applied ethics (as in, e.g., business ethics or medical ethics, where the focus is on setting professional norms of conduct), and normative ethics (establishing general norms for ethical conduct). Here, I am talking primarily about the interplay of meta-ethics and normative ethics.
21 For an expanded discussion of ethical diversity and need to foster the emergence of a global ethical ecosystem, see Hershock (2021: 128–37).
22 On the use of the concepts of attractors, attractor basins and narrative resonances to explain the dynamics of cultural change, see van der Leeuw and Folke (2021).

Works Cited

Aerts, Diederik (2010). "Quantum Particles as Conceptual Entities: A Possible Explanatory Framework for Quantum Theory." *Foundations of Science* 14: 361–411. https://doi.org/10.1007/s10699-009-9166-y

Aerts, Diederik and Massimiliano Sassoli de Bianchi (2018). "Quantum Perspectives on Evolution." In Shyam Wuppuluri and Francisco Antonio Doria (eds.), *The Map and the Territory: Exploring the Foundations of Science, Thought and Reality*. Springer: The Frontiers Collection, 571–95. DOI: 10.1007/978-3-319-72478-2

Alberts, Bruce with Alexander Johnson, Julian Lewis, Martin Raff, Keith Roberts and Peter Walter (2002). *Molecular Biology of the Cell*, 4th edition. New York: Garland Science.

Alter, Torin and Derk Pereboom (2019). "Russellian Monism." *The Stanford Encyclopedia of Philosophy* (Fall 2019 Edition), Edward N. Zalta (ed.) https://plato.stanford.edu/archives/fall2019/entries/russellian-monism/

Arkani-Hamed, Nima and Jaroslav Trnka (2014). "The Amplituhedron." *Journal of High Energy Physics* 30 (10), October 6, 2014.

Atmanspacher, Harald (2020). "Quantum Approaches to Consciousness." In *The Stanford Encyclopedia of Philosophy* (Summer 2020 Edition), Edward N. Zalta (ed.) https://plato.stanford.edu/archives/sum2020/entries/qt-consciousness/

Baars, B.J. (1997). "In the Theatre of Consciousness. Global Workspace Theory, a Rigorous Scientific Theory of Consciousness." *Journal of Consciousness Studies* 4: 292–30.

Baker, Lynne Rudder (2019). "Just What Is Social Ontology?" *Journal of Social Ontology* 5 (1), published online. November 14, 2019. https://www.degruyter.com/view/journals/jso/5/1/article-p1.xml

Barad, Karen (2007). *Meeting the Universe Halfway: Quantum Physics and the Entanglement of Matter and Meaning*. Durham, NC: Duke University Press.

Barrett, F. and R. Griffiths (2017). Classic Hallucinogens and Mystical Experiences: Phenomenology and Neural Correlates. *Current Topics in Behavioral Neurosciences*. [Epub ahead of print]. 10.1007/7854_2017_474 [PMC free article] [PubMed] [CrossRef] [Google Scholar].

Basso, Julia C., Mehda K. Satyal and Rachel Rugh (2021). "Dance on the Brain: Enhancing Intra- and Inter-Brain Synchrony." *Frontiers in Human Neuroscience* 14: 584312. DOI: 10.3389/fnhum.2020.584312

Baxter, William F. (1974). *People or Penguins: The Case for Optimal Pollution*. New York: Columbia University Press.

Bayne, Tim and Olivia Carter (2018). "Dimensions of Consciousness and the Psychedelic State." *Frontiers of the Neuroscience of Consciousness* 4 (1). DOI: 10.1093/nc/niy008

Bekenstein, Jacob D. (2003). "Information in the Holographic Universe." *Scientific American* 289 (2), August 2003: 58–65.

Benjamin, Andrew (2016). *Towards a Relational Ontology: Philosophy's Other Possibility*. Albany, NY: State University of New York Press.

Bennett, Jane (2010). *Vibrant Matter: A Political Ecology of Things*. Durham, NC: Duke University Press.

Bergson, Henri (1911a). *Creative Evolution*, translated by Arthur Mitchell. New York: Henry Holt and Company.

Bergson, Henri (1911b). *Matter and Memory*, translated by Nancy Margaret Paul and W. Scott Palmer. London: George Allen and Unwin.

Bergson, Henri (1935). *Two Sources of Morality and Religion*, translated by R. Ashley Audra and Cloudesley Brereton, with the assistance of W. Horsfall Carter. London: Macmillan and Co., Ltd.

Bird, Alexander (2007). *Nature's Metaphysics: Laws and Properties*. New York: Oxford University Press.

Blackmore, Susan (2010). "Temes: An Emerging Third Replicator," published online on August 23, 2010, as part of the National Humanities Center on the Human Project. https://nationalhumanitiescenter.org/on-the-human/2010/08/temes-an-emerging-third-replicator/

Blackmore, Susan and Emily T. Troscianko (2018). *Consciousness: An Introduction*. London: Routledge.

Block, Ned (1995). "On a Confusion about a Function of Consciousness." *Behavioral Brain Science* 18: 227–47. DOI: 10.1017/S0140525X00038188

Bostrom, Nick (2014). *Superintelligence: Paths, Dangers, Strategies*. Oxford, UK: Oxford University Press.

Boyd, Robert and Peter J. Richerson (2005). *The Origin and Evolution of Cultures*. New York: Oxford University Press.

Braidotti, Rosi (2019). *Posthuman Knowledge*. Cambridge, UK: Polity Press.

Brillouin, Léon (1953). "Negentropy Principle of Information." *Journal of Applied Physics* 24: 1152–63. https://doi.org/10.1063/1.1721463

Bruineberg, Jelle, J. Kiverstein and Eric Rietveld (2018). "The Anticipating Brain Is Not a Scientist: The Free-Energy Principle from an Ecological-Enactive Perspective." *Synthese* 195: 2417–44. DOI: 10.1007/s11229-016-1239-1

Bruineberg, Jelle and Erik Rietveld (2014). "Self-Organization, Free Energy Minimization, and Optimal Grip on a Field of Affordances." *Frontiers in Human Neuroscience* 8: 599. DOI: 10.3389/fnhum.2014.00599

Bubeck, Sébastien with Varun Chandrasekaran, Ronen Eldan, Johannes Gehrke, Eric Horvitz, Ece Kamar, Peter Lee, Yin Tat Lee, Yuanzhi Li, Scott Lundberg, Harsha Nori, Hamid Palangi, Marco Tulio Ribeiro, and Yi Zhang (2023). "Sparks of Artificial General Intelligence: Early Experiments with GPT-4," preprint available at: [2303.12712] Sparks of Artificial General Intelligence: Early Experiments with GPT-4 (arxiv.org) arXiv:2303.12712

Cangelosi, Angelo and Matthew Schlesinger (2015). *Developmental Robotics: From Babies to Robots*. Cambridge, MA: MIT Press.

Cardeña, Etzel and Michael Winkelman (2011). *Altering Consciousness: Multidisciplinary Perspectives*; Volume 1: History, Culture, and the Humanities, Volume 2: Biological and Psychological Perspectives. Santa Barbara, CA: Praeger.

Carhart-Harris, Robin L. (2018). "The Entropic Brain—Revisited." *Neuropharmacology* 142: 167–78.

Carhart-Harris, Robin L. with Suresh Muthukumaraswamy, Leor Roseman, Mendel Kaelen, Wouter Droog, Kevin Murphy, Enzo Tagliazucchi, Eduardo E. Schenberg, Timothy Nest, Csaba Orban, Robert Leech, Luke T. Williams, Tim M. Williams, Mark Bolstridge, Ben Sessa, John McGonigle, Martin I. Sereno, David Nichols, Peter J. Hellyer, Peter Hobden, John Evans, Krish D. Singh, Richard G. Wise, H. Valerie Curran, Amanda Feilding and David J. Nutt (2016). "Neural Correlates of the LSD Experience Revealed by Multimodal Neuroimaging." *Proceedings of the National Academy of Sciences, USA* 113 (17): 4853–8.

Carse, James (1986). *Finite and Infinite Games*. New York: The Free Press.

Carter, Charles W., Jr. and Peter R. Wills (2018). "Interdependence, Reflexivity, Fidelity, Impedance Matching, and the Evolution of Genetic Coding." *Molecular Biology and Evolution* 35 (2), February 2018: 269–86. https://doi.org/10.1093/molbev/msx265

Chaisson, Eric J. (2001). *Cosmic Evolution: The Rise of Complexity in Nature*. Cambridge, MA: Harvard University Press.

Chaisson, Eric J. (2014). "The Natural Science Underlying Big History." *The Scientific World Journal* 2014 (1): 384912. DOI: 10.1155/2014/384912. http://dx.doi.org/10.1155/2014/384912

Chalmers, David J. (1995). "Facing Up to the Problem of Consciousness." *Journal of Consciousness Studies* 2 (3): 200–219.

Chalmers, David J. (1996). *The Conscious Mind*. New York: Oxford University Press.

Chemero, Anthony (2009). *Radical Embodied Cognitive Science*. Cambridge, MA: MIT Press.

Christian, David (2018). *Origin Story: A Big History of Everything*. New York: Little, Brown and Company.

Clark, Andy (2016). *Surfing Uncertainty: Prediction, Action and the Embodied Mind*. New York: Oxford University Press.

Clark, Andy (2017). "Bursting Out: Predictive Brains, Embodied Minds, and the Puzzle of the Evidentiary Veil." *Noûs* 51 (4): 727–53. https://doi.org/10.1111/nous.12140

Cofré, Rodrigo, Ruben Herzog, Pedro Mediano, Juan Piccinini, Fernando E. Rosas, Yonatan Sanz Perl and Enzo Tagliazucchi (2020). "Whole-Brain Models to Explore Altered States of Consciousness from the Bottom Up." *Brain Sciences* 10 (9): 626. https://doi.org/10.3390/brainsci10090626

Coleman, Sam (2006). "Being Realistic: Why Physicalism May Entails Panexperientialism." *Journal of Consciousness Studies* 13 (10–11): 40–2.

Coleman, Sam (2012). "Mental Chemistry1: Combination for Panpsychists." *Dialectica* 66 (1): 137–66.

Connolly, William E. (2002). *Neuropolitics: Thinking, Culture, Speed.* Minneapolis: University of Minnesota Press.

Connolly, William E. (2011). *A World of Becoming.* Durham, NC: Duke University Press.

Connolly, William E. (2014). "Species Evolution and Cultural Freedom." *Political Research Quarterly* 67 (2): 441–52.

Corballis, Michael C. (2011). *The Recursive Mind: The Origins of Human Language, Thought, and Civilization.* Princeton, NJ: Princeton University Press.

Coseru, Christian (2017). "Mind in Indian Buddhist Philosophy." *The Stanford Encyclopedia of Philosophy* (Spring 2017 Edition), Edward N. Zalta (ed.) https://plato.stanford.edu/archives/spr2017/entries/mind-indian-buddhism/

Cowen, Ron (2015). "Space, Time, Entanglement." *Nature* 527, November 19, 2015: 290–3.

Crossley, Nick (2011). *Towards Relational Sociology.* London: Routledge.

Csikszentmihalyi, Mihaly (2008). *Flow: The Psychology of Optimal Experience.* New York: Harper Perennial Classics.

Darwin, Charles (1877). *The Descent of Man*, second edition, with an introduction by Adrian Desmond and James Moore. London: Penguin, 2004.

Dawkins, Richard (1995). *River out of Eden: A Darwinian View of Life.* New York: Basic Books.

Deacon, Terrence (2012). *Incomplete Nature: How Mind Emerged from Matter.* New York: W.W. Norton Press.

Dehaene, Stanislaus, Hakwan Lau, Sid Kouider (2017). "What Is Consciousness, and Could Machines Have It?" *Science* 358: 486–92.

Del Santo, Flavio and Nicolas Gisin (2019). "Physics without Determinism: Alternative Interpretations of Classical Physics." *Physics Review A* 100: 062107. Published December 5, 2019. arXiv:1909.03497v2

Dennett, Daniel C. (1995). *Darwin's Dangerous Idea: Evolution and the Meanings of Life.* New York: Simon and Schuster.

Dennett, Daniel C. (1996). *Brainstorms: Philosophical Essays on Mind and Psychology.* Cambridge, MA: MIT Press.

Di Paolo, Ezequiel A. with Elena Clare Cuffari and Hanne De Jaegher (2018). *Linguistic Bodies: The Continuity between Life and Language.* Cambridge, MA: MIT Press.

Donald, Merlin (1993). *Origins of the Modern Mind: Three Stages in the Evolution of Culture and Cognition.* Cambridge, MA: Harvard University Press.

Donnay, Gabriel F. with Summer K. Rankin, Monica Lopez-Gonzalez, Patpong Jiradejvong and Charles J. Limb (2014). "Neural Substrates of Interactive Musical Improvisation: An fMRI Study of 'Trading Fours' in Jazz." *PLoS ONE* 9 (2): e88665. DOI: 10.1371/journal.pone.0088665

Dos Santos, R., F. Osório, J. Crippa and J. Hallak (2016). "Classical Hallucinogens and Neuroimaging, a Systematic Review of Human Studies: Hallucinogens and Neuroimaging." *Neurosci. Biobehav. Rev.* 71: 715–28. DOI: 10.1016/j.neubiorev.2016.10.026

Dozmorov, Igor M. and D. Dresser (2010). "Immune System as a Sensory System." *International Journal of Biomedical Science* 6 (3), September 2010: 167–75.

Dreyfus, Hubert and Charles Taylor (2015). *Retrieving Realism*. Cambridge, MA: Harvard University Press.

Ellis, Brian and Caroline Lierse (1994). "Dispositional Essentialism." *Australasian Journal of Philosophy* 72: 27–45.

Farber, Paul Lawrence (1994). *The Temptations of Evolutionary Ethics*. Berkeley, CA: University of California Press.

Farisco, Michele with Arleen Salles and Kathinka Evers (2018). "Neuroethics: A Conceptual Approach." *Cambridge Quarterly of Healthcare Ethics* 27: 717–27.

Fauconnier, Gilles and Mark B. Turner (2002). *The Way We Think: Conceptual Blending and the Mind's Hidden Complexities*. New York: Basic Books.

Ferrando, Francesca (2013). "Posthumanism, Transhumanism, Antihumanism, Metahumanism, and New Materialisms: Differences and Relations." *Existenz* 8 (2): 26–32.

Ferrando, Francesca (2019). *Philosophical Posthumanism*. London: Bloomsbury Publishing.

Flannery, Kent and Joyce Marcus (2012). *The Creation of Inequality: How Our Prehistoric Ancestors Set the Stage for Monarchy, Slavery and Empire*. Cambridge, MA: Harvard University Press.

Floridi, Luciano (2007). "Understanding Information Ethics." *APA Newsletter on Philosophy and Computers* 071: 3–12.

Floridi, Luciano (2008a). "Information Ethics: A Reappraisal." *Ethics and Information Technology* 10 (2–3): 189–204.

Floridi, Luciano (2008b). "The Method of Levels of Abstraction." *Minds and Machines* 18 (3), September 2008: 303–29.

Floridi, Luciano (2013). *The Philosophy of Information*. London: Oxford University Press.

Fox C. R. Kieren, Matthew L. Dixon, Savannah Nijeboer, Manesh Girn, James L. Floman, Michael Lifshitz, Melissa Ellamil, Peter Sedlmeier, Kalina Christoff et al. (2016). "Functional Neuroanatomy of Meditation: A Review and Meta-analysis of 78 Functional Neuroimaging Investigations." *Neuroscience & Biobehavioral Reviews* 65: 208–28. DOI: 10.1016/j.neubiorev.2016.03.021

Frischmann, Brett and Evan Selinger (2019). *Re-Engineering Humanity*. New York: Cambridge University Press.

Friston, Karl (2010). "The Free-Energy Principle: A Unified Brain Theory?" *Nature Reviews Neuroscience* 11: 127–38. DOI: 10.1038/nrn2787

Friston, Karl J. and K. E. Stephan (2007). "Free-Energy and the Brain." *Synthese* 159 (3): 417–58. https://doi.org/10.1007/s11229-007-9237-y

Froese, Tom (2018). "Searching for the Conditions of Genuine Intersubjectivity." In Albert Newen, Leon De Bruin, Shaun Galllagher (ed.), *The Oxford Handbook of 4E Cognition*. New York: Oxford University Press, 163–86.

Gabora, Liane (2008). "The Cultural Evolution of Socially Situated Cognition." *Cognitive Systems Research* 9 (1–2): 104–13.

Gabora, Liane (2018). "The Creative Process of Cultural Evolution." In Angela K.Y. Leung, Letty Kwan, Shyhnan Liou (eds.), *Handbook of Culture and Creativity: Basic Processes and Applied Innovations*. Oxford: Oxford University Press, 33–60.

Gabora, Liane (2019). "Creativity: Linchpin in the Quest for a Viable Theory of Cultural Evolution." *Current Opinion in Behavioral Sciences* 27: 77–83.

Gabora, Liane and Cameron Smith (2018). "Two Cognitive Transitions Underlying the Capacity for Cultural Evolution." *Journal of Anthropological Sciences* 96: 27–52.

Gallagher, Shaun (2017). *Enactivist Interventions: Rethinking the Mind*. London: Oxford University Press.

Garcia-Romeu, A. P. and Charles T. Tart (2013). *The Wiley-Blackwell Handbook of Transpersonal Psychology*, first edition. Hoboken, NJ: John Wiley & Sons, Ltd.

Gergen, Kenneth J. (2009). *Relational Being: Beyond Self and Community*. London: Oxford University Press.

Gethin, Rupert (1997). "Cosmology and Meditation: From the Aggañña-Sutta to the Mahāyāna." *History of Religions* 36 (3), February 1997: 183–217.

Gibson, James J. (1979). *The Ecological Approach to Visual Perception*. Boston: Houghton Mifflin.

Gillett, Grant R. (2009a). *Subjectivity and Being Somebody: Human Identity and Neuroethics*. Exeter, UK: Imprint Academic.

Gillett, Grant R. (2009b). "The Subjective Brain, Identity, and Neuroethics." *The American Journal of Bioethics* 9 (9): 5–13.

Gisin, Nicolas (2020). "Real Numbers Are the Hidden Variables of Classical Mechanics." *Quantum Studies: Mathematical Foundations* 7: 197–201.

Goff, Philip (2019). "Did the Universe Design Itself?" *International Journal of the Philosophy of Religion* 85: 99–122.

Goff, Philip (2017). *Consciousness and Fundamental Reality*. New York: Oxford University Press.

Gottlieb, Jacqueline, Pierre-Yves Oudeyer, Manuel Lopes, Adrien Baranes (2013). "Information-Seeking, Curiosity, and Attention: Computational and Neural Mechanisms." *Trends in Cognitive Sciences* 17 (11): 585–93. https://doi.org/10.1016/j.tics.2013.09.00

Graziano, Michael S. A. (2019). *Rethinking Consciousness: A Scientific Theory of Subjective Experience*. New York: Norton and Company.

Grosz, Elizabeth (2008). *Chaos, Territory, Art*. New York: Columbia University Press.

Grosz, Elizabeth (2017). *The Incorporeal: Ontology, Ethics and the Limits of Materialism*. New York: Columbia University Press.

Hagendorff, Thilo (2020). "The Ethics of AI Ethics: An Evaluation of Guidelines." *Minds and Machines*: 99–120. https://doi.org/10.1007/s11023-020-09517-8 (accessed March 8, 2020).

Han, Shihui, Georg Northoff, Kai Vogeley, Bruce E. Wexler, Shinobu Kitayama and Michael E. Varnum (2013). "A Cultural Neuroscience Approach to the Biosocial Nature of the Human Brain." *Annual Review of Psychology* 64: 335–59. DOI: 10.1146/annurev-psych-071112-054629

Harari, Yuval Noah (2015). *Sapiens: A Brief History of Humanity*. London: Vintage.

Harari, Yuval Noah (2016). *Homo Deus: A Brief History of Tomorrow*. London: Vintage.

Harari, Yuval Noah (2017). *Homo Deus: A Brief History of Tomorrow*. London: Penguin/Vintage.

Haraway, Donna (2004). *The Haraway Reader*. New York: Routledge.

Hayles, N. Katherine (2011). "Wrestling with Transhumanism." In Gregory R. Hansell, William Grassie, et al. (eds.), *H+: Transhumanism and Its Critics*. Philadelphia, PA: Metanexus Institute, 215–26.

Hayward, Timothy (1997). "Anthropocentrism: A Misunderstood Problem." *Environmental Values* 6 (1): 49–63.

Henrich, Joseph (2015). *The Secret of Our Success: How Culture Is Driving Human Evolution, Domesticating Our Species, and Making Us Smart*. Princeton, NJ: Princeton University Press.

Hershock, Peter D. (1999). *Reinventing the Wheel: A Buddhist Response to the Information Age*. Albany, NY: State University of New York Press.

Hershock, Peter D. (2006). *Buddhism in the Public Sphere: Reorienting Global Interdependence*. Albany, NY: State University of New York Press.

Hershock, Peter D. (2012). *Valuing Diversity: Buddhist Reflection on Realizing a More Equitable Global Future*. Albany, NY: State University of New York Press.

Hershock, Peter D. (2021). *Buddhism and Intelligent Technology: Toward a More Humane Future*. London: Bloomsbury Academic.

Hershock, Peter D. (2023). "Karma." In Sarah Flavel and Chiara Robbiano (eds.), *Concepts in World Philosophies: A Toolkit for Philosophers*. London: Bloomsbury Academic.

Heyes, Cecilia (2018). "Enquire within: Cultural Evolution and Cognitive Science." *Philosophical Transactions of the Royal Society B* 373: 20170051. http://dx.doi.org/10.1098/rstb.2017.0051

Ho, Mae-Wan (2008). *The Rainbow and the Worm: The Physics of Organism*. Singapore: World Scientific Publishing.

Hobson, J. Allan (2007). "States of Consciousness: Normal and Abnormal." In Philip David Zelazo, Morris Moscovitch and Evan Thompson (eds.), *The Cambridge Handbook of Consciousness*, Cambridge, UK: Cambridge University Press, 435–44.

Hohwy, Jakob (2013). *The Predictive Mind*, first edition. Oxford: Oxford University Press.

Holder, John J. (2013). "A Survey of Early Buddhist Epistemology." In Steven M. Emmanuel (ed.), *A Companion to Buddhist Philosophy*. New York: Wiley-Blackwell.

Hongladarom, Soraj (2020). *The Ethics of AI and Robotics: A Buddhist Viewpoint*. Lanham, MD: Lexington Books.

Hu, Yi with Pan Yafeng, Shi Xinwei, Cai Qing, Li Xianchun and Cheng Xiaojun (2018). "Inter-brain Synchrony and Cooperation Context in Interactive Decision Making." *Biological Psychology* 2018 (133): 54–62.

Hutchins, Edwin (1995). *Cognition in the Wild*. Cambridge, MA: MIT Press.

Hutto, Daniel D. and Erik Myin (2012). *Radicalizing Enactivism: Basic Minds without Content*. Cambridge, MA: MIT Press.

Hutto, Daniel D. and Erik Myin (2017). *Evolving Enactivism: Basic Minds Meet Content*. Cambridge, MA: MIT Press.

Illes, Judy and Sharmin Hossain (eds.) (2017). *Neuroethics: Anticipating the Future*. London: Oxford University Press.

Ingold, Timothy (2021). *Imagining for Real: Essays on Creation, Attention and Correspondence*. London: Routledge.

James, William (1902). *The Varieties of Religious Experience: A Study in Human Nature*. New York: Longmans, Green and Co.

Jullien, Francois (2000). *Detour and Access: Strategies of Meaning in China and Greece*. New York: Zone Books.

Kanai, Ryota, Acer Chang, Yen Yu, Ildefons Magrans de Abril, Martin Biehl and Nicholas Guttenberg (2019). "Information Generation as a Functional Basis of Consciousness." *Neuroscience of Consciousness* 2019 (1): niz016. https://doi.org/10.1093/nc/niz016

Kastrup, Bernardo (2018). "The Universe in Consciousness." *Journal of Consciousness Studies* 25 (5–6): 125–55.

Kasulis, Thomas P. (2002). *Intimacy or Integrity: Philosophy and Cultural Difference*. Honolulu: University of Hawaii Press.

Keppler, Joachim and Itay Shani (2020). "Cosmopsychism and Consciousness Research: A Fresh View on the Causal Mechanisms Underlying Phenomenal States." *Frontiers in Psychology*, March 05, 2020. https://doi.org/10.3389/fpsyg.2020.00371

Kirk, Robert (2019). "Zombies." *The Stanford Encyclopedia of Philosophy*, Edward N. Zalta (ed.), https://plato.stanford.edu/archives/spr2019/entries/zombies/

Koch, Christof (2019). *The Feeling of Life Itself: Why Consciousness Is Widespread but Can't Be Computed*. Cambridge, MA: MIT Press.

Kolodny, Oren and Shimon Edelman (2018). "The Evolution of the Capacity for Language: The Ecological Context and Adaptive Value of a Process of Cognitive Hijacking." p. 6. *Philosophical Transactions of the Royal Society B* 373: 20170052. http://dx.doi.org/10.1098/rstb.2017.0052

Kriegel, Uriah (ed.) (2020). *The Oxford Handbook of the Philosophy of Consciousness*. Oxford, UK: Oxford University Press.

Laland, Kevin N. (2017). *Darwin's Unfinished Symphony: How Culture Made the Human Mind*. Princeton, NJ: Princeton University Press.

Lebedev, A. V., M. Lövdén, G. Rosenthal, A. Feilding, D. J. Nutt and R. L. Carhart-Harris (2015). "Finding the Self by Losing the Self: Neural Correlates of Ego-Dissolution under Psilocybin." *Human Brain Mapping* 36 (8): 3137–53.

LeDoux, Joseph E. with Matthias Michel and Hakwan Lau (2020). "A Little History Goes a Long Way toward Understanding Why We Study Consciousness the Way We Do Today." *Proceedings of the National Academy of Sciences* 117 (13), March 2020: 6976–84. DOI: 10.1073/pnas.19216

Lee, Darrin J. and Edwin Kulubya, Philippe Goldin, Amir Goodarzi, Fady Girgis (2018). "Review of the Neural Oscillations Underlying Meditation." *Frontiers in Neuroscience*, March 26, 2018. https://doi.org/10.3389/fnins.2018.00178

Levin, Michael (2022). "Technological Approach to Mind Everywhere: An Experimentally-Grounded Framework for Understanding Diverse Bodies and Minds." *Frontiers of Systems Neuroscience* 24 (16), March: 768201. DOI: 10.3389/fnsys.2022.768201

Levy, Neil (2007). "Rethinking Neuroethics in Light of the Extended Mind Thesis." *American Journal of Bioethics* 7 (9): 3–11.

Lewens, Tim (2015). *Cultural Evolution: Conceptual Changes*. Oxford, UK: Oxford University Press.

Lewens, Tim (2020). "Cultural Evolution." *The Stanford Encyclopedia of Philosophy*, Edward N. Zalta (ed.). https://plato.stanford.edu/archives/sum2020/entries/evolution-cultural/

Lusthaus, Dan (2000). *Buddhist Phenomenology: A Philosophic Investigation of Yogācāra Buddhism and the Ch'eng wei-shih lun*. London: Curzon Press.

MacCormack, Patricia (2020). *The Ahuman Manifesto: Activism for the End of the Anthropocene*. London: Bloomsbury Academic.

Mackenzie, Matthew (2018). "The Yogācāra Theory of the Three Natures: Internalist and Non-dualist Interpretation." *Comparative Philosophy* 9 (1): 18–31.

Mancuso, Stefano (2018). *The Revolutionary Genius of Plants: A New Understanding of Plant Intelligence and Behavior*. New York: Atria Books.

Manzocco, Roberto (2019). *Transhumanism—Engineering the Human Condition: History, Philosophy and Current Status*. Chichester, UK: Springer Praxis.

Maudlin, Tim (2011). *Quantum Non-locality and Relativity: Metaphysical Intimations of Modern Physics*. West Sussex, UK: Wiley-Blackwell.

Mayor, Adrienne (2019). *Gods and Robots: Myths, Machines and Ancient Dreams of Technology*. Princeton, NJ: Princeton University Press.

McDermott, Rose and Peter K. Hatemi (2020). "Ethics in Field Experimentation: A Call to Establish New Standards to Protect the Public from Unwanted Manipulation and Real Harms." *Proceedings of the National Academy of Sciences of the United States of America* 117 (48): 30014–21.

Megedish, Eli, Assav Halevy, Tomer Shacham, Tom Dvir, Liat Dorvat, Hagai S. Eisenberb (2013). "Entanglement between Photons That Have Never Coexisted." *Physical Review Letters* 110 (21), May 24: 210403. DOI: 10.1103/PhysRevLett.110.210403. Epub 2013 May 22. PMID: 23745845.

Mesoudi, Alex (2011). *Cultural Evolution: How Darwinian Theory Can Explain Human Culture and Synthesize the Social Sciences*. Chicago, IL: University of Chicago Press.

Metzinger, Thomas (2009). *The Ego Tunnel: The Science of the Mind and the Myth of the Self*. New York: Basic Books.

Midgley, Mary (2010). *The Solitary Self: Darwin and the Selfish Gene*. London: Routledge.

Millière, Raphael with Robin L. Carhart-Harris, Leor Roseman, Flynn-Mathis Trautwein and Aviva Berkovich-Ohana (2018). "Psychedelics, Meditation, and Self-Consciousness." *Frontiers in Psychology* 9, Article 1475. https://doi.org/10.3389/fpsyg.2018.01475

Miyagawa, Shigeru; with Cora Lesure and Vitor A. Nóbrega (2018). "Cross-Modality Information Transfer: A Hypothesis about the Relationship among Prehistoric Cave Paintings, Symbolic Thinking, and the Emergence of Language." Frontiers in Psychology vol. 9 115. 20 Feb. 2018.

Morin, Orrin (2016). "Reasons to be Fussy about Cultural Evolution." *Biology and Philosophy* 31: 447–58. DOI: 10.1007/s10539-016-9516-4. Epub 2016 Feb 29. PMID: 27472420; PMCID: PMC4944120.

Morozov, Evgeny (2013). *To Save Everything, Click Here: The Folly of Technological Solutionism*. New York: Public Affairs.

Morton, Timothy (2016). *Dark Ecology: For a Logic of Future Coexistence*. New York: Columbia University Press.

Müller, Viktor and Ulman Lindenberger (2019). "Dynamic Orchestration of Brains and Instruments during Free Guitar Improvisation." *Frontiers in Integrative Neuroscience* 13, Article 50. https://doi.org/10.3389/fnint.2019.00050

Musser, George (2015). *Spooky Action at a Distance: The Phenomenon That Reimagines Space and Time—and What It Means for Black Holes, the Big Bang, and Theories of Everything*. New York: Scientific American/Farrar, Straus and Giroux.

Nagel, Saskia K. and Peter B. Reiner (2018). "Skillful Use of Technologies of Extended Mind Illuminate Practical Paths toward an Ethics of Consciousness." *Frontiers in Psychology* 9, July 2018, Article 1251.

Nagel, Thomas (1986). *The View from Nowhere*. London: Oxford University Press.

Nagel, Thomas (2012). *Mind and Cosmos: Why the Materialist Neo-Darwinian Conception of Nature Is Almost Certainly False*. New York: Oxford University Press.

Newen, Albert with Leon de Bruin and Shaun Gallagher (ed.) (2018). *The Oxford Handbook of 4E Cognition*. Oxford, UK: Oxford University Press.

Nixon, Rob (2011). *Slow Violence and the Environmentalism of the Poor*. Cambridge, MA: Harvard University Press.

Noble, Denis (2015). "Evolution beyond Neo-Darwinism: A New Conceptual Framework." *Journal of Experimental Biology* 2015 (218): 7–13. DOI: 10.1242/jeb.106310

Northoff, Georg (2018). *The Spontaneous Brain: From the Mind–Body to the World–Brain Problem*. Cambridge, MA: MIT Press.

Northoff, Georg (2019). "Lessons from Astronomy and Biology for the Mind-Copernican Revolution in Neuroscience." *Frontiers of Human Neuroscience* 13, September 19: 319. DOI: 10.3389/fnhum.2019.00319. PMID: 31607878; PMCID: PMC6761250.

Nye, David E. (2021). "Harari's World History: Evolution toward Intelligence without Consciousness?" *Technology and Culture* 62 (4): 1219–28. DOI: 10.1353/tech.2021.0160

Ofengenden, Tzofit (2014). "Memory Formation and Belief." *Dialogues in Philosophy, Mental and Neuro Sciences* 7 (2): 34–44.

O'Neil, Cathy (2016). *Weapons of Math Destruction: How Big Data Increases Inequality and Threatens Democracy*. New York: Crown Publishing Group.

Penn, Derek with Keith Holyoak and Daniel Povinelli (2008). "Darwin's Mistake: Explaining the Discontinuity between Human and Nonhuman Minds." *Behavioral and Brain Sciences* 31: 109–78.

Pepperell, Robert (2003). *The Posthuman Condition: Consciousness beyond the Brain*. Bristol, UK: Intellect.

Pérez, Alejandro, Manuel Carreiras and Jon Adoni Duñabeitia (2017). "Brain-to-Brain Entrainment: EEG Interbrain Synchronization while Speaking and Listening." *Scientific Reports* 7 (4190). https://doi.org/10.1038/s41598-017-04464-4

Putnam, Hilary (1992). *Renewing Philosophy*. Cambridge, MA: Harvard University Press.

Quiroga, Rodrigo Quian (2020). *Neuroscience Fiction*. Dallas: BenBella Books.

Ramsey, William (2020). "Eliminative Materialism." In Edward N. Zalta (ed.), *The Stanford Encyclopedia of Philosophy*. https://plato.stanford.edu/archives/sum2020/entries/materialism-eliminative/

Razeto-Barry, Pablo (2012). "Autopoiesis 40 Years Later: A Review and a Reformulation." *Origins of Life and Evolution of Biospheres* 42: 543–67.

Read, Dwight (2008). "Working Memory: A Cognitive Limit to Non-Human Primate Recursive Thinking Prior to Hominid Evolution." *Evolutionary Psychology* 6 (4): 676–714.

Reiner, Peter B. and Saskia K. Nagel (2017). "Technologies of the Extended Mind: Defining the Issues." In Judy Illes and Samsir Hossain (eds.), *Neuroethics: Anticipating the Future*. London: Oxford University Press, 108–22.

Richerson, Peter J. and Morten H. Christiansen (eds.) (2013). *Cultural Evolution: Society, Technology, Language, and Religion*. Cambridge, MA: MIT Press (online UH).

Richerson, Peter J. and Robert Boyd (2005). *Not by Genes Alone: How Culture Transformed Human Evolution*. Chicago: University of Chicago Press.

Robinson, Douglas (2013). *Feeling Extended: Sociality as Extended Body-Becoming-Mind*. Cambridge, MA: MIT Press.

Rommelfanger, Karen S., with Sung-Jin Jeong, Arisa Ema, Tamami Fukushi, Kiyoto Kasai, Khara M. Ramos, Arleen Salles and Ilina Singh (2018). "Neuroethics Questions to Guide Ethical Research in the International Brain." *Neuron* 100, October 10, 2018.

Rosenberg, Gregg (2004). *A Place for Consciousness: Probing the Deep Structure of the Natural World*. New York: Oxford University Press.

Rosiek, Jerry Lee, Jimmy Snyder, Scott L. Pratt (2020). "The New Materialisms and Indigenous Theories of Non-human Agency: Making the Case for Respectful Anti-Colonial Engagement." *Qualitative Inquiry* 26: 331–46.

Rovelli, Carlo (2017). *Reality Is Not What It Seems: The Journey to Quantum Gravity*. New York: Riverhead Books.

Salles, Arleen with Kathinka Evers and Michele Farisco (2019). "Neuroethics and Philosophy in Responsible Research and Innovation: The Case of the Human Brain Project." *Neuroethics* 12: 201–11.

Samorini, Giorgio (2002). *Animals and Psychedelics: The Natural World and the Instinct to Alter Consciousness*. Rochester, VT: Park Street Press.

Sanches de Oliveira, Guilherme and Anthony Chemero (2015). "Against Smallism and Localism." *Studies in Logic, Grammar and Rhetoric* 41 (54): 9–23.

Sanders, Barry and Ivan Illich (1989). *ABC: Alphabetization of the Popular Mind*. New York: Vintage Books.

Savulescu, Julian and Ingmar Persson (2012a). "Moral Enhancement, Freedom and the God Machine." *Monist* 95 (3), July 2012: 399–421.

Savulescu, Julian and Ingmar Persson (2012b). *Unfit for the Future: The Need for Moral Enhancement*. Oxford, UK: Oxford University Press.

Sayre, Kenneth (1976). *Cybernetics and the Philosophy of Mind*. London: Routledge and Keagan Paul.

Schaffer, Jonathan (2009). "Spacetime the One Substance." *Philosophical Studies* 145: 131–48.

Schaffer, Jonathan (2010a). "The Internal Relatedness of All Things." *Mind* 119: 341–76.

Schaffer, Jonathan (2010b). "Monism: The Priority of the Whole." *Philosophical Review* 119 (1): 31–76.

Schlosser, Gerhard (2018). "A Short History of Nearly Every Sense: The Evolutionary History of Vertebrate Sensory Cell Types." *Integrative and Comparative Biology* 58 (2), August 2018: 301–16.

Schneier, Bruce (2018). *Click Here to Kill Everybody: Security and Survival in a Hyper-Connected World*. New York: W.W. Norton.

Schooler, Jonathan W. (2002). "Re-representing Consciousness: Dissociations between Experience and Meta-consciousness." *Trends in Cognitive Sciences* 6 (8): 339–44. DOI: 10.1016/S1364-6613(02)01949-6

Schooler, Jonathan W. and Piotr Winkielman (2011). "Splitting Consciousness: Unconscious, Conscious and Meta-conscious Processes in Social Cognition." *European Review of Social Psychology* 22: 1–35.

Schrodinger, Edwin (1944). *What Is Life? The Physical Aspect of the Living Cell.* Dublin: Dublin Institute for Advanced Studies.

Seager, William (2016). *Theories of Consciousness: An Introduction and Assessment.* New York: Routledge.

Seager, William (2018). "The Philosophical and Scientific Metaphysics of David Bohm." *Entropy* 2018 (20): 493.

Shani, Itay (2015). "Cosmopsychism: A Holistic Approach to the Metaphysics of Experience." *Philosophical Papers* 44 (3): 389–437.

Sherman, Jeremy (2017). *Neither Ghost Nor Machine: The Emergence and Nature of Selves.* New York: Columbia University Press.

Shoemaker, Sydney (1981). "Some Varieties of Functionalism." *Philosophical Topics* 12 (1): 83–118.

Siderits, Mark with Tom Tillemans and Arindam Chakrabarti (eds.) (2011). *Apoha: Buddhist Nominalism and Human Cognition.* New York: Columbia University Press.

Siegel, Ronald K. (1989). *Intoxication: Life in Pursuit of Artificial Paradise.* New York: Dutton.

Smart, John M. (2019). "Evolutionary Development: A Universal Perspective." In G. Georgiev, J. Smart, Martinez C. Flores, M. Price (eds.), *Evolution, Development and Complexity.* New York, NY: Springer Proceedings in Complexity.

Smolin, Lee (2021). "Views, Variety, and Quantum Mechanics." *Quantum Physics,* pre-publication paper, available at: arXiv:2105.03539v1

Solms, M. (2019). "The Hard Problem of Consciousness and the Free Energy Principle." *Frontiers in Psychology* 9, January 30, 2019: 2714. DOI: 10.3389/fpsyg.2018.02714

Specker, Jona with Farah Focquaert, Kasper Raus, Sigrid Sterckx and Maartje Schermer (2014). "The Ethical Desirability of Moral Bioenhancement: A Review of Reasons." *BMC Medical Ethics* 15, January 30, 2019: 67. DOI: 10.1186/1472-6939-15-67

Sterelny, Kim (2012). *The Evolved Apprentice: How Evolution Made Humans Unique.* Cambridge, MA: MIT Press.

Stewart, John E. (2019). "The Origins of Life: The Managed-Metabolism Hypothesis." *Foundations of Science* 24: 171–95. https://doi.org/10.1007/s10699-018-9563-1

Strawson, Galen (2006a). "Realistic Materialism: Why Physicalism Entails Panpsychism." *Journal of Consciousness Studies* 13 (10–11): 3–31.

Strawson, Galen (2006b). *Consciousness and Its Place in Nature: Does Physicalism Entail Panpsychism?*, edited by Anthony Freeman. Charlottesville, VA: Imprint Academic.

Strawson, Galen (2018). "The Consciousness Deniers." *New York Times Review of Books,* March 13, 2018. https://www.nybooks.com/daily/2018/03/13/the-consciousness-deniers/

Stubenberg, Leopold (2018). "Neutral Monism." *The Stanford Encyclopedia of Philosophy*, Edward N. Zalta (ed.). https://plato.stanford.edu/archives/fall2018/entries/neutral-monism/

Tang, Yi-Yuan and Michael I. Posner (2009). "Attention Training and Attention State Training." *Trends in Cognitive Sciences* 13 (5): 222–7.

Tattersall, Ian (2019). "Evolution and Human Cognition." *Aisthesis* 12 (2): 11–18.

Teller, Paul (1986). "Relational Holism and Quantum Mechanics." *The British Journal for the Philosophy of Science* 37 (1), March 1986: 71–81.

Thelen, Esther and Linda B. Smith (1994). *A Dynamic Systems Approach to the Development of Cognition and Action*. Cambridge, MA: MIT Press.

Thompson, Evan (2007). *Mind in Life: Biology, Phenomenology and the Sciences of Man*. Cambridge, UK: Cambridge University Press.

Thompson, Evan (2015). *Waking, Dreaming, Being: Self and Consciousness in Neuroscience, Meditation, and Philosophy*. New York: Columbia University Press.

Tomasello, Michael (2019). *Becoming Human: A Theory of Ontogeny*. Cambridge, MA: Harvard University Belknap Press.

Tononi, Giulio (2008). "Consciousness as Integrated Information: A Provisional Manifesto." *Biological Bulletin* 215, December 2008: 216–42.

Tononi, Giulio (2012). *Phi: A Voyage from the Brain to the Soul*. New York: Pantheon.

Tononi, Giulio and Christof Koch (2015). "Consciousness: Here, There and Everywhere?" *Philosophical Transactions of the Royal Society*. https://royalsocietypublishing.org/doi/10.1098/rstb.2014.0167

Tuan, Yi-Fu (1977). *Space and Place: The Perspective of Experience*. Minneapolis, MN: University of Minnesota Press.

Unger, Roberto Mangabeira and Lee Smolin (2014). *The Singular Universe and the Reality of Time: A Proposal in Natural Philosophy*. Cambridge, UK: Cambridge University Press.

Vaitl, Dieter with Niels Birbaumer, John Gruzelier, Graham Jamieson, Boris Kotchoubey, Andrea Kübler, D. Lehmann, Wolfgang Miltner, Ulrich Ott, Peter Pütz, Gebhard Sammer, Inge Strauch, Ute Strehl, Jiri Wackermann and Thomas Weiss (2005). "Psychobiology of Altered States of Consciousness." *Psychological Bulletin* 131: 98–127. 10.1037/0033-2909.131.1.98

Valencia, Ana Lucia and Tom Froese (2020). "What Binds Us? Inter-brain Neural Synchronization and Its Implications for Theories of Human Consciousness." *Neuroscience of Consciousness*. 2020 Jun 11; 2020 (1): niaa010. https://doi.org/10.1093/nc/niaa010. PMID: 32547787; PMCID: PMC7288734.

Van der Leeuw, Sander and Carl Folke (2021). "The Social Dynamics of Basins of Attraction." *Ecology and Society* 26 (1): 33. https://doi.org/10.5751/ES-12289-260133

Van der Tuin, Iris and Rick Dolphijn (2010). "The Transversality of New Materialism." *Women: A Cultural Review* 21 (2): 153–71.

Varela, Francisco J. and Natalie Depraz (2003). "Imagining: Embodiment, Phenomenology, and Transformation." In Alan Wallace (ed.), *Buddhism and Science: Breaking New Ground.* New York: Columbia University Press: 195–232.

Véliz, Carissa (2021). *Privacy Is Power: Why and How You Should Take Back Control of Your Data.* London: Melville House.

von Rospatt, Alexander (1995). *The Buddhist Doctrine of Momentariness: A Survey of the Origins and Early Phase of This Doctrine Up to Vasubandhu* (Alt- und Neu-Indische Studien 47). Stuttgart: Franz Steiner Verlag.

Walker, Matthew (2017). *Why We Sleep: The New Science of Sleep and Dreams.* New York: Penguin.

Watson, Robert N. (2018). *Cultural Evolution and Its Discontents: Cognitive Overload, Parasitic Cultures, and the Humanistic Cure.* Milton: Taylor & Francis Group.

Wesson, Paul S. (2015). "The Status of Modern Five-Dimensional Gravity (A Short Review: Why Physics Needs the Fifth Dimension)." *International Journal of Modern Physics D* 24 (01): 1530001.

Wesson, Paul S. and James M. Overduin (2015). "Waves and Causality in Higher Dimensions." *Physics Letters B* 750: 302–5.

Wesson, Paul S. and James M. Overduin (2018). *Principles of Space, Time and Matter: Cosmology, Particles and Waves in Five Dimensions.* London: World Scientific.

White, Daniel and Hirofumi Katsuno (2023). "Modelling Emotion, Perfecting Heart: Disassembling Technologies of Affect with an Android Bodhisattva in Japan," preprint copy *Journal of the Royal Anthropological Institute*, forthcoming March 2023.

Whitehead, Alfred North (1929 [1985]). *Process and Reality* (Gifford Lectures 1927–28). New York: Macmillan. Corrected edition, David Ray Griffin and Donald W. Sherburne (eds.). New York: The Free Press, 1985.

Williams, Daniel (2018). "Predictive Processing and the Representation Wars." *Minds & Machines* 28: 141–72.

Wilson, E.O. (1975). *Sociobiology: The New Synthesis.* Cambridge, MA: Harvard University Press.

Wilson, Robert A. (2004). *Boundaries of the Mind.* New York: Cambridge University Press.

Winkelman, Michael J. (2017). "The Mechanisms of Psychedelic Visionary Experiences: Hypotheses from Evolutionary Psychology." *Frontiers in Neuroscience* 11: 539. https://doi.org/10.3389/fnins.2017.00539

Wolfe, Cary (2010). *What Is Posthumanism?* Minneapolis: University of Minnesota Press.

Zelazo, Philip David with Morris Moscovitch and Evan Thompson (eds.) (2007). *The Cambridge Handbook of Consciousness.* Cambridge. UK: Cambridge University Press.

Zeng, Yi, Zhao Yuxuan, Bai Jun and Bo Xu (2018). "Towards Robot Self-Consciousness (II): Brain-Inspired Robot Mirror Neuron System Model and Its Application in Mirror Self-Recognition." *Cognitive Computation* 10: 307–20. https://doi.org/10.1007/s12559-017-9505-1

Ziporyn, Brook (2012). *Ironies of Oneness and Difference: Coherence in Early Chinese Thought: Prolegomena to the Study of Li*. Albany, NY: State University of New York Press.

Ziporyn, Brook (2013). *Beyond Oneness and Difference: Li and Coherence in Chinese Buddhist Thought and Its Antecedents*. Albany, NY: State University of New York Press. https://link.springer.com/article/10.1007/s10339-018-0855-8

Zuboff, Shoshana (2019). *The Age of Surveillance Capitalism: The Fight for a Human Future at the New Frontier of Power*. New York: Public Affairs.

Index

agency 12, 25–28, 45, 85, 134–36, 167
   and brain imaging 121–22
   artificial 2, 89, 98–99
   of matter 100
   quality of 26, 29
   and structure 35
   subjective 78
   temporal scale of 41–43
   without agent 53
Aggañña Sutta 60–62, 64
ālayavijñāna (karmic/storehouse consciousness) 50–53
   and cultural evolution 167–68
   (see also: consciousness, eighth)
Aristotle, 3
artificial intelligence 2, 69, 88–89, 146–47, 176 (see also: intelligence, machine/synthetic)
attention (*manaskāra*; *manasikāra*) 1, 7–8, 10, 14, 30, 38, 107, 164, 166–67, 178
   beyond phenomenal present 166
   as capital 56
   -energy 49, 74, 149, 173
   freedom of 14, 145, 152, 157, 178
   meditatively concentrated (*samādhi*) 57–58
   quality of 55–58
   theories of 35
   training 56
attention economy 13, 142, 146–47, 152
   scope of 54, 97

Barad, Karen 100, 111–13, 132, 137
Bergson, Henri 137–38
Big Bang/Big Bounce 10, 59, 62, 70, 78, 81
Borges, Jorge Luis 6
Bostrom, Nick 158
brain
   in cooperative vs competitive activity 115
   decentering 148–49
   entropy 110, 116
   and free will 121
   hacking 121
   imaging, multiperson 12, 55, 107
   and meditation 110, 115
   as model of econiche 116–17
   and psychedelics 109
   as reducing valve 178
   as social or relationally entangled 118–20, 148, 169
   synchronization 119–20

causality
   and intentionality 46
   nonlinear 5, 38–39, 77
Chalmers, David 19
Chan Buddhism 7, 51, 173
Clark, Andy 117
coevolution 7, 10, 55, 59, 73, 78, 169
   of consciousness and self-awareness 86
   of matter and what matters 61–62, 153
   of sensed and sensing presences 10, 123
   of space of causes and space of reasons 80
cognition (*manovijñāna*) 11, 21, 26, 28, 45, 52, 56, 74, 89, 97
   as interpersonal 120
   and predictive processing 36–37, 81, 117
   as sixth consciousness 165
coherence 2, 13–14, 16, 69, 76, 79, 129, 131, 141, 146, 152, 160, 165, 169
   vs decoherence 12, 140, 153, 157
   evolution of 131–33
   vs incoherence 79, 93
   and presence 57
   qualities of 129, 141, 146, 152
concepts (see also *apoha*; *papañca*) 157, 159
   as exclusions 34–35, 51, 56
Connolly, William E. 128
consciousness

altering/altered 7, 12, 53–55, 95, 127, 129, 139
artificial 11, 69, 85, 98, 104
as coherent differentiation 1, 10–11, 46, 78, 81, 138
colonization of 8, 13, 147, 149, 155
"hard problem" of 13, 19, 25, 29, 35, 41, 69, 76, 130, 135, 139
as illusory 90, 130
infrastructure of 2, 7, 12, 35, 51, 78, 91, 127, 129–30, 140, 146, 159, 169
karmic/eighth (*ālayavijñāna*) 74, 174
machine/robotic 92–100
as medium of significant interdependence 79
and nonduality 7, 17, 29, 32, 91, 100–03, 128, 138–39, 140, 173
nonlocality of 12, 9, 91, 108, 118, 122, 147–48
and physical/phenomenal diffraction patterns 108–09
pure (*amalavijñāna*) 53
qualities of 147
as relational 30, 53, 62
as rhythmic 43
as sensory relation/contact 30, 39–40, 66
subjective/seventh (*kliṣṭamanas* or *manas*) 52–53, 55, 68, 74, 77–78, 96, 100, 167–68, 174
as a *skandha* 27, 30
and technology 150–52
temporality of 38–39, 42–43, 103, 123
waking and sleeping as phases of 43, 54, 96–97
consciousness theories 1–4, 127–129
cosmopanpsychic 10, 63, 79–80
dual aspect 61–62
dualist 29, 80, 128, 158
enactivist 21, 35
4E (embodied, embedded, enacted, extended) 35, 39, 148
functionalist 10, 89–91, 158
global workspace theory (GWT) 11, 89, 108, 165
integrated information theory (IIT) 11, 89, 94–95, 99–100, 108
intelligent design (creationist) 128, 132–34

monist/reductionist (idealist) 10, 65, 130–31
monist/reductionist (physicalist) 10, 70, 128, 130–31, 158
neutral monist (Russellian) 61–62, 137
nondualist 2, 128–29
panpsychist 10, 79
physicalist 10
as theories of mattering 1, 13, 132
coordination 10, 46, 93, 120, 171–72
and cultural evolution 168–69
and life origins 67–69
sentient/sensory 50, 89
voluntary vs instinctual 172
cosmology 70–71
Buddhist 77–78, 81–82, 102–03
creativity 28, 69, 128, 152, 161, 165, 170–71, 173
closed vs open 46–51
Csikszentmihalyi, Mihaly 48

Darwin, Charles 135, 163
Dawkins, Richard 134, 144, 163
Dennett, Daniel 134, 144
Diamond Sutra 31
differentiation
as intrinsic work of consciousness 97
and life origins 67–68
dreaming 43, 54, 90, 96, 107
robotic 98
Dreyfus, Hubert 46

Edison, Thomas 56
emptiness (*śūnyatā*; *suññatā*) 16, 17, 22, 26, 31–32, 34, 63, 73, 76, 81, 101, 129, 156
of five *skandhas* 55
enactivism (see consciousness theories, enactivist)
entropy 3, 81, 171
of brain in altered states of consciousness 109, 116–17
ethics 12–13, 85, 128, 130–31, 133
of consciousness 13–14, 99, 141, 146
diversity of 142, 175
evolution of 142, 175
of moral engineering 143–45
neuroethics 132, 148
origin of 14

evolution 12, 46, 133
  of consciousness 105, 139, 158, 161
  cosmic 61
  cultural 14, 161, 163–172
  ethics, role of 174–78
  hacking 92
  human 134
  intention, role of 137
  lifeform/organic 67, 93, 124, 129, 134–36
experience 5–6, 28–29, 32–34, 44, 60, 65, 70, 79–80, 89–90, 93
  experimental accounts of 15, 19
  and imagination 88
  and intent 80, 95
  optimizing 20–23, 48–50
  robotic, possibility of 98–99
  of self/subjective 7, 24, 26–27, 52, 62, 78, 123
  shared 119
  temporality of (momentary vs continuous) 38–40, 72–76
experimental apparatuses 111–13
  and agential cuts 115, 119–20, 145
  in consciousness studies 114, 139–40

Fazang (643–712) 101
feelings (*vedanā*) 23, 26, 35
  as crucial to sentience 66
Floridi, Luciano 42
freedom 48, 77–78, 122, 143, 158, 172
  of attention 14, 58, 152, 157, 178
  from conceptual boundaries 51
  of intention 14, 58, 152, 157, 176, 178
  temporal 82
freewill 2, 3, 11, 121–22, 132

habit (see *saṃskāra*)
Harari, Yuval 164
Heart Sutra 35
Hutto, David 35
Huxley, Aldous 173

ignorance (*avidyā*) 32, 34–35, 52, 95, 140, 145, 173
imagination 87–89, 104, 107, 161
  machine 88
improvisation 10, 49, 51, 68, 81, 139, 141, 153, 160–61

vs innovation 47
  relational 46–47, 79, 81, 104, 129, 172
intelligence 51, 132–33, 138, 155, 164
  as adaptive conduct 47–48
  arboreal 28
  artificial/machine 2, 11, 36, 69, 89, 91–92, 96, 103, 147, 151–52
  evolutionary 91–92
  human vs machine 146, 151
  synthetic 8, 85, 105
intention (*cetanā*) 4, 7, 14, 22–23, 28, 35, 56–58, 61, 80, 87–88, 113, 120, 122
  and attention-energy 74
  in biocultural evolution 50, 68–69, 135–39, 141, 164, 169, 172–75
  and causal synchrony 46
  and cosmic evolution 79–82, 128
  freedom of 14, 58, 152, 157, 176, 178
  and karma 27–29, 35, 38–39, 73–74, 78–80
  and life process 68
  as relational tension 78
  technological scaling of 150–52
interdependence (*paṭiccasamuppāda*; *pratītyasamutpāda*) 6, 16, 20, 22, 32, 34, 73, 79, 101, 103, 124
  in evolutionary dynamics 64–69, 131–32
  as internal vs external relation 31, 145
  ultimate reality of 22

James, William 56, 106

Kafka, Franz 24
karma 6, 11, 16, 22–23, 26–30, 34, 38–39, 50, 65, 157
  as additional temporal dimension 5, 77–83
  and *ālayavijñāna* 52
  in cosmic evolutionary context 61–62
  and emergent moral order 23
  and event entanglement 51–52, 72–75
  and perception 38
  shared 124

Laṅkāvatāra Sutra 74, 77
Levy, Neil 148
Linji (d.866) 173

Madhyamaka Buddhism 63
matter 3, 33–35, 62, 81, 99, 115, 132, 158
　agency of 100
　in Buddhism 61–63, 65, 78–79
　as definition of point of view 31, 71, 160
　living 67
　meaning of 97, 99–101
　and what matters, nonduality of 17, 32, 59, 95, 111, 115
meditation 9, 11, 19–20, 25, 38, 55, 82
　and brain entropy 109–10, 116
　and brain imaging 114–115
　mindfulness 26, 47, 57, 82
memory 4, 25, 28, 138, 168
　and creativity 47
　and human/cultural evolution 172
Middle Path, Buddhist 3, 64, 133
mind (*citta*) 7–8, 19, 26, 31, 33–35, 52, 60–63, 110, 131, 146, 148, 156, 158, 165
　affective 37
　enactivist theory of 40
　and heartmind 45–46, 50
　and mind-body relation 64, 118–19, 137
　and predictive processing 11, 36–37, 117
Morozov, Evgeny 144
Myin, Erik 35

Nagel, Thomas 24–25
neurocentrism 10, 12, 141
neuroethics 13, 132, 147–48, 151
new materialism 6, 137, 139, 157
nonduality 101–02, 139–41
　of matter and what matters 17
　of physical and mental 29
Northoff, Georg 118, 148

perception (*saṃjña*; *saññā*) 7, 9, 21, 26–27, 34–35, 37–41, 45, 51, 55–56, 60, 106–07
Persson, Ingmar 143
posthumanism 13, 156–59, 161
papañca; *prapañca* (conceptual proliferation) 51, 57
psychedelics 109–10, 116
Putnam, Hillary 137

quantum physics 21, 65, 108, 115, 124, 139, 160
　entanglement 75, 111
　and relational propensities 76–77
　and structural realism 70

reality 3, 12, 74–77, 124–25, 141
　as ambiguous/indeterminate 64, 115
　and diversity 124
　experienced as elaboration of consciousness 95
　of interdependence 22
　physical 81, 136, 161
　smallist account of 63, 103, 111
　and truth in Buddhism 15–16, 129
　virtual 6, 89, 161
representationalism 111–12, 117
responsibility 17, 23, 31, 56–57, 83, 93, 98, 113, 127, 161, 172, 175
　and consciousness theorizing 8, 104
　and responsivity 8, 11, 153
　theft 177
robotics 86, 95, 98

Sakkapañha Sutta 51
saṃskāra/saṅkhāra (habit formations; volitional compounds; patterns of enaction) 32, 35, 91, 110
Savulescu, Julian 143
Seager, William 25
self (*atta*; *atman*) 26, 30, 50–52, 87, 123–24, 129, 132, 140
　without-self (*anatta*; *anatman*) 7, 27, 31, 63, 129
self-awareness 86–88, 89
　and mirror self-recognition test 86
　robotic 86–88, 99
　and seventh consciousness 168
sensation 25, 45, 56, 71–72, 165
smallism (atomism) 63, 103, 111, 130, 139
solutionism 144–45, 147
space-time-matter theory 11, 76–78, 80
Spencer, Herbert 163
Strawson, Galen 62, 130
subjectivity 7, 10–11, 24, 26–27, 52–54, 57, 62, 68, 74, 78, 80, 96, 48, 78, 96, 123–24, 157, 167, 172
　machine/robotic 98–100

Taylor, Charles 46
teleodynamics 128
time/temporality
  dilation 108
  patterning of 5
  scales of and consciousness 4, 36, 38–41
  as two-dimensional 11, 76–78, 103, 122
transhumanism 13, 156–60
truth 15–17
  Buddhist two truths theory 17, 63
  as truing capacity 16
twelvefold chain of codependent origination 32–33, 56

upāya (skillful means; responsive virtuosity) 16

values 74, 116, 124, 147, 161, 165, 171
  as modalities of relational appreciation 45, 102
  organic 68

Whitehead, Alfred North 33–34
Wilson, E.O. 144
Wolfram, Stephen 160

Yogācāra Buddhism 7, 52–53, 63, 96, 100, 109, 160, 167, 180–81

www.ingramcontent.com/pod-product-compliance
Lightning Source LLC
Chambersburg PA
CBHW052110300426
44116CB00010B/1609